GOVERNMENT SURVIVAL IN PARLIAMENTARY DEMOCRACIES

PAUL V. WARWICK

Simon Fraser University

CAMBRIDGE
UNIVERSITY PRESS

CAMBRIDGE UNIVERSITY PRESS
Cambridge, New York, Melbourne, Madrid, Cape Town, Singapore, São Paulo

Cambridge University Press
The Edinburgh Building, Cambridge CB2 8RU, UK

Published in the United States of America by Cambridge University Press, New York

www.cambridge.org
Information on this title: www.cambridge.org/9780521470285

First published 1994
This digitally printed version 2007

A catalogue record for this publication is available from the British Library

Library of Congress Cataloguing in Publication data
Warwick, Paul V.
Government survival in parliamentary democracies / Paul
V. Warwick.
p.   cm.
Includes bibliographical references and index.
ISBN 0-521-47028-5
1. Cabinet system – Europe.   2. No confidence motions – Europe.
I. Title
JN94.A63W37   1995
321.8′043′094 – dc20   94–10920
                                                                CIP

ISBN 978-0-521-47028-5 hardback
ISBN 978-0-521-03831-7 paperback

To BJC

Contents

Tables and figures

FIGURES

Preface

This book has its genesis in a confluence of enticing circumstances: the existence of an important but puzzling phenomenon as old as parliamentary democracy itself, the development over time of a profusion of incompatible explanations for the phenomenon, and the recent emergence of a methodology holding out the promise of resolving the confusion. The phenomenon in question is the well-known tendency for government survival rates to vary enormously both within and across parliamentary systems. If one accepts that the length of time governments survive strongly affects their ability to govern effectively, then it follows that our understanding of parliamentary democracy depends very much on the explanation of this variation. Identifying the correct explanation, however, has not proved to be straightforward. It has often been assumed, to cite one major example, that unbridgeable ideological or policy differences among member parties constitute a prime source of coalition government collapses, yet a recent survey (Laver and Schofield 1990:155) finds no systematic evidence to support the claim. To add fuel to the fire, there appeared in the 1980s a major school of thought that asserted that government dissolutions are essentially random and therefore unamenable to causal analysis. Fortunately, the past few years have also seen the introduction of a statistical methodology, event history analysis, that is capable of reconciling causal and random approaches, and a good deal else as well.

Any methodology is only as good as the data to which it is applied. The empirical investigation of government survival has been inhibited by the tendency for various hypotheses to be tested by their proponents on data sets expressly tailored for that purpose; alternative approaches, especially when they involved factors that are difficult to measure such as ideological diversity, were only rarely investigated. If the potential of event history analysis was to be exploited to the full, a much more comprehensive data set clearly would have to be developed, one that encompassed a variety of ways of defining controversial concepts and a broad range of potential causes. The data set that I created for this study ultimately included, in its largest form, well over 1,200 variables. Many of these, to be sure, were intermediate constructs used to create other variables, alternative versions incorporating different definitions of key concepts, or measurements of the same variable at different times; nevertheless, the range of causal factors remains considerable.

Although this study is concerned mainly with the empirical testing of these potential causes, it would be disingenuous of me to leave the impression that the approach is totally inductive. I have been persuaded for some time that the alleged failure of the ideological diversity hypothesis had less to do with its merits than with the inadequacy of the efforts to test it; a good deal of this study is therefore devoted to developing and testing a range of measures of the concept based on evidence from voters, political "experts," and party electoral manifestos. In other areas, to be sure, the approach is much more inductive; for instance, the introduction of evolving economic conditions, which event history analysis makes possible, proceeds in this fashion because very little work has been done in this area. Despite the inductive quality of much of the investigation, the model that ultimately emerges embodies, I believe, a reasonably coherent view of government survival. In the final chapter I attempt to articulate that view.

I have been aided in this effort by a number of institutions and individuals. A grant from the Social Sciences and Humanities Research Council of Canada gave me time to develop the data set, which incorporates the postwar experiences of sixteen West European parliamentary systems, and to launch the analysis. My knowledge of event history methodology benefited from an extended visit to the European University Institute in Florence, made possible by Professor Jean Blondel. Stanford University, through the auspices of its Center for European Studies, granted me the use of its facilities throughout the 1990–1 academic year. Stephen Easton, an economist at Simon Fraser University, proved an invaluable and tireless ally in the task of sorting out the various ideas, hunches, problems, and conundrums that cropped up in the course of the research. George Tsebelis of the University of California, Los Angeles, offered helpful criticism, especially of the final chapter, in his capacity as a manuscript referee. Kaare Strom of the University of California, San Diego, provided me with a copy of his own data set on parliamentary governments, making it possible for me to undertake some analytical work before my own data were ready. Needless to say, none of these individuals bears any responsibility for the final form of the book. Finally, the *American Political Science Review* (Warwick 1992b), the *American Journal of Political Science* (Warwick 1992c; Warwick and Easton 1992), and *Comparative Political Studies* (Warwick 1992a) allowed me to reproduce portions of the research reported in their pages. Readers who are familiar with those articles will find that what is presented here not only expands upon, but very substantially amends, those earlier efforts.

GOVERNMENT SURVIVAL IN PARLIAMENTARY
DEMOCRACIES

1

Introduction: the government survival debates

The liberal democratic world is composed for the most part of two very different regime types: the presidential and the parliamentary. Needless to say, comparisons between the two have long been a stock-in-trade of political analysts and propagandists. Typically, the presidential system – I take the United States as the prototype – is praised for its elaborate separation and balancing of powers, its constitutionally enshrined protection of individual rights and freedoms, and its governmental stability. There is a price to be paid for these advantages, however, and it is usually seen in the multifarious possibilities for stalemate or deadlock between formally separate institutions of government (Congress vs. president, Senate vs. House of Representatives, etc.). When these stalemates become serious, U.S. observers occasionally turn an admiring eye toward the parliamentary regime of Britain, where the fusion of executive and legislative powers under a disciplined, majoritarian party appears to open the door to rapid and coherent government action – even if the lack of checks on executive power is regretted.

While the "Westminster model" of parliamentary government is highly respected, a similar regard is seldom extended to the parliamentary system of government as a whole; the functioning of what is essentially the same regime type in Italy, for instance, more often elicits criticism or ridicule than praise. This bifurcation in perceptions of parliamentary government stems from the fact that its fundamental principles do not in themselves guarantee that decisive government action will be possible. For governments in parliamentary systems to act decisively – indeed, even to survive – they usually require the support of cohesive and disciplined parliamentary majorities.[1] In systems where such majorities cannot be assembled, the consequence may be not merely policy stalemate (presidentism's dilemma), but also a feature that presidential systems expressly rule out – rapid changes of government. If parliamentary government can seem superior to presidential government at times, it can also seem far worse: not only ineffective but unstable to boot.

This Janus-faced nature of parliamentarism is more than a curiosity to political scientists; to a considerable extent, it provoked the rapid development of the comparative politics subfield in the 1950s and 1960s. Two "real world" concerns were uppermost in the minds of democratic theorists at the time: would democratic government take root in the defeated powers of the Second World War – (West) Germany, Italy, and Japan – and could it be implanted in the numerous new states then emerging from the breakup of colonial empires? The prior experiences of the Axis powers with representative institutions were not auspicious. In Germany, a democratic regime created in the aftermath of the First World War had fallen victim to ideological polarization, party-system fragmentation, and governmental instability before finally succumbing to a Nazi movement bent on territorial expansion. Italy and Japan also had seen parliamentary institutions give way to expansionist authoritarian governments in the interwar period. Despite these experiences, all three countries had become parliamentary democracies in the wake of their military defeats. As for the new states, the predominant tendency was for them to adopt parliamentarism, in part because their erstwhile colonial rulers (usually Britain or France) were themselves parliamentary. The future of liberal democracy – then perceived to be in global conflict with international communism – thus appeared to be intimately tied to the parliamentary model of government, with all the risks that model entailed.

The theoretical lesson taken from the weakness or collapse of democratic regimes in the 1920s and 1930s was that democratic political institutions, at least in their parliamentary versions, do not in themselves guarantee a thriving democracy – something more is involved. Early pioneers of comparative politics, such as Almond and Verba (1963), found that extra ingredient in the concept of political culture. Democratic institutions, in their view, required democratic or "civic" attitudes and orientations – tolerance of dissent, bonds of solidarity across political divisions, emotional attachment to the regime – to sustain them. It became important, therefore, to examine cultures as well as institutions and to assess the "fit" between the two. This connection was seen not just by political scientists but also by policy makers. In Europe, both the determined effort in West Germany to inculcate democratic values through the school system and the establishment in France of a hybrid parliamentary-presidential regime in 1958 (the Fifth Republic) may be interpreted as efforts to improve the fit between political culture and democratic institutions.

Tracing the source of parliamentarism's divergent outcomes to society's cultural foundations possesses a strong intuitive appeal; after all, how could one expect a democratic regime to function stably and effectively if its citizens are not guided in their political behavior by democratic values and orientations? Nevertheless, on closer examination, the connection between the political orientations of the average citizen and the functioning of parliamentary government became somewhat murky, given that (1) most citizens have relatively little involvement in politics and (2) the political elites who operate the system often do not share mass political orientations. There were, in addition, the very successes of West Germany in transforming cultural values (Conradt 1980) and of France in institutional engineering to get around them to be reckoned with; neither is particularly compatible with a strong interpretation of the constraining role of culture.

Political culturalists were not oblivious to the need to establish a more tangible linkage between mass political attitudes and elite institutional functioning. For the most part, the interpretation they favored was that cultural traits such as political distrust, intolerance, and the lack of overarching bonds of solidarity undermine democratic functioning because they reflect a society divided along fundamental lines.[2] Given the opportunity, societies composed of hostile, distrusting subgroups typically tend to produce party systems mirroring these divisions, and where no subgroup is majoritarian, it may be very difficult to find sufficient interparty agreement on policy issues to generate stable coalition governments. In such circumstances, the result is likely to be governments that fall apart quickly because they cannot agree on what to do, or else occupy power only so long as they agree to do nothing.

This interpretation of parliamentarism's darker face, although very popular, has never gained universal acceptance. Its most persistent challenger is a perspective that views politics in the Italian and French parliamentary republics in a fundamentally opposed way. Where the standard interpretation sees ideological divisiveness as a fundamental characteristic of parliamentary life in these regimes, exponents of this latter view see collegiality; where the first view sees instability, they see stability, even excessive stability. The key for this school is the actual behavior of parliamentarians. Although ideological differences may appear to be highly developed and strongly articulated in these systems, various observers (Jouvenel 1914; Leites 1959; Lapalombara 1987) have noted that relations among parliamentarians of different parties are guided by elaborate rules of courtesy and respect; the advancement of careers, not the cultivation of principle, appears to be the true goal of political life. More significantly, beneath the apparent instability of governments lies a profound stability of ministers. Governments change frequently but they are made up largely of the same parties and the same individuals. The politeness of parliamentary life reflects this reality; cabinet ministers may disagree with their coalition partners, yet their conduct is tempered by an awareness that they will probably have to collaborate with them in future governments. Indeed, the very stability of ministers may provoke the largely epiphenomenal instability of governments: because party leaders know that their support will be needed to form future coalition governments, they may defect from the present one all the more easily. Governmental instability, in this view, is more often the result of the jockeying for position in the next government than it is a question of policy differences, and the fundamental weakness of these regimes is more likely to be not extreme instability, but extreme stability induced by the relative absence of turnover in governmental personnel.

These two interpretations seem diametrically opposed, but the gap may not be as unbridgeable as it appears. For one thing, it is possible to argue that the elaborate rules of courtesy and the pervasive careerism manifest in the parliamentary arenas of these regimes are consequences of the intense political divisions among parties and the resultant inability of any one party to achieve its political program – in other words, that policy gridlock induces a displacement of objectives.[3] For another, since even supporters of the more "benign" perspective would be reluctant to describe these regimes as models of democratic governance, it may be suspected that the differences in interpretation have more to do with different usages of the term *stability* than with different evaluations of the systems themselves. Sartori (1976), in a classic study of party systems, provided a framework that clarifies these points.

The thrust of Sartori's approach is to divide competitive party systems into two basic types, each with its own "mechanics." The first type, which comprises two-party systems and moderate pluralist (three- to five-party) systems, is "bipolar" in its operation: two sides, composed of either single parties or coalitions of parties, compete with each other for political power. In this competition, each side moderates its political position in an attempt to win a majority of parliamentary seats in general elections; and the result, at least over the long term, will usually be an alternation in power between the two. This type corresponds, generally speaking, to the stable and effective variant of parliamentary government.

The second type identified by Sartori characterizes party systems that are fragmented (usually more than five significant parties) and polarized ideologically. Its most essential structural feature is the existence of sizable "antisystem" parties at both extremes of the Left–Right political spectrum. Because antisystem parties are usually considered unacceptable as coalition partners, governing majorities must be formed from the remaining prosystem parties. The result is perpetual rule from the center. Coalitions composed of the center plus the moderate Right may alternate with coalitions of the center plus the moderate Left, but as long as the extremes of Right and Left are large, the center itself must remain in power. Even so, governmental instability is rife in these systems. Governments collapse easily because they necessarily include diverse coalition partners (given the ideological polarization of the entire system) and because many of these partners know they risk little in abandoning governments as their advantage dictates: their chances of returning to office are excellent.

In policy terms, the consequence of perpetual center rule is immobilism: the divisions within governing coalitions, the fact that they usually contain one or more parties committed to the status quo, and the lack of a viable alternative waiting in the wings all ensure that government action will be difficult to come by. Rather than focusing on policy, therefore, coalition partners or potential coalition partners turn their attention to things that can be achieved: career advancement, patronage allocation, logrolling on the less charged issues, and so forth. From this follows the distinction between the "visible" politics of ideological rhetoric and the "invisible" (and thus apparently more fundamental) politics of polite pragmatism that fascinates students of the parliamentary scene and disgusts partisans of its various ideological tendencies.

Sartori's analysis of polarized pluralism not only accommodates manifestations of both ideological and pragmatic political behavior; it also encompasses both stability and instability. Simply put, the instability resides in the high rate of government turnover, whereas the stability refers to the high probability that subsequent governments will resemble their predecessors in party composition and ministerial personnel. *Immobilism* is probably a better term for the latter characteristic because it references not only the continuity in personnel but the policy stalemate as well. This stalemate is important in Sartori's analysis because it contributes to a migration of popular support toward the antisystem parties and thus to the overall instability of this type of parliamentary system – its instability in a larger sense.

From the observation that parliamentary systems seem to subdivide into stable, effective Westminster-style variants and chaotic, immobilist "Italian" types, we have moved to a consideration of cultural characteristics, the societal divisions they reflect, and the very different party-system types that result from both. In Sartori's framework, the Janus-faced nature of parliamentarism is traced to one key intervening factor, the bifurcation in the mechanics of competitive party systems. The absense of disciplined, majoritarian parties or coalitions identified earlier as a major impediment to effective government in some parliamentary systems is thereby accounted for as an intrinsic feature of their party systems.

The very Manicheanism of the framework, so appealing from a theoretical standpoint because of its lack of ambiguity, involves a price, however: vulnerability at an empirical level. While it can be plausibly argued that the German Weimar Republic (1919–33) and the French Fourth Republic (1946–58), whose party systems displayed all the basic characteristics of polarized pluralism, were weak regimes that commanded little popular support and fell easily in crisis situations, the present Italian regime has defied predictions of an early demise. The destabilizing tendency of Italian voters to migrate to the political extremes, which Sartori demonstrated for the period before 1975, has largely waned since that time; even the present corruption crisis feeds calls for reform of the system rather than its dissolution. Like the French Third Republic (1875–1940), the Italian parliamentary regime has displayed a staying power, despite the periods of economic difficulty and political turmoil, that sustains the more benign interpretation of its government instability.

Another indication that the dichotomy between moderate and polarized pluralism may be too extreme can be found in comparative data on government durations. Table 1.1 presents, in ascending order, the mean durations of governments in sixteen West European parliamentary democracies for the postwar period up till 1989.[4] Although the order of regimes clearly progresses from polarized pluralist systems (Fourth Republic France and Italy) to moderate pluralist systems, there is no sharp break in the series. Rather, the list of mean durations resembles a continuum with no obvious place to draw a distinction between stable and unstable systems. The real world does not seem as clear-cut as the theory would lead us to expect.

These observations do not in themselves invalidate Sartori's party-system framework, but they do suggest the need for further empirical study of the determinants of government survival across a diverse set of parliamentary systems. If the benign or pragmatic interpretation of government instability is to be effectively countered, convincing evidence would have to be produced that issues of ideology or policy undermine the ability of governments to survive in office and implement policies. Sartori's analysis follows, and systematizes, a long-standing hypothesis that identifies the ideological diversity within governments as crucial

Table 1.1. *Mean government duration in sixteen West European parliamentary systems (1945-89)*

Country	Period	Mean duration in days
France (Fourth Republic)	1945-58	141.6
Italy	1948-89	251.0
Portugal	1976-89	312.3
Finland	1947-89	319.1
Belgium	1946-89	450.4
Denmark	1945-89	578.5
Netherlands	1946-89	649.7
West Germany	1949-89	671.0
Sweden	1948-89	744.6
Norway	1945-89	753.7
Iceland	1947-89	779.2
Austria	1945-89	800.6
United Kingdom	1945-89	850.2
Spain	1979-89	925.8
Ireland	1948-89	935.0
Luxembourg	1945-89	1,106.6

Note: These data are based on the CDS definition of governments, discussed in Chapter 2. Alternative definitions produce only slight changes in the means.

in this regard, yet largely because this factor is inherently so difficult to measure, its empirical connection with government survival has only rarely been investigated.

Nor is this the only plausible linkage between ideology and government survival. Game-theoretic models, which have become common in recent years, posit an alternative means by which the ideological or policy positions of parties may affect the survival of governing coalitions. The basic premise of these models is that coalitions fall apart, not because their members cannot agree among themselves, but because the larger parliamentary environment affords at least one member party the possibility of entering an alternative coalition whose policy position will be more favorable to itself. In other words, it is not the difficulties within existing coalitions so much as it is the prospects of better deals elsewhere that lead parties to terminate coalitions. This is a very different hypothesis from the ideological diversity hypothesis, but it, too, has received little empirical investigation. Moreover, none of it has been conducted in direct confrontation with the ideological diversity hypothesis.

Other hypotheses could be mentioned at this point, but the ones introduced so far are sufficient to establish the conclusion that theoretical work on government survival has run ahead of empirical testing. A great deal of energy has been expended over the past twenty-five years to develop theories and models that can account for (or explain away) variations in government survival in and across parliamentary regimes, but relatively little has been established in a rigorous manner. The consequences of this situation are serious: it means, among other things, that we still cannot be sure whether to interpret governmental instability as epiphenomenal or fundamental to system performance. This study's primary objective is to redress this imbalance.

THE DEBATE OVER THE NATURE OF THE PHENOMENON

The preceding discussion raises some very basic questions about the sources of government survival in parliamentary regimes, but behind them lurks an even more basic one: is causality involved at all? The scholarly debate as characterized in the preceding section rests on the assumption that survival in office depends on one or more causal processes that, in principle, are identifiable through further empirical work. From this perspective, the fact that researchers continue to disagree over the role ideology or policy plays in government survival is attributable to nothing more than the difficulties of measuring accurately the ideological positions of parties. The unspoken premise is that government survival must be approached from a causal perspective, even if every suspected cause cannot readily be measured.

Most of the empirical work done on government survival since the 1960s conforms to this basic epistemological stance. It has repeatedly been shown that majority governments survive longer than minority ones (Blondel 1968; Sanders and Herman 1977) and that minimal winning governments – governments that need all of their member parties to command a parliamentary majority – are more long-lived than other governments (Laver 1974). Dodd (1976) demonstrated that duration increases as governments approach the minimal winning condition. If the incentive of holding onto power keeps coalitions together, it has also been shown – in fairly rudimentary ways – that ideological diversity may have the opposite effect. Axelrod (1970) combined the minimal winning condition with the stipulation that the coalition members be adjacent on a Left–Right continuum and found that these "minimal connected winning" coalitions lasted significantly longer. De Swaan (1973) reported some explanatory value in replacing the connectedness criterion with that of minimal range on the Left–Right continuum. I produced evidence indicating that the involvement of both socialist and nonsocialist parties or clerical and nonclerical parties in governing coalitions undermines their durability (Warwick 1979). That bargaining complexity is inimical to longevity is suggested by evidence that party-system fragmentation is associated with shorter durations (Taylor and Herman 1971; Sanders and Herman 1977). Finally, Robertson (1983a, 1983b, 1983c) reported evidence that economic conditions, especially unemployment levels, are statistically linked to government survival. This list of reported relationships is not exhaustive, but it does reflect the overall correspondence between empirical findings and commonsense causality.

Notwithstanding the common sense, the causal focus of this research came under fundamental attack in the 1980s from a group of scholars headed by E. C. Browne. Their starting point was the observation that "with one exception, none of these studies has been able to explain more than 20 to 30 percent of the variation in government or coalition duration. This is not a very impressive result for more than ten years of empirical work" (Browne, Frendreis, and Gleiber 1986:630). Against the orthodox view that further progress depends only on better measures of some of the independent variables, Browne et al. (1986:634) argued that "the existing methodology has, perhaps, reached an upper level of predictability." Rather than develop a better methodology to advance the process of causal explanation, they suggested instead that the search for causes be abandoned.

The reason Browne and his associates did not advocate the search for a better methodology is very simple: they do not believe the methodology is the problem. In their view, the inability of independent variables such as those cited earlier to explain large amounts of variance in government duration relates to the fact that they all reference government or parliamentary attributes whose values are fixed or set at the time a government takes office; none takes account of the (subsequent) events that actually bring governments down. The kind of events they had in mind include political scandals, international crises, illnesses or deaths of prime ministers, and the like. The important feature of government-toppling events such as these is that they occur independently of any parliamentary or government characteristics and therefore cannot be explained by them. Indeed, since events such as these are essentially random with respect to the parliamentary arena, the occurrence of government terminations must be random as well. Thus, given the stochastic nature of the underlying process, the search for causes – no matter how sophisticated it becomes – is bound to come up short.

The "events" hypothesis marks a very important turning point in the study of government survival because it destroyed the complacency that surrounded previous research on the issue. The search for systematic relationships between government duration and various proposed independent variables assumes that systematic relationships must exist; if the underlying process is random, however, it would mean not only that the search is ultimately bound to fail, but also that there may be no way to account for the very different outcomes observed in different parliamentary systems. Taking the events hypothesis to its logical extreme implies that whether a given parliamentary system experiences short-lived or long-lived governments is purely a matter of chance.[5] A central feature of democratic politics, in other words, would escape systematic explanation.

The events theorists probably never intended their hypothesis to be taken that far. The empirical analyses they performed revealed that only four of twelve countries tested had distributions of government durations consistent with the assumption of an underlying process of random collapses (Browne et al. 1986:643). Moreover, the four countries in question – Belgium, Finland, Italy, and Israel – are all among the more unstable countries in their sample.[6] This pattern suggests that the parliamentary systems whose governments lack the characteristics associated with durability are the ones most at risk to government-threatening events; conversely, governments with the requisite characteristics may be relatively immune from them. Browne, Frendreis, and Gleiber (1986:645–7) not only acknowledged this point; they presented evidence that the four countries conforming to the events hypothesis have significantly higher mean levels of certain traits previously shown to be associated with instability, including (1) the number of parties in government, (2) the spanning of my socialist–nonsocialist and clerical–secular cleavage lines, and (3) nonminimal winning status. In their words,

We are driven to the conclusion that the quality of cabinets we have called "inherent stability," while weak as an explanatory factor conditioning duration in all countries, is variable across countries and sufficiently strong in some countries to introduce a systematic (as opposed to perfectly random) element into the timing of cabinet dissolutions." (Browne et al. 1986:649)

This concession may seem grudging, but it was achieved at great cost to the events theorists. Previously, the interpretation was that differences among countries in dissolution rates were due to "country-specific idiosyncratic attributes" (Browne, Gleiber, and Mashoba 1984:24); now they were willing to admit that systematic factors were involved. The difference is crucial because, while idiosyncratic differences among systems may not be amenable to comparative analysis, systematic factors in principle are. Moreover, it means that any valid explanation of government survival or dissolution must at least temper the impact of random outside events with a consideration of general governmental attributes the possession of which provides protection from their destabilizing potential. The events hypothesis raised a new consideration; it did not invalidate the old epistemology. Nevertheless, that new consideration turned out to have immense implications for future research.

THE UNIFICATION OF PERSPECTIVES

The epistemological debate as cast by the events theorists centered on the question: which is more important in determining how long governments stay in power – random outside events or the structural features of governments and/or parliaments that may provide protection from them? This focus found play in a dispute between the events theorists and myself over which types of government termination ought to be considered as valid for the purposes of analysis. My earlier empirical work on survival in parliamentary regimes had excluded any government "whose termination was unconnected with the idea of instability" (Warwick 1979:468). This exclusion principally concerned governments that took office sometime after the beginning of a parliamentary term and ended with the arrival of the next regularly scheduled elections; the rationale was that it is impossible to say how long these governments would have lasted if the requirement of new elections had not forced their end.[7] Browne, Frendreis, and Gleiber (1984) objected that these exclusions were unwarranted and may have served to enhance the explained variance above the 20–30% range of other studies. Easton and I responded that Browne et al.'s inclusion of these cases had the contrary effect of introducing an unjustified degree of randomness into the data (Warwick and Easton 1992).[8]

The reasoning behind this counterclaim is as follows. Since the arrival of regular elections is unconnected with any government attributes, the distribution of durations brought on by regular elections is bound to appear random or uncaused. But elections whose timing is established in advance by statute cannot reasonably be considered to be random events that just crop up and topple governments. Not only is their occurrence not random, but even the events theorists do not treat them as "events" in the sense of their hypothesis: to have done so would have required considering a government that wins an election and stays in power as having survived the challenge imposed by the outside environment. Instead, the events theorists defined each election as marking the end of the government that encountered it, regardless of its outcome.[9]

Clearly, the punctuation of government durations by regularly scheduled elections posed a dilemma for both the causal and the stochastic approaches. If it was undesirable in principle to exclude any category of government termination from the analysis, it also seemed inappropriate to treat these situations as equivalent to terminations brought on by parliamentary defeat, coalition disintegration, and the like. What was required was some means of including them in the analysis, as Browne and his associates insisted, but of treating them as "special." What was true of this skirmish was true of the larger debate as well. Although proponents of the two approaches bickered vehemently (Browne, Frendreis, and Gleiber 1988; Strom 1988), it was difficult to avoid the conclusion that future progress would require some means of combining the two perspectives. There was plenty of evidence that certain attributes provide "inherent stability" to governments, but by the same token, was it not also reasonable to suppose that unanticipated outside events must occasionally bring down governments, particularly those that lack the appropriate attributes? Rather than debate which perspective was the more fundamental, a more productive strategy would be to explore what could be achieved if both perspectives were allied in some fashion.[10]

The methodology to handle this challenge was, in fact, waiting in the wings. It goes by different names in different fields: in medicine it is survival analysis; in engineering, reliability analysis; in economics, duration analysis; in sociology, event history analysis. In all applications, it consists essentially of explaining the "hazard rate," or the rate at which terminating events occur (people die, machines break down, episodes end, transitions from one state to another occur), as a function of a set of independent variables and an underlying termination rate. This underlying rate may be defined so as to capture systematic changes in the rate of termination over time or to mirror a process of random terminations, such as the events theorists postulated. In addition, terminations that are deemed to be artificial, such as those imposed on governments by the electoral timetable, can be adjusted statistically to correct for any bias they convey.

The first application of event history analysis to the government survival issue was undertaken by King, Alt, Burns, and Laver (1990). Their effort at unifying causal and stochastic approaches consisted basically of inserting causal factors or attributes into the events framework. The events theorists had reasoned that if terminations are caused by random outside events, there would be no reason to suppose a government more likely to end on any one day as opposed to any other; in other words, a government's risk of termination should be approximately constant over its lifetime. Since the frequency distribution of durations in a data set prepared by Strom[11] displayed a shape that was consistent with this assumption, King et al. accepted the argument that a process of random collapses was involved. However, rather than assuming, as the events theorists had, that each country possesses a unique hazard or termination rate owing to its "idiosyncratic attributes," they made the hazard rate a log-linear function of a set of independent variables. As we shall see in Chapter 2, this is equivalent to explaining duration as a product of the independent variables and an exponentially distributed error term.

The solution to the issue of what to do with governments whose periods in office were cut short by regular elections is equally elegant. In examining the Strom data set, King and associates also noticed an unusual concentration of cases that had terminated at or just after thirty-six months in power. They reasoned that thirty-six months must be the point at which government dissolutions begin to occur in anticipation of approaching elections. On this basis, they decided that the durations of governments that began immediately after general elections and lasted until within twelve months of the next elections ought to be adjusted statistically for this effect. How this is done in event history analysis is developed in the next chapter; suffice it to say here that the technique involves treating the "true" durations as at least as great as the recorded durations – in other words, leaving open the possibility that these governments would have lasted longer if regular elections had not come along when they did. Thus, in the King et al., or KABL, model, no cases are excluded, but the durations of some governments are treated statistically as less informative than others, reflecting the disruptive impact of elections on government duration data.

It is ironic that the events theorists' foray into the field of government stability, which began by criticizing the existing (regression) methodology of "attributes" studies and ended up by rejecting the causal epistemology itself, should have stimulated the adoption of a new methodology much better attuned to the causal analysis of the issue. Nevertheless, the upshot of the debate between attributes theorists and "stochasticists" was a result beyond what either side anticipated: the introduction of an approach that supercedes the need to choose between attributes and random events and that has the flexibility to handle cases that fit neither of the previous frameworks satisfactorily. If, as the next section will argue, there are shortcomings in the KABL model, it nevertheless illustrates the capacity of event history analysis to overcome difficult obstacles that have inhibited the empirical investigation of government survival.

The principal value of the KABL model of government dissolution is that it showed the way in which certain issues that had divided attributes theorists and events theorists could be resolved. However, it did not itself resolve all of those issues. The deficiencies in the model that are discussed next are not presented to minimize the contribution of King and his colleagues, but rather to illustrate the extraordinary potential of event history methodology – a potential this study will attempt to exploit.

The model that King et al. developed with the aid of the Strom data set contains seven independent variables. Of these, four are dichotomous: investiture, majority status, postelection status, and caretaker status. They indicate, respectively, whether or not a government (1) had to undergo a vote of investiture, (2) was majoritarian, (3) was the first government formed after an election, and (4) was a caretaker government. A fifth variable, formation attempts, registers the number of failed attempts that preceded the successful formation of a government. Finally, there are two continuous variables: fractionalization (a measure of the number and size of parties in the parliament) and polarization (the proportion of parliamentary seats held by extremist parties).

The principal success of this set of independent variables is in accounting for differences in termination rates among parliamentary systems; King and associates were able to show that no significant improvement, statistically speaking, results from adding "idiosyncratic" differences among countries to the model.[12] This finding represents a vindication of the concession made by Browne et al. that systematic factors may, after all, account for these cross-system differences. What the model fails to do is address fully the import of their criticism of the fixed nature of attributes used in causal studies: clearly, all seven independent variables in the KABL model take on their values at or before the time of government formation. It is true that the model incorporates the possibility that random events occurring during a government's lifetime bring about its demise (through the assumption of an underlying exponential distribution of durations), but fixed and random effects are not the only possibilities. Although the events hypothesis tends to conjure up the image of totally random and unexpected government-toppling events, such as an unanticipated international crisis, a government may also be brought down by much more orderly and foreseeable processes that take place during its lifetime – a worsening of the economy, for example. Factors such as the state of the economy are neither fixed nor random; they represent potential influences that change with time but may affect government survival in very systematic ways.[13]

One of the strengths of event history analysis is that it permits the assessment of the impact of "time-varying covariates," that is, variables that take on different values over the lifetime of a case. This type of analysis is not the same as a time-series regression analysis in which different cases represent values of the same dependent and independent variables at different times. Rather, the time variation in event history analysis takes place within single cases. This means that any variable whose changing values over time can be measured, for example, economic indicators, can be introduced into the analysis as a potential cause; there is no reason to relegate such effects to the random component in the model.

There is another kind of time-varying effect that is distinguishable from that produced by random events and indeed can be considered a rival to the events interpretation. This effect pertains to the underlying termination rate or "baseline hazard." Earlier, I noted that King and his associates accepted the events theorists' assumption of a constant hazard on the basis of the shape of the frequency distribution of durations in the sample they used. However, as Chapter 2 will demonstrate, there are a number of different hazard-rate assumptions that could have produced a frequency distribution with that shape. Fortunately, there is no need to assume a particular hazard function on the basis of the distribution of durations (or the plausibility of preexisting hypotheses) because more reliable means of assessing the underlying process are available.

It is important to realize what a nonconstant underlying hazard, if it exists, would mean: instead of a process of random terminations, there would be a rate of termination that changes systematically over time. It may be that certain factors exert their strongest effect relatively early on in the lifetimes of governments; once past this hurdle, survival may then become less difficult. Other factors may operate in the opposite way, primarily affecting relatively long-lived governments. More complex patterns are also possible. One can readily appreciate that, as a practical matter, effects of this sort may be difficult to measure directly, but their existence and relative importance can be assessed quantitatively through an estimation of the baseline hazard. The capacity to assess time-varying effects whose causes are themselves unknown is one of the most remarkable features of event history analysis.

A third area in which the KABL model seems deficient is in its choice of fixed covariates. It is relatively easy to interpret the findings that majority governments and those formed immediately after elections are advantaged in terms of survival and that caretaker governments and those that must undergo investiture votes are disadvantaged; the latter two factors are regarded by King et al. as "control" (as opposed to causal) variables in any case. But what of the causal roles of the remaining independent variables – formation attempts, fractionalization, and polarization? What makes it difficult to interpret the causal impact on government survival of variables such as the latter two, in particular, is that they clearly reference characteristics of parliaments, not governments. King et al. suggest that all three variables reflect the complexity of the bargaining environment in the parliament, but they never explain precisely how a complex bargaining environment would act to curtail the longevity of governments formed in it.

Possibilities may, of course, be suggested. One favored by Laver and Schofield (1990) is that the complex array of parties and party positions in some parliaments makes it difficult to arrive at an optimal coalition solution and increases the likelihood that small perturbations (events) in the environment will redistribute the parties' bargaining power and thereby upset any solution that has been reached.

This argument embodies the game-theoretic assumption that parties will remain in existing coalitions, however unworkable they may be, until more attractive coalitional alternatives present themselves. Another possibility is that a complex bargaining environment simply means a party system highly divided along ideological/policy lines. It is worth recalling in this regard that the pivotal feature of Sartori's polarized pluralist systems is the strong presence of antisystem parties; this is, after all, what the polarization variable measures. In Sartori's framework, however, antisystem parties are not a direct cause of government instability or immobilism. Instead, their impact is mediated by another factor: the necessity, given the parliamentary weight of the antisystem parties, to form prosystem governments that are themselves ideologically diverse in order to command a parliamentary majority. In this interpretation, the real culprit is the ideological diversity contained within coalition governments, a factor not measured in the Strom data set.

In making this observation, the intention is not to discredit King et al.'s theoretical orientation; rather, the point is that their independent variables are not very informative about what actually is going on. King et al. (1990:848–9) clearly mean to subsume their results under the Laver and Schofield argument, but as we have seen, an interpretation in terms of ideological divisions within governments may account for the results just as well. If we are to make progress in explaining government survival, a necessary step must be to avoid, wherever possible, the use of proxy variables whose connection with underlying theoretical arguments is unclear or ambiguous and undertake a more direct testing of hypothesized causes.

ORGANIZATION OF THE BOOK

The first section of this chapter developed the suggestion that theoretical work on the sources of government survival in parliamentary regimes has run ahead of the empirical testing needed to support it; subsequent sections have attempted to show that an appropriate statistical methodology – event history analysis – is now available to remedy the situation. Although the events theorists undoubtedly were justified in pointing to the limitations in the types of factors the attributes theorists had tested and in the results they had obtained, the introduction of this methodology means that these limitations need no longer apply. In what follows, I outline the manner in which this study attempts to overcome them.

Chapter 2 contains a brief introduction to the concepts and techniques of event history analysis that are most relevant in the investigation. Particular attention is paid to the distinction between the partial likelihood method, which ignores both the nature and the effect of the baseline hazard function, and the method of maximum likelihood estimation, which requires that the nature of the baseline hazard be known or assumed. For our purposes, both techniques are valuable, the former to track down relevant independent variables, the latter to combine these causes with the underlying tendencies expressed by the baseline hazard function.

Chapter 2 also discusses the nature of the data set that has been prepared for this enterprise. This data set covers the sixteen European parliamentary democracies listed in Table 1.1 from the resumption of normal politics after the Second World

War until 1989. The watchword that guided its development was comprehensiveness: I have attempted both to incorporate a very broad range of potential influences on government survival and to allow for every reasonable way in which key concepts might be defined. For example, the data set contains six different definitions of a government, from the most narrow (which includes only parties in the cabinet) to the most comprehensive (which adds parties that declare their willingness or are known to be willing to support or abstain in favor of the cabinet). Since much of the debate over government survival has involved how concepts should be defined, one of the goals of this study is to identify relationships that do not depend on these kinds of considerations.

In Chapter 3, the focus shifts to the examination of the possible causal roles of a wide variety of parliamentary and government attributes, most of which have been proposed in earlier studies. These studies by and large have tended to concentrate on the particular independent variables of interest to the investigators, rather than testing those factors against the full range of available rivals. As the work of King and associates illustrates, there has also been a tendency to mix parliamentary and government characteristics indiscriminately, without questioning very closely how a characteristic of parliamentary systems could have a direct effect on the survival of governments. In this chapter, I examine the relative roles of both types of attributes and use the continued presence of parliamentary properties in the model as an indicator of what remains to be achieved.

Chapter 4 expands the search for causes beyond the standard range of government and parliamentary attributes to incorporate what is probably the most elusive of potential causes, the ideological diversity within governments. As we have seen, there is a major line of interpretation that culminates in the thesis that ideological diversity within governments brings about their downfall; there are also, it should be added, many doubters of this proposition. Ideological diversity has been neglected in empirical studies largely because it is inherently so difficult to operationalize, but the situation needs to be addressed in some fashion. In this study, measures of the ideological diversity within governments are developed using a wide variety of sources, including voter-based definitions of the ideological positions of parties, expert scales of party positions, and measures of party positions derived from content analyses of party platforms. The objective is to undertake the most comprehensive test ever attempted of the hypothesis linking ideological diversity to government survival.

No matter how elaborate the measurement of fixed attributes, they can never provide a complete explanation of government survival. Clearly, developments that occur during the lifetimes of governments must also be taken into account, and foremost among these are changes in the economy. Chapter 5 introduces a dynamic element to the investigation by examining the effect that changing levels of consumer prices, unemployment, and gross domestic product per capita have on the fortunes of parliamentary governments.

The preceding analyses are undertaken without assuming any particular shape to the baseline hazard function. In Chapter 6, the method of analysis changes from partial likelihood to maximum likelihood estimation, and the underlying rate of termination becomes the focus of attention. Is this rate constant over the lifetimes of governments, as the hypothesis of random government-ending events predicts, or is there a trend of increasing or decreasing survivability over time? This second type of dynamic effect is one of the most difficult to tease out, but it is also the effect about which we have the least prior information and therefore, perhaps, the most curiosity.

The model that emerges from the analyses of Chapter 3 through 6 is fundamentally at variance with earlier models rooted in the game-theoretic tradition, including the KABL model. Given that its derivation – like those of its predecessors – rests on a particular conceptualization of the subject matter, it is important that the model's robustness with respect to alternative conceptualizations be tested. Chapter 7 exploits the definitional options built into the data set in order to test the model's robustness when definitions of governments, durations, and valid terminations are varied. Also explored in this chapter is the validity of the variables in the model – do they really measure what they are intended to measure? – and the model's overall explanatory power.

Chapter 8 attempts to put the myriad empirical findings of the preceding five chapters into perspective. What have we been able to discover concerning the fixed and dynamic determinants of government survival? How do these findings relate to the theoretical literature on government survival, and what amendments to that literature, if any, do they suggest? Most important, can the findings of this study provide a better understanding of the differences in the functioning of parliamentary regimes in countries such as Britain and Italy? It is no exaggeration to say that the value of this undertaking must ultimately be judged by its success in accounting for the two faces of parliamentary government.

2

The quantitative study of government survival

The rapid evolution in research on parliamentary government survival in recent years has involved a major shift in methodology from regression approaches to event history analysis. This shift brings with it several advantages, including a more satisfactory treatment of "artificial" government terminations, the possibility of incorporating time-varying covariates, and the capacity to estimate the effects of unmeasured time-dependent factors. It also involves the loss of a familiar signpost of empirical success for political scientists, the coefficient of determination (R^2). Because event history methodology is relatively unknown in political science, this chapter presents a brief development of its guiding principles and the manner in which it will be utilized for the investigation of government survival.

THE "EVENTS" METHODOLOGY

The most suitable way of introducing event history analysis in the present context is to trace the steps that led to its emergence in the government survival literature. The purposes of orienting the discussion in this manner are threefold: (1) to add methodological substance to the review of recent developments presented in the previous chapter, (2) to specify more precisely the nature of the deficiencies in that work, and (3) to indicate the ways in which these deficiencies will be tackled in this study. Because the discussion keeps technical details to a minimum, interested readers may wish to consult other sources, such as Tuma and Hannan (1984), Kiefer (1988), and Blossfeld, Hamerle, and Mayer (1989), for more complete treatments.

We begin with the initial (and unintended) stimulus, the "events" hypothesis advanced by Browne, Frendreis, and Gleiber (1984, 1986, 1988). The essence of this hypothesis, it will be recalled, is that government terminations occur as a result of critical events cropping up unpredictably in the environments of governments. The implication is that researchers should no longer concern themselves with explaining government survival but instead turn their attention to modeling its randomness.

To see how this modeling may be effected, imagine that each government is at risk of termination from the moment of its inception. Clearly, there is some (unconditional) probability that a government will fall on its first day in office, on its second day, and so forth. This gives rise to (1) a probability density function of terminations $f(t)$, which records the probability of termination for any duration time t, and (2) an associated cumulative distribution function $F(t)$, which records the probability of termination at any duration time up to time t. A related conceptualization addresses the question: Given that government i has lasted t_i months, what is the probability that it will terminate at that point? This characterization, which focuses on the *conditional* probability of termination, generates the hazard function. Since $F(t)$ gives the probability that an actual duration t_i is less than some value t, one can also define a survivor function S, $S(t) = 1 - F(t)$, as the probability that t_i equals or exceeds the value t. The hazard rate λ, the conditional rate at which terminations occur at time t, can then be defined as[1]

$$\lambda(t) = f(t)/S(t). \tag{2.1}$$

The hazard rate, or conditional rate of termination, is the central concept in event history analysis; in most applications, it constitutes the dependent variable. No displacement of objectives is involved in casting the analysis in terms of hazard rates rather than duration values because the two are intimately linked: high hazard rates imply short durations and vice versa. To generate a model of the distribution of durations or times to termination, however, it is necessary to make some assumption concerning the nature of the underlying process of terminations. The assumption the events theorists made is that given the randomness of government-toppling events, terminations should occur at a rate that is constant over duration time. In other words, they hypothesized that governments are no more likely to fall on their first day than on their twentieth (given that they have made it to twenty days), or on any other day. This assumption describes a Poisson process of terminal events in which the implied distribution of government durations is exponential:[2]

$$f(t) = \lambda \exp(-\lambda t), \tag{2.2}$$

with the corresponding survivor function

$$S(t) = \exp(-\lambda t). \tag{2.3}$$

Notice that the only parameter in the functions defining $f(t)$ and $S(t)$ is λ, the hazard rate.

That a constant rate of termination should result in a negative or declining exponential distribution of government durations may seem surprising, but its plausibility can be demonstrated with a simple example. Suppose there are a hundred governments under examination and the underlying termination or hazard rate is one-tenth per day.[3] On this basis, we would expect ten governments to fall on the first day. However, the number of surviving governments becomes smaller with each successive day. By the time there are only ten governments left, the hazard rate leads us to expect just one termination per day. Thus, on the assumption of a constant termination rate, the largest number of terminations should occur on the first day, with progressively fewer terminations per day over time. Note that this decline in the daily frequency of terminations is not linear; rather, it becomes ever more gradual as the number of surviving governments diminishes. To reach the point at which the number of terminations per day has fallen from ten to one, for example, requires about twenty-two days. This pattern is characteristic of a negative exponential distribution.

Browne et al. (1986) tested the events hypothesis by assessing, in each of twelve parliamentary democracies, whether the distribution of surviving governments over various duration intervals resembles that produced by the survivor function defined in Equation (2.3), with λ taken as the inverse of the average duration of governments for that country.[4] In contrast to most previous attributes studies, they included both single-party governments and coalition governments (since causal factors are not being considered, there is no longer any reason to distinguish the two situations). Their results, as noted earlier, provided only partial support for the hypothesis: the distributions did not differ significantly (at the .05 level) in just four of those countries – Belgium, Finland, Italy, and Israel.

On the assumption that government-challenging events occur in all parliamentary systems, the failure of the events hypothesis in most systems indicates that there must be factors that allow governments in those systems to withstand challenges that might have toppled governments in the less stable systems. In statistical terms, this means that independent variables must be brought into the picture in some fashion. The solution proposed by King et al. (1990) met this need: it consisted of an event history model that incorporated a set of independent variables or covariates while retaining the notion that the underlying distribution of durations is exponential, consistent with the events hypothesis. The key change that permitted this unification of approaches was to make the hazard rate a function of a set of covariates.

In the King et al., or KABL, model the expected duration $E(t)$ is modeled as

$$E(t) = \exp(\beta'x), \tag{2.4}$$

where x is a (column) vector of covariates and β is a (column) vector of associated coefficients. In the absence of any a priori information on the nature of the relationship, the log-linear specification was chosen because, unlike a linear specification, it precludes negative predicted values for duration. As in the events model, the hazard rate is taken as the inverse of the mean or expected duration:

$$\lambda = 1/E(t) = \exp(-\beta'x). \tag{2.5}$$

The log-linear specification here serves to prevent λ from taking on negative values (hazard rates, by definition, can never be negative).

The task now is to obtain point estimates of the β coefficients. This is done by maximum likelihood estimation (MLE), which generates estimates that maximize the probability or likelihood of getting the sample data in question. Assuming that individual durations are independent of one another, the overall likelihood for the sample is simply the product of the likelihoods of the individual cases:

$$L(\beta \mid t) = \prod_{i=1}^{n} f(t_i, \beta)$$

$$= \prod_{i=1}^{n} \lambda_i \exp(-\lambda_i t_i)$$

$$= \prod_{i=1}^{n} \exp(-\beta' x_i) \exp[-\exp(-\beta' x_i) t_i], \tag{2.6}$$

where the product $\prod$ is taken with respect to the observations $i = 1, \ldots, n$. In practice, it is more convenient to maximize the logarithm of the likelihood function, $L^* = \ln L(\beta \mid t)$:

$$L^*(\beta \mid t) = \sum_{i=1}^{n} \{-\beta' x_i - t_i \exp(-\beta' x_i)\}. \tag{2.7}$$

This solution elegantly combines causal and events perspectives by fitting covariates into an exponentially based likelihood function, but what of the problem of governments that end with regular elections? We have seen that regular elections are not random events that topple governments; rather, they are preset limits to which even the most durable of governments must succumb, by definition if not in reality. In most such cases, it is reasonable to assume that the government would have continued in office had that limit not been reached. Since our interest is with what causes governments of collapse, the question really is: How long would these governments have lasted if regular elections had not come along when they did?

It is, of course, impossible to answer this question with any precision, but we can get around the problem by assessing their likelihoods with the survivor function $S(t)$, rather than with the density $f(t)$. The survivor function in this situation represents the probability that the "true" durations (those that would have occurred if regular elections had not intervened) would have equaled or exceeded the observed durations; using it is equivalent to assuming that the true durations would have been at least as great as the observed durations and would have conformed to the same (exponential) distribution as durations that were not terminated in this fashion. Cases that are so treated are known as *censored* cases and are commonly found in duration or survival studies. Using a dummy variable d to allocate uncensored ($d = 1$) and censored ($d = 0$) cases to $f(t)$ or $S(t)$, respectively, the log-likelihood function with censoring becomes

$$L^*(\beta \mid t) = \sum_{i=1}^{n} d_i \ln f(t_i, \beta) + \sum_{i=1}^{n} (1 - d_i) \ln S(t_i, \beta)$$

$$= \sum_{i=1}^{n} d_i [-\beta' x_i - \exp(-\beta' x_i) t_i] + \sum_{i=1}^{n} (1 - d_i)[(-\beta' x_i) t_i]. \tag{2.8}$$

King and associates assessed this model on the Strom data set, which covers fifteen postwar parliamentary democracies. Arguing that the analysis should extend to the complete universe of governments, they rejected the events theorists' practice of excluding noninvested governments and caretaker governments;[5] instead, they introduced dummy "control" variables to register any significant differences in the hazard rates of these types of government. On the assumption that the concentration of terminations they observed at about thirty-six months (see Chapter 1) reflects a tendency for governments nearing the end of their term to leave power at a time that appears to be to their electoral advantage, they censored all cases whose durations reached twelve months of the maximum possible term of office (the "constitutional interelection period" or CIEP). With these specifications, they were successful in showing significant effects on the hazard rate from seven covariates, including the caretaker and investiture dummy variables.

CHALLENGING THE ASSUMPTIONS

There can be little doubt that the KABL model marked an important step forward in research on this topic. It has always been evident that there are systematic factors that influence governmental survival (that majority governments last longer than minority governments, for instance) and that random, unforeseeable events can occasionally provoke government collapses. (The fall of the Italian government following the hijacking of the *Achille Lauro* in 1985 is a good example.) The incorporation of these two facets of reality within a single model should bring to an end much pointless debate over whether to adopt a stochastic or a causal framework. Although the event-history approach is clearly an appropriate way to reconcile the two perspectives, however, I noted in the preceding chapter that the particular reconciliation advanced by King et al. raises certain concerns.

Some of these concerns can be illustrated by placing the KABL model in a larger context. The model partakes of a common formulation in event history analysis that conceives of the hazard rate as a log-linear function of a set of covariates and an underlying trend, known as the baseline hazard. The general form of this model is

$$\lambda(t) = \exp(\beta'x(t))\lambda_0(t), \qquad (2.9)$$

where $\lambda_0(t)$ is the baseline hazard.[6]

This formulation expands on the KABL model in two very important respects: it allows both the covariates x and the baseline hazard $\lambda_0(t)$ to vary over the lifetimes of governments. The stipulation that the covariates x may be time-varying means that the rate of government termination at any duration time t can be related to, say, economic conditions prevailing at t, rather than to average economic conditions pertaining to the government's period in office or to any other fixed value. It is this feature that allows the model to assess the effects on survival of systematic developments or trends occurring during the lifetimes of governments.

The other novel component of the model, the baseline hazard $\lambda_0(t)$, is intended to capture the underlying trend in the hazard once the effects of all measured covariates, both fixed and time-varying, have been taken into account. Given the linkage between hazard rates and duration values, the specification of a baseline hazard is equivalent to specifying an underlying distribution for the duration values; in this sense it is akin to specifying the distribution of the disturbance term in regression analysis. Theoretical premises and/or empirical evidence typically provide the grounds for choosing a particular baseline hazard. The exponential specification employed by King and his associates, for example, follows from the belief that random outside events generate the baseline hazard. This specification, however, is merely the simplest of a wide variety that might have been made.

The general model thus suggests two areas in which the KABL model may be deficient: its omission of time-varying covariates and its assumption of a constant baseline hazard. Since much of this study deals with the selection of an appropriate set of both fixed and time-varying covariates, the following subsection concentrates on the issue of the underlying distribution.

The distribution assumption

The assumption made by the events theorists and by King et al. that the times to government termination are drawn from an exponential distribution is attractive because it fits the theoretical argument attributing terminations to random events that follow a Poisson process. But there are many potential candidates for modeling duration data, and interpretative appeal should not be the sole criterion for selection. To add further weight to their choice, King et al. pointed to the (smoothed) shape of the empirical distribution of durations. This justification can be assessed with the aid of Figure 2.1, which plots the frequency distribution of durations in the Strom data set.[7] Each point in the figure represents the proportion of all durations, measured along the vertical axis, associated with a particular duration value on the horizontal axis. The exponential distribution that fits these data is plotted as a solid line. Although the fit of the exponential seems to be reasonable on visual inspection, there are a number of other distributions whose density functions are sufficiently similar so as to appear to fit the actual observations. To make this point graphically, two other density functions are plotted in Figure 2.1: the Weibull and the log-logistic.[8] What becomes very evident in examining the figure is that the plot of the duration frequencies offers little guidance in identifying which distribution might be generating the sample.

A clearer differentiation among distributions can often be detected in the graphs of their hazard functions. The simplest is the hazard function for an exponential distribution, which, as noted earlier, is constant over time. All other distributions have hazards that vary with time, a property known as *duration dependence*. For example, the Weibull distribution may exhibit either positive (an increasing hazard rate) or negative duration dependence (a falling hazard rate). The log-logistic is somewhat more complex: it can display a hazard rate that increases initially and then falls. The distinctiveness of these patterns can be seen clearly in Figure 2.2, which plots the estimated hazard functions associated with the densities of Figure 2.1.

A natural inference from Figure 2.2 is that the first step in any analysis ought to be the plotting of hazard rates against duration time in order to assess the presence

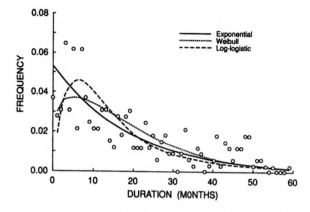

Figure 2.1. Duration frequencies with three fitted distributions (Strom data).

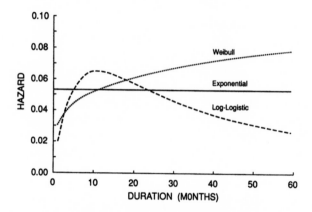

Figure 2.2. Estimated hazard functions for three distributions (Strom data).

and nature of any duration dependency effect. Although this can be done fairly easily, it would be of limited usefulness since we are really interested in the baseline hazard, not the overall hazard. To assess the shape of the baseline hazard, we must be able to disentangle it from the effects of the covariates. Fortunately, there is an event history method that is especially well suited to assist in this task. The method in question is Cox's (1972, 1975) partial likelihood (PL) method, which is capable of estimating covariate effects without knowledge of the nature of the baseline hazard. Because of this feature, the PL method will be used extensively in the next three chapters to sort out possible covariate influences. Once these have been identified, graphic and other methods will be enlisted to assess the nature of the underlying hazard.

The PL method conforms to the supposition that the overall hazard is the product of covariate influences and a baseline hazard as defined in equation (2.9). A key simplifying assumption of that formulation is that the baseline hazard depends only on duration time, which implies that it does not vary across individual cases.[9] The significance of the assumption is that it allows a likelihood function to be constructed solely from the $\exp(\beta'\mathbf{x})$ term – hence the name "partial likelihood."

The PL method begins by ordering all cases according to their durations and then asking of each case: What is the probability that it terminated at its duration time, given that it survived till that time? Since the hazard for a case at any time t represents its conditional probability of terminating at that time, the probability that case i is the one that terminates at time t_i is given by the ratio of its hazard rate at t_i to the sum of the corresponding hazards for all cases that have survived up to time t_i. Provided the baseline hazard is indeed identical for all surviving cases at time t_i, this ratio reduces to

$$\frac{\exp(\beta'\mathbf{x}_i(t_i))}{\sum_{v \in R(t_i)} \exp(\beta'\mathbf{x}_v(t_i))}, \tag{2.10}$$

where $R(t_i)$ is the *risk set* or set of all cases surviving up to time t_i.[10]

The PL likelihood function consists of the product of these conditional probabilities over all cases in the sample. It increases in value to the extent that the likelihood of any case i terminating at time t_i, indicated by $\exp(\beta'\mathbf{x}_i(t_i))$, is large relative to the sum of the corresponding likelihoods for the cases still at risk of termination. Thus, the estimation procedure selects βs to maximize the probability that cases terminating when they did had a high probability of doing so, given their covariate values, compared with the pool of cases lasting at least as long as they lasted.

The PL technique provides a highly convenient method of determining the effect of various covariates on the hazard rate without specifying the nature of the baseline hazard function. Nevertheless, it does depend critically on the assumption that the same baseline hazard (whatever its nature) characterizes all cases. In Chapter 6, where the nature of the baseline hazard comes under scrutiny, this assumption will be examined in detail. For the time being, it will simply be assumed that the data to be described meet this condition in order to examine covariate effects.

One aspect of the PL method that remains to be considered is censoring. Since the true duration of a censored case is unknown, no probability along the lines of equation (2.10) can be estimated. However, any censored case can figure in the risk set of all noncensored cases whose durations are at least as long as its recorded duration. Thus, in the overall log-likelihood, censored cases enter in the denominator of the summation but not in the numerator. This method is different from that employed in ML models, but the two methods do have one feature in common: neither can tell us which cases should be censored. This suggests another area in which the KABL model may be deficient – its choice of a censoring regime.

The censoring issue

King et al. (1990:853–4) censored all durations greater than or equal to CIEP minus twelve months on the assumption that governments may have resigned in anticipation of approaching elections. At face value the assumption appears too

Table 2.1. *A comparison of the effects of censoring regimes on log-likelihoods (exponential models)*

Censoring regime	Total number of cases	Number of censored cases	Log-likelihood
No censoring	312	0	-1,195.6
Parliamentary defeats/ threatened defeats	312	49	-1,057.3
Political resignations	312	90	-935.1

Note: These results were computed using the econometrics computer program SHAZAM, Version 6.1, on the Strom data set. All models include fourteen country dummy variables.

sweeping: the phenomenon of early terminations for electoral advantage is well known in some countries in the sample (e.g., Britain, Canada) but is disallowed in others (e.g., Sweden, Norway). King et al. (1990:860) justified the assumption by showing that the use of this censoring regime causes the overall log-likelihood for a model with country dummies as independent variables to improve significantly. Unfortunately, this justification is not valid.

As noted earlier, the effect of censoring a case in the KABL model is to place it in the $S(t)$ part of the right-hand side of equation (2.8) instead of the $f(t)$ part. Whether this increases or decreases the likelihood depends on whether $S(t)$ is greater than $f(t)$ for that case. In an exponential model, the only difference between the formulas for the two functions is that $f(t)$ has an extra λ term, as equations (2.2) and (2.3) show. Therefore, $S(t)$ will exceed $f(t)$, and the overall likelihood will be increased by censoring a case, whenever λ for that case is less than unity. But λ is the instantaneous rate of collapse at any time t, and it will normally be less than unity. Therefore, in general, censoring will improve the overall likelihood.

To illustrate the point, Table 2.1 presents the results of reestimations of the KABL model using the same data set with three different censoring regimes: (1) no censoring at all, (2) censoring of governments that fell because of defeat or threatened defeat in the parliament, and (3) censoring of governments that re-signed for political reasons.[11] The latter two categories are chosen because they represent situations that clearly should *not* be censored: parliamentary defeats and political resignations are valid terminations under any definition of the term. Nevertheless, the results presented in Table 2.1 show that even these unjustifiable censoring regimes produce improvements in the log-likelihood, the improvement being roughly proportional to the number of censored cases.

This finding, which also holds when the Weibull and log-logistic distributions are used, raises a very difficult issue, one that apparently has not been addressed in the likelihood estimation literature. In most applications, the censoring regime itself is not a matter of judgment: a study runs a certain length of time and cases still surviving at that point are censored. In the Strom data set, there are no such cases. Rather, cases are censored when their recorded terminations are deemed to be "artificial." But what should count as artificial? One could argue, for instance, that terminations created when governments add extra coalition members should be censored; after all, if they had not expanded their size, these governments might have been at greater risk, but they probably would not have collapsed immediately. In the case of King et al.'s censoring regime, one may question the decision to censor only those governments that formed at or near the beginning of a CIEP and terminated within twelve months of regular elections, rather than censoring all governments that terminated within twelve months of regular elections. If the idea is that regular elections stop short a government that would otherwise have lasted longer, surely this should be applied to governments formed in midterm as well.

Since there is no statistical criterion for selecting a censoring regime, the choice inevitably falls to the judgment of the researcher. In this study, a censoring scheme will be developed based upon the idea that terminations are artificial if they do not implicate the viability of the governments in question. The development of this scheme depends substantially on the larger issue of how the cases themselves ought to be defined and it will be presented in that context.

DATA CHOICES AND OPTIONS

The most intuitively appealing criterion for the definition of cases is to fit them as closely as possible to the way they are defined officially (i.e., by the rules or conventions of the regime in question). Regrettably, this criterion may not always make theoretical sense. For instance, both the events theorists and Strom record a government termination in cases where a government wins an election and continues on in office; the theoretical justification is that the bargaining situation in the parliament that sustains the government has changed, even if the government has not. Another situation where, arguably, real-world and theoretical meanings bifurcate concerns the composition of governments: normally only parties that take positions in the government are considered part of the government, but it may make better theoretical sense to count parties that commit themselves to support the government in the parliament (without entering the cabinet) as well. These "support parties" may have no formal voice in policy making, but major government policies will usually have to meet with their approval if the government is to survive in office.

Data sets constructed to test theories of government formation or survival invariably are based on a particular set of fairly arbitrary decisions of this sort. The data set developed for this study, whose scope is indicated in Table 1.1, attempts to escape this constraint: wherever feasible, alternative definitions have been incorporated into the design. The purpose behind this decision is to permit tests of whether key results that emerge from the empirical analysis are artifacts of the way concepts have been defined. There is a cost associated with this flexibility, however: it results in a relatively large and complex data set. In this section, the definitional constraints and options that generate this complexity are outlined.

Government duration. A government typically begins when it is appointed by a head of state. In some European countries, a government or the individual designated to head it must surmount a second hurdle: a formal parliamentary vote of investiture. Although some earlier studies viewed investiture (where required) as the start of a government, the present data set incorporates King et al.'s recommendation that all governments, including noninvested and caretaker governments, be considered in order to maximize comprehensiveness. Investiture therefore becomes a government's first parliamentary test rather than its formal beginning. Nevertheless, the design of the data set does allow noninvested and caretaker governments to be separated out for analytic purposes.

The issue of what should constitute a government termination is less clear-cut. A variety of alternatives have been proposed (Lijphart 1984), but the most useful appears to be the formulation proposed by Browne, Gleiber, and Mashoba (1984:7). Their definition, henceforth referred to as the BGM definition, registers a government termination whenever (1) parliamentary elections are held, (2) the head of government changes, (3) the party composition of the government changes, or (4) the government tenders its resignation, which is accepted by the head of state.[12] The intent of this list is to reference situations that involve a "failure to maintain the integrity of a coalition bargain" (Browne, Gleiber, and Mashoba 1984:6). The integrity criterion seems to fit all of the situations reasonably well with the possible exception of the first: in what sense, one may ask, does the reelection of a government mark a failure of governmental integrity?

The answer offered by Browne, Gleiber, and Mashoba is that elections, including those the government wins, change the strengths of the various coalition partners and may alter the "issue environment" as well. Whether this can be held to constitute a coalition government failure in every instance seems doubtful; it certainly seems inappropriate for victorious single-party majority governments, which are also included in the present data set. What is characteristic of all situations in the list, on the other hand, is that they each describe, if not a true termination, at least a disruption sufficiently serious to make it difficult to view the government as continuing on the same basis as before. Disrupted durations present no particular problem in event history analysis since they can be handled through censoring. The notion of a disruption or discontinuity will therefore serve as the basis for registering the end of a government, with censoring applied to distinguish between true terminations and those that seem artificial or definitional. The nature of this distinction is discussed in the next subsection.

The four situations contained in the BGM definition will be taken to mark government-terminating disruptions, with one partial exception. Implicit in the situations is the principle that the termination of a government is unaffected by the composition of the government that succeeds it; in other words, a government termination remains a termination even if the upshot is the re-formation of essentially the same government (i.e., the same prime minister and party composition).[13] The idea that the occurrence of a termination should not be determined by events that take place subsequent to it is a sensible one, but it is violated in the fourth situation, which counts only resignations accepted by a head of state. The data set's domain includes several instances in which a prime minister submitted his government's resignation, the head of state asked other parliamentary leaders to attempt to form governments, these attempts failed, and the head of state then asked the resigning government to re-form itself. To avoid passing over situations such as these, the standard adopted in this study is that a termination has occurred whenever a government submits its resignation, regardless of the head of state's reaction. In deference to Browne, Gleiber, and Mashoba, however, the data have been coded according to both versions of this criterion. The consequences of using the "accepted resignations only" version will be explored in Chapter 7.

Types of termination. At various stages, I have pointed to situations encompassed by the BGM definition that do not seem to involve true government terminations, as the term is usually understood. The most noteworthy case concerns governments that have reached the end of their statutory terms of office; even if the governments in question should lose the subsequent elections, most observers would agree that the terminations would not have the same meaning as, say, a defeat on a motion of nonconfidence or a resignation due to disagreements within a governing coalition. The resignation of a head of government evokes a similar dilemma. A prime minister may leave office for political reasons, suggesting the unpopularity or unmanageability of the government as it is presently constituted, or because of purely personal circumstances, such as advanced age (genuine or nondiplomatic), illness, or death. Another example would be a coalition government that loses a "surplus" member party and continues in office relatively unaffected, or adds a member party well in advance of any threat to its existence. It is possible to argue in both these circumstances that treating them as terminal is excessively harsh.

The appropriate statistical corrective for terminations that are deemed artificial is to censor them, that is, to treat the terminal dates as establishing minimum duration values rather than exact durations. The advantage of this strategy is that it introduces an intermediate category between survival and collapse, thereby obviating the need to treat every significant disruption – for example, regularly scheduled elections – as implying a government failure. As the preceding section illustrates, however, the determination of which terminations to censor is necessarily a matter of judgment. To minimize arbitrariness, this decision should be based on a complete inventory of terminations and made in accordance with some reasonable definition of artificiality. Table 2.2 contains a categorization of terminations derived principally from *Keesing's Contemporary Archives* (1945–90) for this purpose. Because the concern of this study is with the systematic causes of government survival or collapse, the criterion that will be applied is that a duration is considered artificially short or truncated if external circumstances induced a termination on a government whose viability was not immediately at issue.[14]

The application of this criterion results in the censoring of a case if its termination (1) is caused by, or occurs voluntarily within a year of, elections that were scheduled before it took office, (2) results from the death or illness of a prime min-

Table 2.2. *End type: a typology of government terminations*

End type number	Nature of termination
0	Resignation: voluntary; no indication of political problems or pressures
1	Electoral: statutory; within twelve months of and related to end of CIEP (assumed unless indications exist of some other motivation)
2	Electoral: political; elections motivated by internal political difficulties
3	Electoral: voluntary; government under no substantial pressure to resign (e.g., a new prime minister takes over and holds elections; apparently voluntary elections held more than twelve months early)
4	Death or resignation due to illness of head of government
5	Constitutional/technical; due to customs/rules/needs of the system
6	Governmental: addition of coalition members with no formal resignation
7	Governmental: addition of coalition members with a formal resignation
8	Governmental: resignation of prime minister/cabinet for political reasons
9	Governmental: resignation of prime minister/cabinet because of scandal, impropriety, breach of trust (leaks)
10	Parliamentary: defeat or threatened defeat of government
11	Governmental: resignation of prime minister/cabinet for "external" reasons such as social crisis, foreign incident, or referendum loss
12	Governmental: resignation of caretaker government
13	Electoral: provoked by external circumstances
14	Governments not terminated by December 31, 1989
15	Electoral: caretaker governments only; elections arranged before caretaker government took office in order to find a replacement

ister, (3) is imposed by constitutional rules or customs, or (4) has not occurred by the end of the observation period (December 31, 1989). The relevant categories in Table 2.2 are 1, 4, 5, 14, and 15. The time frame included in the first-mentioned category is designed to accommodate King et al.'s hypothesis that governments may dissolve themselves at a convenient moment in anticipation of upcoming elections, but it specifically excludes governments that were defeated or resigned under political pressure. Another point to note is that the censoring categories do not include terminations defined by the addition of one or more parties to the government. The rationale here is that although such changes may not have involved government viability in an immediate sense, they probably do reflect issues of viability more generally; unlike terminations covered by the selected categories, they cannot be regarded as the result of externally imposed circumstances.

A final noteworthy characteristic of the censoring regime adopted here is that it removes some of the randomness that comprises the essence of the events interpretation. In other words, the scheme forces attention back on the systematic causes of government termination, adjusting extraneous terminations for their lack of relevance to the subject at hand rather than treating them as the grist of parliamentary government life. Since this choice imposes a particular orientation on the research, the results produced with various alternative censoring regimes will also be considered in Chapter 7.

Government composition. The definition of government composition raises two issues: what are the relevant units that are represented in governments, and how broadly should government membership be defined? The standard approach to the first issue is to take parliamentary parties as the appropriate units, but as Laver (1989:304–5) points out, some parties may be so faction-ridden that it would be misleading to regard them as single actors. Although this argument carries weight, especially with respect to notoriously factionalized parties like the Italian Christian Democrats, recorded information invariably treats parties as single entities. For example, election manifestos and other data that provide the raw material for the development of ideological scales in Chapter 4 are presented only for entire political parties. In addition, it is significant that parties do act as units when it comes to forming coalitions and governments, regardless of the internal disagreements that may have accompanied the decisions to do so.

For these reasons, parties are taken as the relevant constituent units for governments and parliaments in this study. In operational terms, a party is considered to exist if it is listed as such in election results or other reports in the principal data source, *Kessing's Contemporary Archives.* This means, for example, that the Flemish and Walloon fragments of the principal political parties in Belgium are considered as separate entities from the times of the various party splits. The most difficult case to classify under this rule is undoubtedly the Christian Democratic Union–Christian Social Union alliance in West Germany, which *Keesing's* presents inconsistently. Because these two parties always act together, do not compete with each other, and are regarded as one in previous research, they are treated in the same fashion in this study.

A greater challenge is presented by the issue of government membership. The simplest solution is to define government membership in terms of presence in the cabinet, but as noted earlier, the line between government and opposition becomes blurred for parties that agree to support cabinets but do not take up cabinet positions. In the case where a one-party minority cabinet negotiates a formal alliance with a party whose support would assure a parliamentary majority, there may be little to distinguish it from a full-fledged coalition government. At the other extreme is the situation of a small party isolated on one side, ideologically speaking, of a minority government: it may have little choice but to support the government because, although it does not stand to gain much in the way of policy concessions, it disagrees even more with the rest of the opposition. In such a case, to refer to the two parties as a governing coalition may seem hyperbolic. An added complexity involves situations, not uncommon in Italy, in which a noncabinet party agrees only to abstain in votes implicating the government's survival. The willingness to abstain may be highly valued by the cabinet, but one may question whether such lukewarm commitment can reasonably be counted as membership in the government.

A central issue in deciding whether various degrees of commitment on the part of noncabinet parties ought to qualify them as members of the governing coalition concerns how essential these parties are to the cabinet's majority. A noncabinet party whose support establishes a parliamentary majority for the cabinet is likely to be in a bargaining position of some strength, one that may well approach that of a cabinet member. Conversely, a superfluous support party may have little or no effect on the government. To evaluate the essentiality of various forms of commitment, four main versions of government membership were defined:

1. Cabinet parties only (C): includes parties as members of the government only if they take cabinet positions
2. Cabinet plus formal support parties (CFS): includes cabinet parties plus parties that formally ally with the cabinet
3. Cabinet plus declared support parties (CDS): includes cabinet parties, formally allied parties, plus any parties that openly declare that they intend to support the cabinet
4. Cabinet plus all support parties (CAS): includes all of the preceding plus parties that have not declared but are known to be government supporters

In addition, two subsidiary versions of government membership may be proposed to take account of abstaining parties:

5. Cabinet plus declared support and abstention parties (CDSA): includes all of version 3 plus parties that openly declare that they will abstain in favor of the cabinet
6. Cabinet plus all support and abstention parties (CASA): includes all of version 4 plus parties that openly declare that they will abstain or are known to be willing to abstain in favor of the government

Implementing this scheme obviously requires a great deal of information on the individual governments of the sixteen parliamentary systems covered in this study. This information was derived primarily from *Keesing's*, although other sources, including De Swaan (1973), Browne and Dreijmanis (1982), von Beyme (1984), Pridham (1986), and Strom (1990a), as well as various country-specific sources, were also consulted.[15] With the available information, it becomes possible to determine the extent to which extracabinet support was necessary for a government's majority status. The results of these calculations are summarized for the four principal definitions of a government in Table 2.3. Because each successive definition builds on its predecessor, the first three rows of the table give the effect on ma-

Table 2.3. *Support parties and majority status of governments*

Nature of expansion in support	Total number of governments	Number originally minoritarian	Number that became majoritarian
Addition of formal support parties	25	17 (68.0)	13 (76.5)
Addition of declared support parties	19	17 (94.7)	15 (88.2)
Addition of undeclared support parties	26	24 (92.3)	21 (87.5)
Addition of any kind of support	67[a]	57 (85.1)	49 (86.0)

Note: Numbers in parentheses are percentages.
[a]This total does not equal the sum of the first three categories because some governments received support of more than one type.

jority status engendered by each successive expansion of the meaning of government membership. The basic pattern, reproduced at every stage of this expansion, is that cabinets taking on parliamentary supporters tend to be nonmajoritarian to begin with and to become majoritarian with the addition of their supporters. As the fourth row shows, the overall effect is striking: 85.1% of cabinets that received support of some kind required support to command a parliamentary majority, and in 86.0% of those cases, the support received was sufficient to create the majority.

Table 2.3 indicates that external support is seldom superfluous, and one may reasonably assume that it is usually offered at a price in terms of government policy. This suggests that it is appropriate to consider support parties as part of the governing coalition. However, the evidence must be regarded as less compelling in the case of undeclared support parties simply because the identification of these parties is very subjective; in particular, numerous examples of covert support could have been overlooked. For this reason, the main body of the analysis in this study will be conducted on a data subset that incorporates the CDS (cabinet plus formal and declared support parties) definition of government membership. Nevertheless, in view of the controversial nature of this issue, data subsets have been created to embody each of the other three main definitions as well, and these alternative data subsets will be utilized to test the principal findings generated by that analysis. Since the willingness to abstain in favor of a government represents a tenuous commitment at best, complete data subsets were not prepared to encompass abstaining parties as government members; however, the majority and minimal winning statuses of governments have been calculated with as well as without their commitments so that the role played by those commitments in government survival can be determined.

CONCLUDING REMARKS

The thrust of the analysis proposed in this study is to open doors, both methodologically and in terms of the data themselves. The methodological opening is made possible by event history analysis, which not only provides methods of adjusting for terminations deemed artificial, but also allows the effects of time-varying covariates and unmeasured time trends to be estimated. Exactly how the time dimension is incorporated into the models will be explained in due course.

Although the advantages of event history analysis will become increasingly clear as the analysis proceeds, it is appropriate to note that its adoption may not be totally without cost. The principal cost in the eyes of many political scientists will be the absence of any statistic indicating the proportion of the dependent variable's variance that is accounted for by the covariates. ML and PL estimation do provide goodness-of-fit statistics: estimated coefficients in the models come with standard errors, for example, and the statistical value of adding covariates to any model is indicated by the significance of the resulting improvement in the overall log-likelihood. Nevertheless, there is no log-likelihood value that indicates total explanation, and it is therefore impossible to test the events theorists' allegation that government survival has a maximum explainability of 20–30%. Although this loss may seem substantial, it needs to be tempered by the consideration that the R^2 statistic of regression analysis can be profoundly misleading, so much so that some methodologists (e.g., King 1986) have recommended against its use. In addition, there are other means, presented in Chapter 7, by which the capacity of the model developed in this study to explain government survival can be assessed.

The expansion of options on the data side is equally significant. In addition to the introduction of such time-varying factors as inflation, unemployment, and growth in gross domestic product, this study incorporates a sizable variety of ideological diversity measures as well as a comprehensive set of fixed covariates, including many proposed in earlier studies. In fact, the number of distinct independent variables available for analytic purposes amounts to well over a hundred. Choices in such matters as which terminations to censor, how broadly to define government membership, and whether to count unaccepted resignations must also be factored into the picture. In Chapters 3 through 7, we take up the task of navigating through this profusion of options and possibilities; the hope is that it results in a corresponding improvement in our capacity to explain government survival in parliamentary regimes.

3

Basic attributes and government survival

Most empirical investigations of government survival have relied on fairly simple sets of fixed attributes of governments, party systems, and/or regimes as their causal factors. Not only are time-varying influences omitted from these studies, but factors based on the ideological or policy positions of parties in the government are also absent. While it is my intention to introduce these considerations to the analysis, their contribution can be assessed most readily if we start with co-variates of the type utilized in earlier work.

As we have seen, the most important recent example of that work was conducted by King et al. (1990), using a data set created by Strom (1985, 1990a). The set of covariates that will be evaluated in this chapter corresponds closely to that considered in the KABL study; some covariates suggested by other research are included as well. Although the selection of covariates is similar, the sequence in which they will be evaluated is not. King et al.'s procedure was to start with country or regime attributes, then add party structure attributes and, finally, attributes of the governments themselves. The position adopted here is that the immediate causes of government survival ought to reside mainly with the governments themselves; if party or parliamentary system factors play a role, it is often because they influence or constrain the composition of governments. Therefore, rather than working from the outside in, I shall begin with the factors closest to survival, the characteristics or attributes of governments.

GOVERNMENT ATTRIBUTES AND GOVERNMENT SURVIVAL

Apart from ideological diversity, four attributes of governments may be suggested as influences on government survival: majority status, postelection status, caretaker status, and government size.[1] The first attribute, *majority status,* is a dichotomous variable registering whether the government commands a parliamentary majority; by the very logic of parliamentary government, majority governments should be more long-lived than minority ones, other things being equal.[2] Because the CDS data subset is to be utilized for this analysis, government membership extends to all parties that enter the cabinet or openly agree to support it. This means, inter alia, that some governments that are formally minoritarian will be treated as majority governments. As discussed in the preceding chapter, the intent here is to evaluate potential causes of government termination on the basis of a reasonable interpretation of the government's actual parliamentary support; alternative definitions will be considered at a later point.

The next two variables are "controls" utilized in the KABL study. *Postelection status* is a dichotomous variable registering whether the government is the first to be formed after an election. King et al. categorize this covariate as a control (rather than a causal factor) on the argument that only the first government after an election has the opportunity to survive the full constitutional interelection period or CIEP, all other governments being constrained to shorter durations. This rationale for the covariate does not apply in the present study since all terminations brought on by statutory elections (not just those involving durations of greater than three years) will be censored to adjust for that constraint. It is possible, however, that postelection governments benefit from a "honeymoon effect": legislators may be more reluctant to bring postelection governments down because they reflect, in some fashion, the electorate's will. Once the postelection government has fallen, it may become "open season" on subsequent governments formed during the same CIEP.

The second of the KABL control variables, *caretaker status,* fits the category more readily. Caretaker governments, which take office during difficult periods on an interim basis until a regular government can be formed, clearly are a different species of government.[3] In the past, the usual practice has been to discard them, but King et al. argue convincingly that a better strategy is to include them but to control for their shorter durations by means of a dummy variable. This is the practice that is followed here. Nevertheless, caretaker governments that have no identifiable party composition cannot be evaluated on attributes such as majority status and therefore become excluded from the analysis because of missing data. This situation affects ten of the twenty-four caretaker governments in the CDS data set.

The final covariate proposed in this category is the size of the government, as reflected in its number of member parties. The rationale for this factor is that as the membership of the government grows, the task of reaching agreement among government parties increases and, with it, the chances of a government breakdown. Since bargaining among members is the driving principle, it stands to reason that the relative sizes of the parties ought to be taken into consideration as well: small parties will have less bargaining weight and therefore less ability to stake out and maintain distinct bargaining positions, generally speaking. A useful index that incorporates the relative sizes of parties as well as their numbers is Laakso and Taagepera's (1979) "effective number of parties." The analysis that follows will use the effective number of parties in the government or *effective government size* as its primary measure, although the simple number of government parties (*government size*) will also be considered. The computational formula for effective government size may be found in the Appendix, which contains a codebook of variables employed in this study.

The first step in the data analysis is to enter these four covariates in PL analysis of the hazard rates underlying government terminations. The results produced

Table 3.1. *Fixed nonideological attributes and government survival*

	Model			
	1	2	3	4
Government attributes				
Majority status	-0.91 (0.15)	-0.87 (0.16)	-1.27 (0.21)	-1.08 (0.17)
Postelection status	-0.89 (0.14)	-0.98 (0.16)	0.55 (0.16)	-0.55 (0.16)
Caretaker status	0.91 (0.47)	0.93 (0.48)	0.45 (0.49)	—
Effective government size	0.35 (0.06)	0.33 (0.06)	0.38 (0.14)	0.21 (0.06)
Government formation attributes				
Crisis duration	—	0.00 (0.00)	—	—
Formation attempts	—	0.13 (0.05)	0.13 (0.05)	—
Parliamentary attributes				
Investiture	—	—	0.38 (0.17)	0.47 (0.16)
Electoral responsiveness	—	—	0.86 (0.41)	—
Electoral volatility	—	—	-1.19 (1.08)	—
Opposition concentration	—	—	0.39 (0.32)	—
Effective party-system size	—	—	-0.32 (0.24)	—
Effective prosystem size	—	—	0.17 (0.33)	—
Polarization	—	—	4.36 (1.38)	3.49 (0.64)
Returnability	—	—	1.80 (0.50)	1.58 (0.49)
Number of dimensions	—	—	0.12 (0.16)	—
Log-likelihood	-1,176.9	-1,158.4	-1,021.7	-1,028.7
Number of cases	364	359	331	331

Note: Coefficients are PL estimates (standard errors in parentheses).

by this procedure are presented as model 1 of Table 3.1.[4] In interpreting the roles played by each of the covariates in the model, it is important to remember that the log-linear model specification implies that a coefficient must be exponentiated to determine its effect on the hazard or conditional rate of termination. Thus, the coefficient of 0.35 associated with effective government size in model 1 indicates that a one-unit increase in the effective number of government parties is associated with an increase in the hazard of 41.9% (since $e^{0.35} = 1.419$). Similarly, the majority status coefficient of -0.91 means that the attainment of that status will lead, ceteris paribus, to a lowering of the hazard rate to about 40.3% ($e^{-0.91} = 0.403$) of its value for minority governments, a very considerable improvement in expected duration indeed.

Model 1 reveals a set of findings that conform very closely to what one would expect: majority governments and postelection governments tend to be associated with lower termination rates and hence longer durations, while caretaker governments and governments with higher effective numbers of member parties imply higher hazards or shorter durations. The standard errors indicate that all covariate coefficients are significant at the .05 level, which constitutes the standard that will be used throughout this study.[5]

The next category of potential causes to be considered is composed of two covariates that relate to circumstances preceding the government's formation. The first, *crisis duration,* measures the length of the preformation "crisis" period, that is, the number of days between the termination of the preceding government and the formation of the present one. The second covariate, *the number of formation attempts,* records the number of times during this period that an individual was assigned the task of forming a government and failed to do so. Although King et al. (1990:858–9) list both of these covariates as cabinet attributes, they interpret them as indicators of the state of the bargaining environment, a party-system characteristic. The covariates are treated here as intermediate in causal proximity, not so close as true government attributes, but perhaps closer than other party-system factors that are not tied to any particular government.

What bargaining-environment states these variables are meant to reflect in the KABL model is unclear. King et al. (1990:858) view crisis duration as indicative of the "difficulty in forming a government, bargaining complexity, and thus shorter cabinet duration." As for the number of formation attempts, they argue that "The more foiled attempts, the more complex the bargaining environment, and the shorter should be the cabinet durations" (859). These observations seem to suggest that high levels of the variables reflect a parliamentary party system in which it is difficult to find enough agreement among parties to form a viable government coalition. If so, however, it is not obvious that instability should be the result, since it could be argued that the very difficulty in forming viable coalitions would tend to oblige government parties to stick with the existing coalition.[6] As we shall see, an interpretation that is more consistent with King et al.'s theoretical premises would view these covariates, especially formation attempts, as indicators of the opposite: an environment rich in possible alternative coalitions.

The effect of including crisis duration and the number of formation attempts in the specification is given in model 2 of Table 3.1. The model shows that a significant additional impact on termination rates is derived only from formation attempts, which are linked with higher hazard rates. Both the absence of a significant association with crisis duration and the positive connection with formation attempts affirm King et al.'s findings, although the former goes against Strom's (1985:748) earlier regression-based results. The fact that the coefficients associated with the four government attributes are scarcely affected by the inclusion of the two intermediate covariates indicates that the number of formation attempts adds to the explanatory power of those factors, rather than substituting for it.

THE PARLIAMENTARY ARENA

Apart from the six government-centered covariates already considered, a wide variety of attributes relating to parliamentary systems or to the structure of party systems in parliaments may also be proposed as potential causes. In this section, nine such factors, most of them utilized in the King et al. study, are investigated.[7] These factors are described next and summarized, along with the government-based factors, in Table 3.2; further information on their construction is presented in the Appendix.

Investiture is a dichotomous covariate indicating whether the system in question requires a formal vote of investiture for either the head of government (prime minister) or the entire cabinet. As with caretaker governments, governments that did not survive investiture votes were usually excluded from earlier studies; this study follows King et al. in including all governments and treating investiture votes as tests that may provoke very early terminations for governments that are obliged to undergo them.

Electoral volatility (Pederson 1979; Shamir 1984) is an index of the extent to which the party composition of parliaments changes from one election to the next. According to Strom (1990a:46–7), volatility reflects voter willingness to change party allegiances and hence the degree to which parties need to concern themselves with voter reactions to their performance. Since government membership tends to cost votes, higher levels of volatility should be associated with shorter government durations. King et al.'s (1990:857) interpretation is somewhat different: they see electoral volatility as indicative of unstable bargaining environments. The consequence again should be higher rates of government termination.

Electoral responsiveness (Strom 1985, 1990a) measures the proportion of parties entering cabinets that also increased their share of parliamentary seats in the most recent elections, calculated over decade-length intervals for each system.[8] Responsiveness is hypothesized to affect government survival because responsive systems translate the electoral "punishment" of incumbents into a lack of access to government in the future, thereby creating an incentive for early withdrawal from (unpopular) governments (King et al. 1990:857–8; Strom 1990a:45–8).

Opposition concentration (Strom 1985, 1990a) records the largest proportion of noncabinet legislators concentrated in a single bloc on either the left or the right of the cabinet. The idea is that a concentrated opposition will find it easier to unite against the cabinet than one that is split between opponents to the left of the cabinet and those to the right; greater opposition concentration should therefore be associated with higher hazard rates. Unlike the majority status and government size variables, the opposition is considered here to include all noncabinet parties on the argument that even parties committed to supporting the present cabinet may be tempted by the lure of holding office in a new one.[9]

Polarization measures the proportion of parliamentary seats controlled by extremist or antisystem parties. The definition of extremism follows Powell (1982:233–4), who treated parties as extremist if they represented (1) a well-

Table 3.2. *A summary of government and parliamentary attributes*

Government attributes

Majority status	Majority or minority status of government
Postelection status	Is the government the first after an election?
Caretaker status	Is the government a caretaker government?
Government size	Simple number of parties (including formal/ declared support parties)
Effective government size	Effective number of parties in government, defined as the inverse of the sum of squared party proportions of government seats (Laakso-Taagepera 1979)

Government formation attributes

Crisis duration	Length of time from termination of previous government until formation of present one
Formation attempts	Number of failed formation attempts that preceded government's formation
Formation attempts including refusals	Number of failed formation attempts, including invitations that were declined

Parliamentary/party-system attributes

Investiture	Is a formal vote of investiture required?
Electoral responsiveness	Proportion of parties for which electoral gains in seats led to government participation in next parliament, calculated by decade and system
Electoral volatility	Party-system volatility across elections, defined as one-half the sum of proportional changes in party strengths from previous parliament to present one
Opposition concentration 1	Proportion of opposition (noncabinet) seats concentrated to left or right of cabinet
Opposition concentration 2	Proportion of opposition (noncabinet) seats concentrated anywhere on Left-Right scale
Polarization	Proportion of seats held by extremist parties (as defined by Powell 1982)
Effective party-system size	Effective number of parties in the parliamentary party system (Laakso-Taagepera)
Effective prosystem size	Effective number of prosystem or nonextremist parties in the parliament (Laakso-Taagepera)

Table 3.2 (*continued*)

Returnability	Proportion of government parties represented in the next government following a collapse or early termination, calculated by system
Returnability, weighted	Proportion of government seats represented in the next government following a collapse or early termination, calculated by system
Number of dimensions	Number of issue dimensions (as defined by Lijphart 1984)

developed nondemocratic ideology, (2) a proposal to alter national boundaries fundamentally, or (3) diffuse protest, alienation, or distrust of the political system.[10] In King et al.'s framework, high levels of polarization indicate bargaining complexity, which tends to undermine government survival. As noted in Chapter 1, high polarization may instead reflect difficulties in forming majority governments that are sufficiently homogeneous in ideological or policy terms to endure. Both interpretations imply that polarization should be associated with higher hazards or shorter durations.

Returnability is a new measure suggested by the second interpretation of polarization. To the extent that the presence of extremist or antisystem parties in a parliament reduces the range of viable coalition governments, the probability that any member of an outgoing government will participate in the government that replaces it is likely to increase. Where the antisystem presence is substantial, therefore, member parties may be tempted to defect from an uncomfortably diverse coalition government in the expectation that they will have to be included in its successor – with, perhaps, some greater leverage on policy issues that matter to them. In any case, they will have demonstrated to their supporters their commitment to principle at relatively little risk – in terms of office holding – to themselves. The returnability covariate attempts to measure this propensity by recording, for each system, the overall proportion of government parties that returned to power immediately following collapses or politically motivated terminations. For practical purposes, all noncensored terminations (see Chapter 2) are considered to meet this standard. It is assumed that the returnability value for each system reflects an underlying likelihood that is known to its parliamentary actors throughout the period.[11]

Effective party-system size is the Laakso-Taagepera measure of the effective number of parties in the parliamentary party system. Its construction is identical to that of effective government size, except that all the parties in the parliament rather than just those in the government are included. It is closely related to – in fact it contains the same information as – Rae's (1971) fractionalization index, which King et al. used to measure party-system size, but has the advantage of producing values that are more easily interpreted. For example, a party system split between three equally sized parties would have a value of 3 as its effective number of parties, whereas its fractionalization value would be .67.

Party-system size was interpreted by King et al. as an indicator of the complexity of the bargaining system in the parliament. Since extremist parties are normally excluded from bargaining over government formation or support, it could be argued that a more appropriate measure would be the *effective prosystem size,* that is, the effective number of prosystem or nonextremist parties in the parliament. In creating this variable, prosystem parties were defined as parties not considered to be extremist according to Powell's criteria.

The final covariate to be considered here is *the number of dimensions.* This variable was advanced by Grofman (1989) to explain the relationship between survival and the size of the party system. His argument is that the number of issue dimensions ought to be considered as temporally prior to the number of parties; nevertheless, as Taagepera and Shugart (1989:98) point out, "Depending on the circumstances, causality could flow in either direction." For this reason, it will be considered as a possible direct influence on government survival. Following Grofman, the identification of issue dimensions was taken from Lijphart (1984).

A preliminary evaluation of the contribution these covariates bring to the explanation of government survival can be found in model 3 of Table 3.1, which presents the results from a PL analysis incorporating the five significant government-related covariates identified in model 2 plus the nine parliamentary and party-system covariates just described. The standard errors associated with the coefficients indicate that four of the nine new covariates – investiture, polarization, electoral responsiveness, and returnability – play a statistically significant role in government survival. As one would expect, all four covariates are associated with higher hazard rates (shorter durations). Interestingly, of the five government-related covariates in the model, only one – caretaker status – is reduced to statistical insignificance by the addition of the parliamentary and party-system covariates.

It is evident that Model 3 contains too many covariates: fully six of the fourteen covariate coefficients fall below the .05 level of significance. The question is: Which covariates should be removed? The simplest procedure would be to eliminate all insignificant covariates, but this could be profoundly misleading if the roles played by any of the covariates are altered by the presence of other covariates that are themselves insignificant. Nor does theory give us much guidance: all covariates are plausible influences on government survival, but no theories provide a clear indication of the causal ordering among them.

In the absence of clear theoretical guidelines, we inevitably must fall back on statistical criteria. The most suitable statistical method in the present circumstances is a backward-elimination stepwise procedure. This procedure first eliminates the covariate that makes the least significant net contribution to the overall log-likelihood and reestimates the model, then it repeats that process iteratively until the model contains only covariates that provide a significant net contribution to the log-likelihood.[12] This selection criterion is not foolproof, given the complexity of the interrelations that may exist among the covariates, but it takes greater cognizance of these interrelations than does the strategy of eliminating all insignificant linkages at once.[13]

The results of the stepwise procedure applied to model 3 are given as model 4 of Table 3.1. Of the fourteen covariates, eight have been eliminated. The loss of six of these – caretaker status, electoral volatility, opposition concentration, effective party-system size, effective prosystem size, and the number of dimensions – was expected: they are all highly insignificant in model 3. Less anticipated is the elimination of the number of formation attempts and electoral responsiveness. This result, although unexpected, is not an artifact of the order in which covariates were removed in the backward-elimination procedure: not only does neither of these covariates contribute significantly to the overall log-likelihood of a model containing the six remaining significant covariates, but if entered separately in such a model, neither of their estimated coefficients produces a significant t-value.[14]

Perhaps the most noteworthy feature of this reduction in model size is the elimination of effective party-system size as well as a related measure of bargaining-environment complexity, effective prosystem size. This finding directly contradicts the King et al. study, which reported a strong positive linkage between party-system size (as measured by fractionalization) and the hazard rate. What seems to have happened is that the effect conveyed in the KABL model by party-system size has now been picked up by effective government size, leaving only a spurious remaining effect. This is indicated not only by the high correlation between effective government size and the effective party-system size ($r = .77$), but also by the fact that when the former is excluded from the model, the latter enters with a significant positive coefficient.[15]

All in all, model 4 appears to be a reasonable "downsizing" of model 3. That model, however, was fashioned to some extent by the strategy of considering government attributes first, then government-related attributes, and finally extragovernment covariates. It would be instructive, therefore, to see what would happen if a purely statistical criterion, without any imposed priority ordering, were utilized. This can be done either by applying a backward-elimination stepwise procedure to the complete set of covariates or by employing a forward-entry stepwise procedure, which iteratively selects covariates for entry into the model based on their net contribution to the log-likelihood.

Apart from providing a means of assessing the impact of the priority ordering that governs models 1 to 3, these procedures would also allow the testing of alternative versions of some of the covariates. Four of the fourteen covariates listed in Table 3.1 readily admit of alternative versions: effective government size, returnability, the number of formation attempts, and opposition concentration.[16] Concerning government size, it is evident that the concept could be measured by the simple number of government parties rather than the effective or weighted number. The issue of weighting also points to an alternative version of returnability: instead of determining the overall proportion of governing parties that return following premature termination in each system, one could assess the proportion of government *seats* that are represented in successor governments; in other words, weight the parties by their respective parliamentary sizes. This alternative version will be known as *returnability-weighted*. The number of formation attempts allows for a second version if one counts not only the failed attempts but also the number of times an individual refused a head of state's invitation to form a government; if these refusals reflect the difficulties inherent in the bargaining environment, then a *formation attempts including refusals* covariate might be a better measure of the underlying phenomenon. Finally, opposition concentration measures the proportion of opposition seats concentrated to the left or right of the cabinet, but if the idea is that an ideologically contiguous opposition can more readily unite against the cabinet, then there is no compelling reason why it has to be located toward the extremes: even an opposition bloc located in the center of the spectrum could exploit its size and coherence. *Opposition concentration 2* measures the proportion of opposition seats concentrated in any ideologically contiguous bloc.

The tests to be conducted consist of (1) entering all covariates, including the four alternative versions, in the model and allowing the stepwise PL procedure to eliminate insignificant covariates iteratively until only those that provide a significant net contribution to the log-likelihood remain, and (2) entering no covariates initially, but allowing the stepwise procedure to select covariates iteratively according to the size of their net contribution to the log-likelihood until all covariates that can make a significant net contribution have been entered. As noted earlier, such theory-blind procedures run the risk that important relationships may be missed because they are distorted or suppressed by other covariates. Nevertheless, the tests can be valuable in determining whether the selection procedure used to derive model 4 imposed any particular biases, warranted or not, on the final outcome, as well as whether alternative versions of some of the covariates perform better than their original versions.

The results of these tests can be stated very simply: with one very minor exception, both tests reproduced model 4. The exception concerns the size of the government: the backward-elimination method entered effective government size, whereas the forward-entry procedure selected the simple government size measure in its stead. The two covariates correlate very highly with each other ($r = .88$), and the substitution of one for the other has a negligible effect on the other estimated coefficients in the model. In the analyses that follow, I shall continue to use effective government size because it results in a model with a marginally higher log-likelihood ($-1,028.7$ vs. $-1,029.0$); for practical purposes, however, the two covariates are interchangeable. As for the other alternative versions, only opposition concentration 2 performed better than its original version, but neither entered the model significantly.

The reemergence of model 4 under these different covariate selection rules provides us with some confidence that the six covariates in the model represent a good choice from the standpoint of accounting for government survival. The theoretical import of this combination of government and extragovernment attributes remains to be considered, however. We have already seen that the role of polarization can be subsumed under two very different theories; other ambiguities may also exist. These and related issues are taken up in the next section, which evaluates the results produced thus far.

INTERPRETING THE MODEL

The KABL model provides a useful standard against which the results of the present analysis may be compared and evaluated. The covariates of the KABL model fall into three basic categories. The first consists of two covariates, majority status and investiture, that derive from rules of the political system. The basic criterion for survival in parliamentary systems privileges majority governments over minority ones, in general, and the existence of an investiture requirement in some systems presents their governments with an early challenge to their survival. A second category comprises two control variables, postelection status and caretaker status, intended to separate out classes of cases that may reasonably be expected to behave differently from the rest. Finally, there are the bargaining-complexity indicators that constitute the core of King et al.'s theoretical account: the number of formation attempts, party-system size (fractionalization), and polarization.

The greatest degree of similarity between the two models relates to the first category: both majority status and investiture also figure in the model developed in this chapter. Nevertheless, the explanation King et al. offer for the role of investiture – that it represents an early test of survival that some governments may not pass – does not appear to be valid. This may be demonstrated by rerunning the forward-entry and backward-elimination procedures only on those governments that did not fail an investiture test. If investiture affects government termination rates for the reasons they suggest, then it should no longer have a significant negative impact once these governments have been excluded.

In performing this test, three covariates – crisis duration, formation attempts, and formation attempts including refusals – were redefined so that governments failing investiture votes are treated as failed formation attempts; in other respects, the tests remain as described in the preceding section. Given that there are only ten governments excluded from the tests, it is not surprising that the overall results, presented in model 2 of Table 3.3, are very similar to those generated from the full sample (model 1).[17] What is perhaps more surprising is that investiture emerges with nearly as large and significant a coefficient as it previously displayed (0.40 vs. 0.44). Evidently, the association of investiture requirements with shorter survivals is not due to governments failing to survive the challenge that such requirements impose.

The control-variable category of the KABL model is replicated only partially in model 4 of Table 3.1: governments formed after elections do have greater longevity than other governments, but the disadvantage experienced by the small number of caretaker governments is not sufficient, once party-system factors are controlled, to achieve statistical significance. As noted earlier, the interpretation of postelection status is not as clear-cut as it seemed in the King et al. study since

Table 3.3. *Exploring the investiture and postelection effects*

	All cases (model 1)		Invested governments only[a] (model 2)		All cases[b] (model 3)	
Covariates						
Majority status	-1.11	(0.16)	-1.00	(0.17)	-1.12	(0.17)
Postelection status	-0.61	(0.15)	-0.61	(0.15)	-0.65	(0.16)
Investiture	0.44	(0.15)	0.40	(0.15)	0.47	(0.16)
Effective government size	0.20	(0.06)	0.21	(0.06)	0.20	(0.06)
Returnability	1.60	(0.47)	1.47	(0.47)	1.52	(0.49)
Polarization	3.54	(0.62)	3.41	(0.64)	3.59	(0.66)
Reelected government	—		—		0.21	(0.24)
Log-likelihood	-1,120.1		-1,074.5		-1,062.6	
Number of cases	360		350		345	

Note: Coefficients are PL estimates (standard errors in parentheses).
[a]Invested governments are governments that did not fail investiture votes (including governments that did not have to face investiture votes).
[b]Fifteen cases are lost because reelected government cannot be defined for the first government in every country sample.

the shorter time available to subsequent governments should be compensated for in this analysis by the censoring of all terminations occasioned by statutory elections. It may be, however, that the postelection effect is an artifact of the decision to treat all elections as terminal events, even when the same government continues in power after an election. In situations where an election does not mark a true rupture, the government's subsequent longevity may have nothing to do with the election but instead reflect some other factors intrinsic to itself. This possibility can be tested by the introduction of another dichotomous control variable, *reelected government*, representing whether the postelection government was a continuation of the government that held power before the election.[18] As model 3 of Table 3.3 indicates, the addition of this covariate has almost no influence on the postelection role. By elimination, then, it appears that there may well be a honeymoon effect, a tendency among legislators and parties to be more patient with or tolerant of governments that follow, and often issue from, the electorate's verdict.

The final and theoretically most important category of the KABL model comprises the three bargaining-environment indicators. King et al. do not spell out the theoretical premises of their bargaining-environment approach in any detail, but they do refer to an explanation advanced by Laver and Schofield (1990). Like the events hypothesis, this explanation begins with the occurrence of random outside events. These events are viewed in the Laver–Schofield account as perturbations in the environment that occasionally lead not directly to government collapses, but rather to changes in the parliamentary strengths of the various parties or in their policies. In relatively simple party systems, these changes seldom affect the fundamental bargaining power of the parties and therefore do not tempt parties to alter coalition arrangements. In complex "multipolar" systems, however, even small changes in these domains are likely to reallocate bargaining power and encourage attempts to renegotiate coalitions or to form new ones. Whenever these attempts are successful, government survival is sacrificed.

The covariate that fits this interpretation most readily is the size of the party system, which, whether measured with Rae's fractionalization or Laakso and Taagepera's effective number of parties, registers the number and size of parties in the parliamentary party system. In party systems with a higher weighted or effective size, it is reasonable to assume that the opportunities for government members to find or build more attractive alternative coalitions will be correspondingly greater (ceteris paribus).

Less clear is the role of the number of formation attempts. As noted earlier, King et al. take this variable as indicative of the difficulty or complexity of the bargaining environment. If a complex bargaining environment is one that contains obstacles to successful coalition formation, then presumably such an environment would provide fewer alternative coalitions to tempt government parties. On this reasoning, a complex bargaining environment would tend to discourage defections and thereby foster long-lived governments – precisely the opposite of what King et al. found. One way to salvage the bargaining-environment approach would be to stand the argument on its head by interpreting multiple formation attempts as indicative of a party system replete with viable coalitions and hence ample opportunities for members of one coalition to defect to alternative coalitions offering better payoffs. This, in fact, is the tack taken by Schofield and Laver (1990:162).

Preserving the interpretation with respect to the final bargaining-complexity indicator, polarization, is not so straightforward. Laver and Schofield believe that the polarization variable reflects the overall complexity of party positions in the party system; the more complex this array, the more vulnerable the distribution of bargaining power to slight perturbations. But what the variable actually measures is the proportion of parliamentary seats held by extremist parties, and since extremist parties are normally considered unsuitable coalition partners by prosystem parties – "non-coalitionable" in Laver and Schofield's (1990:200–1) terms – their presence should narrow the range of coalition alternatives, other things being equal. Thus, the bargaining-complexity thesis could lead one to expect either a negative or a positive connection between polarization and the hazard rate, depending on whether the polarization measure more closely reflects extremist party presence or total party-system complexity.

Like the KABL model, the final model developed here shows polarization as having a positive effect on the rate of government termination. But this need not mean that a bargaining-environment interpretation of this variable's role is the correct one, for this result would also be expected under the ideological diversity interpretation. The focus of that interpretation is on the difficulties that party systems with a strong extremist or antisystem presence tend to experience in putting together ideologically coherent or workable coalition governments. Given the noncoalitionable status of extremist parties, governments formed in such systems usually must either encompass an ideologically diverse array of prosystem parties and/or settle for being minoritarian; either way, they are vulnerable to early collapse or termination. Apart from accounting for the sign of the polarization coefficient, this explanation has the advantage of locating the proximate cause of government survival in a particular government attribute, rather than associating it with a general feature of the larger parliamentary environment.

Concerning the other two alleged bargaining-complexity indicators, the present analysis offers little support for their hypothesized causal roles. The number of formation attempts, which barely achieved the .05 significance level in the KABL model, fails to meet that standard in this data set (if entered, its significance level would be .10). Differences between the samples probably explain the discrepancy; in any case, the covariate must be deemed a very indirect indicator of the state of the bargaining environment at best. As for party-system size, measured here by the effective number of parliamentary parties, it also fails to enter the model, but for a very different reason. King et al.'s interest in size or fractionalization extended only to the size of the party system; they never tested the size of the government. Once government size is taken into consideration, however, it eliminates the significant role played by effective party-system size, indicating that large party systems tend to experience greater instability because the governments they produce are themselves large. This refinement on the KABL model implies that if there is validity to the bargaining-environment idea, it is the bargaining environment within the government that matters, not the larger parliamentary bargaining environment.

The bargaining environment also figures in the interpretation of a covariate that was not tested by King et al., returnability, but in a very different way. A high returnability score suggests a bargaining environment in which the availability of alternative coalitions is low; that it should be associated with higher levels of government turnover implies that parties defect when the chances of being invited back into the same or a similar coalition government are good. Given that there is always some risk of not being invited back (the nondefecting members may decide to form a minority government rather than invite the defector back in, for instance), one may suppose that government parties would not defect even where the returnability rate is high unless they are sufficiently dissatisfied with the present government to run the risk. This may mean that the policy positions of the coalition members are so different that policy outputs satisfactory to all government members are difficult to come by. Thus, returnability, like polarization, may be indirectly indicative of tensions within governing coalitions based on policy differences or ideological diversity.

The exploration of the role played in government survival by ideological diversity within governments constitutes the subject matter of the next chapter. If the possibilities raised in the preceding paragraphs have validity, one would expect that the coefficients associated with two of the covariates in the model – effective government size and polarization – will be eliminated, or at least substantially reduced, with the addition of covariates measuring the phenomenon. As we shall see, this is precisely what occurs.

4

The role of ideology

In Chapter 1, I suggested that the findings of the KABL model may be understood in terms of an approach that emphasizes the causal role of policy or ideological differences within governments. From this perspective, a large extremist presence in a parliament, as measured by the polarization variable, affects government survival primarily because it raises the proportion of prosystem seats that would have to be represented in any majority government – and hence, on average, the government's ideological diversity. By the same token, the number of failed formation attempts, although barely significant in the KABL model, could be seen as an indirect – and therefore weak – indicator of the existence of serious ideological divisions among potential coalition partners. Even the role of party-system size (fractionalization) may be mediated by ideological diversity: in a fragmented party system, the number of member parties required for a government to command a majority tends to be greater, and with greater numbers of government members may come greater ideological diversity.

The model developed in the preceding chapter moves the analysis a couple of steps further in this direction by eliminating the role of formation attempts and, more important, by replacing effective party-system size with effective government size, a change that is directly supportive of the interpretation. Nevertheless, the interpretation's viability cannot be established convincingly unless the ideological diversity within governments is introduced directly into the analysis. Despite its potential theoretical importance, the concept has received remarkably little attention in the empirical literature; the Strom data set, for example, includes no policy- or ideology-based measures. The present chapter addresses this deficiency by developing measures of ideological diversity from a variety of available sources, including voter-based definitions of the ideological positions of parties, expert estimates of party positions, and assessments of party positions derived from a coding of postwar party platforms. Event-history methodology is then employed to test the ability of these measures to account for governmental survival, particularly when the government and parliamentary influences identified in Chapter 3 are taken into consideration. The ultimate goal is to determine the extent to which the association of survival with alleged bargaining-system indicators is explicable in terms of their common linkage to the ideological diversity within governments.

THE PROBLEMATIC STATUS OF POLARIZATION

The doubts that have been raised thus far concerning the appropriateness of polarization as a bargaining-complexity indicator have been conceptual in nature: on the face of it, the presence of extremist parties seems as likely to reflect the scarcity as the availability of coalition alternatives. Before beginning the development and testing of ideological diversity measures, therefore, it would be useful to show that there are empirical grounds for questioning whether the polarization variable measures precisely what the bargaining-environment theorists believe it measures – the overall complexity of the parliamentary bargaining system.

In the bargaining-complexity interpretation, polarization is an indirect measure: it takes the size of the extremist presence in a parliament as indicative of the ideological polarization of the entire parliamentary party system. If total party-system polarization is indeed what the variable reflects, then presumably a more direct measurement of the concept would play an even stronger causal role in accounting for government survival. Direct measurement of party-system polarization may be attempted in a number of ways. One approach would be to derive a measure from expert judgments of party positions along a Left–Right dimension, such as the Left–Right political scales developed by Castles and Mair (1984) for West European party systems. Alternatively, one could base the measurement on the mean Left–Right positions of party supporters as elicited by various public opinion surveys. A more elaborate tactic would be to utilize party scales covering a variety of different issue or ideological dimensions to calculate an average polarization measure across all dimensions relevant to each party system.[1] Let us consider these alternatives in turn.

Castles and Mair (1984) developed a series of ten-point Left–Right scales for West European democracies based on judgments elicited from surveys of expert observers.[2] Different systems have different ranges across the ten-point scale, as one might expect, but the concept of ideological polarization cannot be based on the ideological range of the party system alone. For instance, a party system may range from extreme left-wing parties to right-wing parties, but if the extreme parties occupy just 1 or 2% of parliamentary seats, their effect on the functioning of the system would be virtually negligible. If these parties are sizable, however, the consequences may be very different. One straightforward method of representing both the ideological positions and the sizes of parties in a party system is to calculate the system's "ideological standard deviation," defined as

$$\sqrt{\sum_{i=1}^{n} p_i (x_i - \bar{x})^2}$$

where p_i is party i's proportion of parliamentary seats, x_i is its position on the ideological scale in question, $\bar{x}$ is the weighted mean position of parties on that scale ($\sum p_i x_i$), and the summations are over the n parties in the parliament (Dodd 1976:105–6).

Table 4.1. *Testing alternative measures of party-system polarization*

	Model					
	1		2		3	
Covariates						
Majority status	-1.13	(0.20)	-1.52	(0.23)	-1.16	(0.17)
Postelection status	-0.51	(0.17)	-0.71	(0.17)	-0.58	(0.15)
Effective government size	0.24	(0.09)	0.25	(0.10)	0.21	(0.06)
Investiture	0.36	(0.17)	0.59	(0.18)	0.58	(0.18)
Returnability	1.67	(0.52)	1.60	(0.72)	1.73	(0.48)
Polarization	3.78	(0.71)	2.19	(0.84)	2.80	(0.78)
Polarization, Castles and Mair (1984)	-0.21	(0.29)	—		—	
Polarization, voter-defined scales	—		0.38	(0.29)	—	
Degree of cleavage conflict, Dodd (1976)	—		—		0.56	(0.33)
Log-likelihood		-873.8		-845.4		-1,079.3
Number of cases		288		272		349

Note: Coefficients are PL estimates (standard errors in parentheses).

A polarization variable based on the standard deviations of party systems along Castle and Mair's Left–Right scales would clearly be a more comprehensive measure of total party-system polarization than the variable used thus far, which considers only the presence of extremist parties. The question is, can it do a better job of accounting for government survival? Since the object is to choose between two purported measures of the same concept, an appropriate means of addressing this question is to include both measures, along with the other significant covariates from model 4 of Table 3.1, in a forward-entry stepwise PL analysis and observe which covariates are selected for entry. In fact, the results of this test reproduced the earlier model: all covariates entered significantly except the polarization measure derived from the Castles and Mair scales. Given that the order in which the covariates were selected in the stepwise procedure could have affected the choice between the two polarization measures, the stronger role of the original polarization measure can be checked by entering all covariates simultaneously in a PL model. The outcome, reported in model 1 of Table 4.1, shows only the Castles and Mair version of polarization to be insignificant.

Since there is no reason to believe that the rankings of parties provided by experts are flawless, other sources, such as the judgments of party supporters, may also be utilized. Beginning in 1973, biannual Eurobarometer surveys of European Community countries have regularly asked respondents to place themselves on a ten-point Left–Right scale. Sani and Sartori (1983) have demonstrated that the mean positions of party supporters on this type of scale can provide reasonable estimates of party locations. Applying this procedure to the Eurobarometer 6 survey of 1976 (Rabier and Inglehart 1978) yielded estimates of party positions for eight West European party systems. Because Spain and Portugal were not included in that survey, the Left–Right positions of their parties were calculated from a later survey, the 1985 Eurobarometer 24 (Rabier, Riffault, and Inglehart 1986).[3] Finally, party positions for two countries not included in the Eurobarometer surveys, Austria and Finland, were estimated from Barnes et al.'s (1979) Political Action surveys, which included the same Left–Right self-placement item.[4] In this manner, it was possible to develop a standard deviation measure of polarization based on voter-defined Left–Right party scales for all systems in the sample except four: the French Fourth Republic, Iceland, Norway, and Sweden.

This voter-based polarization measure would appear to be more "empirical," or at least less impressionistic or subjective, than its expert-based alternative, but that is no guarantee that it will perform better against the original polarization variable. In fact, in PL analyses identical to those performed using the expert-based version, the same basic outcome prevailed: only the original six covariates were selected for entry in a forward-entry stepwise procedure. Moreover, as model 2 of Table 4.1 shows, the voter-based polarization measure alone is insignificant when all seven covariates are entered simultaneously.

Since two polarization measures based on Left–Right party scales have failed to displace the original polarization variable as an influence on government survival, a better strategy might be to develop a version that measures polarization along more than one issue or ideological dimension. Such a measure was proposed some time ago by Dodd (1976:100–6). In constructing his *degree of cleavage conflict* variable, Dodd first located individual parties in each system on up to four "cleavage dimensions": economic conflict, clericalism, regime support, and miscellaneous (country-specific). Each cleavage dimension consisted of a fifteen-point scale grouped into five main categories, corresponding roughly to extreme Left (-7 to -5), moderate Left (-4 to -2), center (-1 to 1), moderate Right (2 to 4), and extreme Right (5 to 7). For the most part, these categories were defined in terms of their support for (1) fundamental or radical change, (2) moderate restructuring, (3) preserving the status quo, (4) moderate opposition to the Left and the present system, and (5) reactionary opposition to the Left and the present system, respectively. The three-point range within each main category allowed for the fine-tuning of party locations to reflect slight leanings to the left or right within each basic rubric. Dodd then computed the parliamentary standard deviations for all cleavage dimensions present in each system and averaged those values to produce a mean level of cleavage conflict or ideological polarization per parliament.

The degree of cleavage conflict (DCC) measure is undoubtedly the most sophisticated attempt to capture total party-system polarization ever attempted, but can it outperform the original polarization variable? Once again, PL analyses yield an essentially negative verdict: a DCC variable constructed from Dodd's three general cleavage dimensions proved unable to enter the model in a stepwise PL procedure once polarization is in the model. When entered simultaneously with polarization and the other relevant covariates, its coefficient, shown in model 3 of Table 4.1, does (just) achieve statistical significance in a one-tailed test, but its presence does not significantly improve the overall log-likelihood, suggesting that its role is due in part to a sharing of the effect conveyed by one or more other covariates in the model, most probably polarization.

The failure of any of these alternative measures to displace the original polarization variable in its capacity to account for government survival is puzzling if all four variables are indeed measuring the same underlying concept, the ideological polarization of the parliamentary party system.[5] But suppose the original polarization covariate really reflects exactly what it records: the extremist or antisystem presence in the parliament. Although the presence of extremist parties and total ideological polarization are related – all four polarization variables intercorrelate significantly – they may not represent exactly the same thing. A hypothetical example will make this clear. Imagine a relatively polarized party system in which a left-wing party or bloc of parties competes against a right-wing counterpart. Although the system itself is polarized, governments might be long-lived provided the blocs themselves are reasonably homogeneous on policy matters. If the Left and Right extremes of the party spectrum are dominated by noncoalitionable parties, however, this scenario dissipates: government members must now be chosen from the prosystem sector alone. The consequence may be that ideological enemies, such as socialists and conservatives, must coalesce if majority governments are to be formed at all. Longevity in office would hardly be expected in such circumstances.

These alternatives, of course, are reminiscent of Sartori's distinction between moderate and polarized pluralism, which was discussed in Chapter 1. The key point about polarized pluralist systems is that they include not just parties that are ideologically distant from one another, but parties that cannot be included in government even with their prosystem neighbors. This makes an enormous difference for the dynamics of coalition formation and maintenance. Relatively homogeneous Left and Right blocs cannot compete for parliamentary control; instead, coalitions must form around the political center, uniting often amorphous and diverse collections of parties and ideologies to amass majority support. If minority status is to be avoided, ideological diversity becomes the rule – and governmental instability may be the result.

THE ROLE OF IDEOLOGICAL DIVERSITY

We have clearly reached the stage where ideological diversity must be introduced directly into the analysis. To effect a thorough testing of this elusive concept, I have created some forty different measures from expert, party manifesto, and survey sources. The basic information derived from each source is a set of scales – usually one per country – registering party positions on one or more ideological dimensions. In all, four basic ideological dimensions are involved: Left–Right, clerical–secular, regime support, and materialist–postmaterialist.[6]

Two versions of the final ideological diversity measure were constructed from each scale: a range version, which assesses the total range of a government on the scale, and a standard deviation version, which weights the scale positions of the government parties by their relative parliamentary strengths. The range versions of each measure are intended to assess the possibility that the full expanse of the diversity within governments is what counts for survival, regardless of the relative strengths of the parties contributing to that diversity.[7] The standard deviation versions incorporate the alternative hypothesis that the sizes of the various government members as well as their ideological positions are important. Regrettably, there are no scales to measure ideological divisions within individual parties; as a result, single-party governments receive a value of zero on all measures.

In view of the relatively large number of variables under consideration, the analysis will proceed in two stages. In the first stage, the explanatory roles played by alternative measures of diversity along the same dimension or derived from the same source will be compared. The best measures from each of these analyses will then be tested against one another in the second stage. Because the first stage is concerned with the evaluation of alternative measures of the same concept, I will take the best measure of diversity in each instance to be the one that relates most strongly to the rate of termination. This will be determined by specifying the alternative measures in a forward-entry stepwise PL analysis. Most of the covariates already shown to have significant effects on survival will also be included in these analyses so that the contributions of the various ideological diversity measures are assessed relative to other causal factors. However, the two possible bargaining-complexity measures (polarization and effective government size) will be excluded for the time being, since they can be properly tested against ideological diversity only after all significant aspects of the latter concept have been identified.

The Left–Right dimension

Expert-based measures. There are four expert sources that provide definitions of party positions on a Left–Right or socioeconomic dimension over a broad range of West European party systems: Dodd's (1976) economic conflict scales; Browne, Gleiber, and Mashoba's (1984) refinement of the Dodd scales; a dichotomous socialist–bourgeois categorization based on Warwick (1979); and Castles and Mair's (1984) Left–Right political scales. With separate range and standard deviation versions, these scales generated eight different ideological diversity measures.

The high levels of intercorrelation that exist among these measures (generally above .75) suggest that they may all be indicating an underlying dimension of Left–Right diversity. To test for this possibility, separate principal components analyses were performed on the range and standard deviation versions of these measures. In each case, a single dominant principal component emerged, accounting for 85.5% and 88.5% of the variance, respectively. These high levels of explained variance support the hypothesis that the first principal components assess an underlying dimension of Left–Right diversity common to the original mea-

Table 4.2. *The composition of Left-Right ideological diversity measures*

Source scales	Missing systems	Combined measure	Missing systems
Expert scales			
Castles and Mair's Left-Right political (CM)	France, Luxembourg, Iceland, Portugal		
Dodd's economic conflict (D1)	Portugal, Spain	Expert Left-Right diversity	Portugal, Spain[a]
Browne, Gleiber, and Mashoba's economic conflict (BGM)	Portugal, Spain		
Socialist-bourgeois dichotomy (SD)	None		
Party Manifestos Project (PMP) scales			
First principal component of PMP	Finland, Iceland, Portugal, Spain		
First discriminant function of D1	Finland, Iceland, Portugal, Spain	PMP Left-Right diversity	Finland, Spain, Iceland, Portugal
First discriminant function of BGM	Finland, Iceland, Portugal, Spain		
First discriminant function of SB	Finland, Iceland, Portugal, Spain		

Note: All measures of ideological diversity derived from these sources were created in both range and standard deviation versions.
[a]Expert Left-Right diversity scores for systems for which the CM scales are missing were calculated from the other three sources.

sures; moreover, because they in effect ignore the idiosyncrasies pertaining to individual source measures, they are likely to provide better measures of the phenomenon than the latter can provide by themselves. For this reason, the factor scores from the first principal components will constitute our initial measures of Left–Right ideological diversity within governments; they are labeled here as the range and standard deviation versions of *expert Left–Right diversity*. The sources employed and countries covered by these composite measures are summarized in Table 4.2.

A second potentially valuable source of information on party positions is the coding of party platforms undertaken by the European Consortium on Political Research's Parties Manifestos Project (PMP) (Budge, Robertson, and Hearl 1986), which encompasses twelve of the sixteen countries in the sample over most elections of the postwar era (Finland, Iceland, Portugal, and Spain are omitted).[8] For each party and election that it covers, the PMP data set registers the proportion of manifesto statements allocated to each of fifty-five subject categories. In West European systems, one would expect the most important dimension spanning party manifesto data to be a Left–Right one. A principal components analysis of these data, using a scheme that weights each country equally, sustains this expectation: the first principal component orders parties in a recognizably Left–Right fashion in all countries. The party positions on this dimension were therefore employed to generate range and standard deviation versions of a Left–Right diversity measure.

One potential weakness of data derived from country-specific sources is that they may not produce good comparative results. This appears to be true of the PMP data set. For instance, Italy is normally considered to have a polarized party system, yet the range of Italian party positions derived from the principal components analysis of the PMP data turns out to be much smaller than that for certain other systems normally considered less polarized, including Norway and Sweden. In this situation, a better strategy might be to utilize the PMP data as a tool to refine other scales, rather than as a source for scales in its own right. Discriminant analysis is a valuable technique in this regard because it can be employed to calculate linear combinations of the PMP variables that, under certain assumptions, optimally discriminate among the categories of other scales. These linear combinations can then be used to generate "predicted" party positions that may represent party ideological positions more accurately than do the original scales.[9] One aspect of this enhanced accuracy is that countries no longer receive just one set of scale positions for the entire 1945–89 period; instead, the party positions are adjusted for each election coded in the PMP data set according to the party manifestos issued at that time.

Figure 4.1 illustrates this procedure for the case of Italy in 1983. The first scale in the figure reproduces Browne, Gleiber, and Mashoba's (1984) Italian party system scale. The second scale collapses this array into its five basic categories (extreme Left, moderate Left, center, moderate Right, and extreme Right) to provide the "target" categories for the discriminant analysis. For purposes of comparison, the party positions for 1983 generated by the first principal component of the PMP data are given in the third scale. Although the ordering appears to be approximately Left–Right, the parties are clustered very close to one another, suggesting that the party platforms in themselves do not distinguish among the parties very efficaciously. When the PMP data are utilized in the discriminant analysis of the second scale, however, the result, shown in the fourth scale, is a much better-spaced and more intuitively plausible array.

In addition to the Browne, Gleiber, and Mashoba scales, discriminant analyses were performed on the Dodd scales and the socialist–bourgeois dichotomy; the

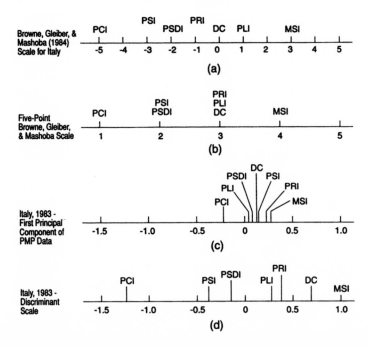

Figure 4.1. Generating a Left–Right party scale for Italy (1983). Only parties available for all scales are shown. Abbreviations: PCI, Communist Party; PSI, Socialist Party; PSDI, Social Democratic Party; PLI, Liberal Party; DC, Christian Democratic Party; PRI, Republican Party; MSI, Italian Social Movement; PMP, Party Manifestos Project.

predicted party positions were then employed to produce a new set of Left–Right diversity measures. It will come as little surprise, given the fact that the original scales were all "refined" by the same data, that these measures are even more highly intercorrelated than were the previous set. They are also highly correlated with the measures derived from the first principal component of the PMP data. This suggests that a strong underlying commonality might be revealed in principal components analyses of the range and standard deviation variants of these measures. Explained variances of 92.4% (range variants) and 93.1% (standard deviation variants) for the first principal components confirm this expectation. These components, which will be labeled as range and standard deviation versions of a PMP *Left–Right diversity* index, provide our second basic measure of Left–Right diversity; their sources and coverage are also listed in Table 4.2.

The outcome of this extensive exercise in data manipulation is two measures of Left–Right ideological diversity within governments, each combining the contributions of four different sources and each computed in both range and standard deviation versions. To determine which measure best explains the rate of termination, all four covariates were included in a forward-entry stepwise PL analysis, along with majority status, postelection status, investiture, and returnability. This analysis revealed the strongest contenders to be the range versions of expert Left–Right diversity and PMP Left–Right diversity: each of them enters the model (along with the four nonideological covariates) with approximately the same statistical significance. Moreover, once either is in the model, no other Left–Right diversity measure enters significantly. These results suggest that neither the refinement in measurement represented by the standard deviation versions nor the refinement added by the party manifesto data contribute very much to the explanation of government survival. Since the PMP version is available for a noticeably smaller number of cases, it might seem preferable to abandon it at this point, but we do not yet know how either of these covariates interacts with other ideological diversity measures that may prove relevant to government survival. For the time being, therefore, both covariates will be retained for further analysis. The effect of adding one of the alternatives, PMP Left–Right diversity, can be seen in a comparison of Models 1 and 2 of Table 4.3.

Voter-based measures. Just as the Eurobarometer 6, Eurobarometer 24, and Political Action surveys could be utilized to generate measures of ideological polarization for twelve West European party systems, so they can be used to provide measures of the ideological diversity within governments in those systems. As with the expert and manifesto measures, two versions of *voter Left–Right diversity* were created, one based on the ideological range of the government and the other on its standard deviation. Again, it was the range version that proved to be more closely related to government survival: only it, together with the four nonideological covariates, entered the model in a forward-entry stepwise procedure. The resultant five-covariate model is given as model 3 of Table 4.3.

Other dimensions

The clerical–secular dimension. After the Left–Right dimension, the clerical–secular distinction has undoubtedly attracted the most attention in the literature on West European party systems. Fewer efforts have been made to develop party scales for this dimension, however, and the analysis will be based on just two: Dodd's clerical scales and a clerical–secular dichotomy based on Warwick (1979). Discriminant analyses were employed to refine each set of scales with the PMP data, as before, and measures of ideological diversity derived from both the original scales and the refined scales were computed in range and standard deviation versions. The result is eight different measures of clerical–secular diversity within governments.

In a stepwise PL analysis that included the four nonideological covariates plus these eight alternative measures of clerical–secular diversity, the range version of the measure based on Dodd's clerical scales was the only clerical–secular diversity variable to enter the model significantly.[10] Given the finer distinctions they embody, it is not surprising that the Dodd scales prove to be superior source material to the clerical–secular dichotomy; more striking, perhaps, is the finding that both the weighting of ideological positions by party sizes and the refinement of

Table 4.3. *Ideological diversity and government survival*

	Model						
	1	2	3	4	5	6	7
Nonideological attributes							
Majority status	-1.20	-1.48	-1.99	-1.70	-1.33	-1.67	-1.76
	(0.18)	(0.19)	(0.23)	(0.22)	(0.18)	(0.21)	(0.21)
Postelection status	-0.77	-0.80	-0.87	-0.66	-0.59	-0.70	-0.60
	(0.16)	(0.16)	(0.16)	(0.17)	(0.17)	(0.18)	(0.17)
Investiture	0.88	0.91	0.65	0.74	0.69	0.58	0.68
	(0.17)	(0.16)	(0.15)	((0.17)	(0.17)	(0.16)	(0.18)
Returnability	2.29	2.12	2.40	1.61	2.18	2.68	1.63
	(0.46)	(0.46)	(0.55)	(0.49)	(0.46)	(0.59)	(0.49)
Ideological diversity measures							
PMP Left-Right diversity (range)	—	0.35	—	—	—	—	0.25
		(0.08)					(0.08)
Voter Left-Right diversity (range)	—	—	0.30	—	—	—	—
			(0.06)				
Dodd clerical-secular diversity (range)	—	—	—	0.26	—	—	0.15
				(0.06)			(0.06)
Dodd regime-support diversity (range)	—	—	—	—	0.24	—	0.17
					(0.05)		(0.06)
Postmaterialist diversity (SD)	—	—	—	—	—	5.31	—
						(1.53)	
Log-likelihood	-867.6	-857.6	-850.1	-855.8	-886.0	-751.5	-846.7
Number of cases	284	284	271	284	292	241	284

Note: Coefficients are PL estimates (standard errors in parentheses).

the Dodd scales with party manifesto data hindered rather than helped the capacity of this type of diversity to account for government survival. The contribution of the range version of *Dodd clerical–secular diversity* is given in model 4 of Table 4.3.

The regime-support dimension. Another ideological dimension commonly held to characterize some European party systems is the regime-support dimension; it distinguishes parties according to their commitment to the parliamentary system itself. As with the clerical–secular dimension, the only sources for this dimension are the Dodd scales and a dichotomous antisystem–prosystem dichotomy based on Warwick (1979). Range and standard deviation measures were produced from both scales.

Because so few countries had any governments that spanned the prosystem–antisystem dichotomy (i.e., included antisystem parties), there is little point in applying discriminant analyses to the dichotomous scale. The Dodd scale, which characterizes parties according to their degree of regime support, is a suitable object for this type of refinement, however, and both range and standard deviation versions of a PMP-refined Dodd scale were computed. This brings the total number of alternative measures of government diversity along the regime-support dimension to six.

PL analyses analogous to those performed for the clerical–secular diversity measures indicated that the range version of the measure based on the (unrefined) Dodd scales is the most closely related to the hazard rate; no other measure of the concept played a significant role. Given that few governments show any diversity on the dichotomous measure, it was to be expected that a version based on the Dodd scales would turn out to perform the best. Once again, neither the added information represented by the standard deviation versions nor that provided by the manifesto data proved to be of any value. The contribution of the range version of the *Dodd regime-support diversity* measure appears in model 5 of Table 4.3.

The materialist–postmaterialist dimension. The final dimension that will be considered is the materialist–postmaterialist dimension identified most closely with Inglehart (1977, 1990). There is no expert coding of party positions on this issue, but it is possible to derive party positions indirectly from public opinion surveys. Each of the surveys utilized earlier to develop voter-based measures of Left–Right diversity also includes Inglehart's three-point materialist–postmaterialist values index. Materialist–postmaterialist party scales can be constructed from these sources by taking the mean score of each party's supporters on the index as an indicator of that party's position. Two sets of scales were created in this fashion, one using Eurobarometer 6 and the other using Eurobarometer 24; each was supplemented with scales for Finland and Austria calculated from the Political Action survey data.[11] When range and standard deviation versions of the *postmaterialist diversity* measures developed from these sets of scales were tested in a stepwise PL analysis, the standard deviation version of the measure incorporating Eurobarometer 24 proved to be the only one to enter the model significantly. Its contribution is indicated in model 6 of Table 4.3.

Partial and total effects

Thus far we have considered separately the effects on government termination rates of ideological diversity along four distinct dimensions and found significant relationships for each dimension. These dimensions are not independent of one another, however. Anticlerical parties tend to be concentrated on the left of the political spectrum, for example, and antisystem parties, although occasionally found on the extreme right, are more often located in the postwar era on the extreme left. The key test therefore consists of assessing the impact of the various ideological diversity covariates relative to one another.

Six measures of ideological diversity have been identified in the preceding analyses as potentially significant influences on government survival: the range versions of expert, PMP, and voter Left–Right diversity, the range versions of Dodd clerical–secular and Dodd regime-support diversity, and the standard deviation version of postmaterialist diversity based on Eurobarometer 24. When these measures were included along with the four nonideological covariates in a forward-entry PL analysis, all covariates entered the model significantly with the exceptions of expert Left–Right diversity, voter Left–Right diversity, and postmaterialist diversity. The first exclusion indicates that although both the discriminant and nondiscriminant versions of the expert Left–Right measure performed equally well in the first-stage analysis, the refinement provided by the PMP data does contribute additional explanatory power once the other ideological covariates are taken into account; the PMP version also performs better than the voter-derived measure.[12] As for the postmaterialism dimension, it may well be an increasingly important dimension in West European politics, but it appears that party differences on it have not been an important source of government terminations over the postwar era to 1989. The final model produced by this analysis is given as model 7 of Table 4.3.[13]

Model 7 indicates that the Left–Right, clerical–secular, and regime-support dimensions of ideological diversity all make significant independent contributions to the explanation of government survival. But the very fact that ideological diversity is partitioned into three separate dimensions raises another consideration. We have seen that each of the ideological diversity covariates in the model is more closely related to survival than any of its alternatives, but this in itself does not establish that their combined effect outweighs that which would be produced by combined measures generated from other scales. Earlier, I noted that Dodd measured the cleavage conflict of a party system by averaging standard deviation values across all of his dimensions; an adaptation of that practice would be to create a total ideological diversity index by summing ideological diversity values derived from the three Dodd cleavage dimensions used here. This can be done both for the range and standard deviation measures of ideological diversity based on the original Dodd scales and for the corresponding measures based on the scales as modified by the discriminant analyses. Concerning the other type of scale common to all three dimensions – the Left–Right, clerical–secular, and regime-support dichotomies – diversity values can also be summed across dimensions to produce a total cleavage diversity index in both range and standard deviation versions.

To test these combined indices against the ideological diversity covariates identified in model 7, we require a method of combining the latter into a single index. The simplest method is to sum the three covariates, using the coefficients listed in the model as weights. Although other methods could be used, this method has the advantage not only of simplicity but of nonintrusiveness: the index receives a coefficient of 1.00 when entered into model 7 in place of its components, but all other estimated coefficients remain the same. The question to be addressed is: How well does this index perform in comparison with the six others just described?

The index proposed for the three ideological diversity covariates in model 7 conveys the maximum contribution that the three covariates can provide to the explanation of government survival, controlling for the other covariates in the model. When tested against the other proposed indexes of total ideological diversity in a forward-entry stepwise PL procedure, it proved to have by far the most significant net impact on the dependent variable; moreover, once it is in the model, no other index is able to enter the model significantly.[14] It appears, then, that the three ideological diversity measures of model 7 represent, individually and in combination, the best measurement of the concept that can be derived from the sources collected for this study.

The ideological locations of governments

The analyses undertaken in this section have assumed that if ideology affects government survival, it must do so by means of its diversity within governments. It is possible, however, that another aspect of ideology plays a role: the ideological *positions* of governments. In this subsection, we consider whether rates of termination vary significantly with the leftward or rightward position of governments.

The import of this issue is to shift the emphasis from the ideological range or standard deviation of a government to its ideological mean or "center of gravity." Each of the Left–Right scales employed earlier to develop diversity measures can also be used to generate mean Left–Right positions for governments. To capture fully the idea of a government's center of gravity, the mean positions were calculated so as to take into account not only the Left–Right positions of the member parties, but also their relative sizes; the final values are thus weighted means.

As was the case with the diversity measures derived from these scales, the mean positions computed from the different Left–Right scales intercorrelate very highly. This suggests that principal components analysis may be used to generate good overall measures of Left–Right positions. Two such composite measures were developed: one based on the Left–Right scales that contributed to expert Left–Right diversity (CM, D1, BGM, and SB) and the second based on the source scales for PMP Left–Right diversity (PMP1, D1D, BGMD, SBD). The first measure, which may be labeled *expert Left–Right position*, derives from a principal component that accounts for 93.7% of the variance of its sources; the second, PMP *Left–Right position*, comes from a principal component with 89.4% explained variance to its credit.

Although the high levels of explained variance suggest a large measure of agreement among sources on Left–Right positions, these positions appear not to matter at all for government survival: PL analyses indicate that neither expert Left–Right position nor its PMP-enhanced counterpart has any significant role to play. This is true when these measures were tested in bivariate relationships with the rate of government termination as well as when they were entered in PL models along with the significant covariates identified earlier.[15] Evidently, what counts for government survival is not where a government is centered on the Left–Right spectrum, but rather how far it ranges along that and other spectra.

BARGAINING ENVIRONMENT OR IDEOLOGICAL DIVERSITY?

The extensive analyses of the preceding section have identified significant independent effects on the rate of termination from three distinct dimensions of ideological diversity within governments: Left–Right, clerical–secular, and regime support. The question that must now be addressed is how well these relationships hold up against the bargaining-complexity interpretation. That interpretation, it will be recalled, sees instability as emanating from the capacity of small changes in party policies or parliamentary strengths to affect the distribution of bargaining power in complex multipolar systems, thereby creating incentives for some parties to alter coalition arrangements. Despite the apparent plausibility of the account, evidence has already appeared that challenges the hypothesized roles of its two main indicators of bargaining-environment complexity – effective party-system size and polarization.

The challenge involving effective party-system size is an empirical one: although it represents a straightforward operationalization of the complexity of the parliamentary bargaining environment, the analyses of Chapter 3 saw it displaced as a determinant of survival by effective government size. As for polarization, the challenge relates not to the existence of an effect on termination rates – there clearly is a very strong one – but rather to its interpretation. Polarization's superior ability to account for government survival vis-à-vis more sophisticated and comprehensive indicators suggests that its operationalization in terms of the presence of extremist parties is crucial to its performance; yet extremist parties are normally noncoalitionable, and their presence ought to simplify the bargaining environment and result in a *reduction* in governmental instability – precisely the opposite of what has been found.

These concerns bring us to the ideological diversity hypothesis. The essence of this interpretation is that governments terminate because they contain member parties that cannot agree with one another on government policy. Polarization plays an indirect, though powerful, role in this account because it indicates the root cause: the size of the extremist or antisystem presence in the parliament. The greater the antisystem presence, the more necessary it becomes to involve most of the remaining party spectrum if a prosystem majority government is to be formed. Because this remaining spectrum itself covers a wide ideological range, however, coalitions formed on this basis tend to be ideologically diverse. Terminations may be facilitated by member parties' knowledge that their chances of returning to office in the next government are good, given the parliamentary weight of the noncoalitionable parties, but policy differences among members of ideologically diverse governments remain central to the explanation of government survival.

One advantage of the ideological diversity perspective is that it provides a consistent interpretation of the strong positive link between polarization and the hazard rate. If the interpretation is correct, however, this connection should disappear or be substantially reduced once the more immediate causes, returnability and ideological diversity, are introduced into the analysis. As for effective government size, its effect, too, should disappear; under the hypothesis, it is not the effective number of government parties but the ideological differences among them that count.

These expectations are tested in a series of PL models given in Table 4.4. Model 1 repeats the six-covariate model (model 4) of Table 3.1, calculated on the basis of all available cases. Since the use of the PMP data restricts the available data noticeably, the model is reestimated on the basis of this reduced data set in model 2. Although coefficient values are affected to some extent by the reduction in cases, the key finding is that all coefficients remain significant in model 2. This result greatly facilitates the task of evaluating the two rival hypotheses.

Let us consider the role of returnability first. If returnability is left out of either of these models, the principal result is a very sizable strengthening of the coefficient associated with polarization. In model 2, for example, the polarization coefficient would increase from 3.65 to 4.47 with returnability excluded. This means that polarization's effect on the hazard rate has already been reduced by the presence of returnability in these models. The point to note about this result is that it is consistent with the hypothesis that the strong presence of antisystem parties curtails opportunities for alternation in power and leaves prosystem parties free to defect in the knowledge that they are very likely to return to power – along with most of their coalition partners – in the next government.

The evidence that the antisystem presence in the parliament is associated with lower levels of party turnover in government does not establish the main plank of the ideological diversity hypothesis, which is that governments terminate because of ideological differences. That plank can be established only by introducing ideological diversity directly into model 2. Given that three different measures of ideological diversity enter significantly into model 7 of Table 4.3, the total role of ideological diversity will be assessed (as before) by means of a weighted summation. The weights that will be used are given in model 3, which reports the effects of the three ideological diversity covariates plus majority status.[16] If the index constructed with these weights were substituted for its constituent covariates in model 3, it would receive a coefficient of 1.00; when entered along with the four nonbargaining covariates, model 4 shows that its coefficient drops to 0.67. The critical question is: What happens when polarization and effective government size are also entered into the model?

The results of this test are presented in model 5. The most striking finding is that the presence of the ideological diversity index causes effective government size to be reduced to statistical insignificance. Apparently, the effective number of parties in the government, which replaced the party-system size effect reported by King et al., is itself merely a surrogate for the government's ideological diversity. Model 6 reestimates the model, excluding the insignificant covariate.

The expectation that polarization's role in explaining rates of termination will turn out to be attributable to ideological diversity is also sustained in large measure by models 5 and 6: the presence of the ideological diversity index lowers polarization's coefficient from 3.65 in model 2 to 2.50 in model 6. It is noteworthy

Table 4.4. *Bargaining-environment versus ideological diversity hypotheses:
preliminary tests*

	Model					
	1	2	3	4	5	6
Covariates						
Majority status	-1.11	-1.07	-1.60	-1.73	-1.37	-1.39
	(0.16)	(0.19)	(0.21)	(0.20)	(0.23)	(0.23)
Postelection status	-0.61	-0.57	—	-0.55	-0.51	-0.49
	(0.15)	(0.17)		(0.17)	(0.17)	(0.17)
Investiture	0.44	0.54	—	0.62	0.50	0.49
	(0.15)	(0.18)		(0.17)	(0.19)	(0.19)
Effective government size	0.20	0.18	—	—	0.11	—
	(0.06)	(0.06)			(0.07)	
Returnability	1.60	1.44	—	1.62	1.34	1.30
	(0.47)	(0.51)		(0.48)	(0.51)	(0.50)
Polarization	3.54	3.65	—	—	2.62	2.50
	(0.62)	(0.69)			(0.83)	(0.82)
Ideological diversity index	—	—	—	0.67	0.34	0.43
				(0.11)	(0.14)	(0.13)
PMP Left-Right diversity	—	—	0.19	—	—	—
			(0.08)			
Dodd clerical-secular diversity	—	—	0.26	—	—	—
			(0.06)			
Dodd regime-support diversity	—	—	0.30	—	—	—
			(0.05)			
Log-likelihood	-1,120.1	-844.9	-866.4	-847.9	-842.2	-843.3
Number of cases	360	284	284	284	284	284

Note: Coefficients are PL estimates (standard errors in parentheses).

that the index's coefficient is also lowered considerably, from 0.67 (model 4) to 0.43 (model 6). These results indicate that the two covariates overlap in their abilities to account for survival and that the PL procedure has divided the shared effect between them.

Given that this allocation is done according to statistical rather than theoretical criteria, one might be tempted to argue on theoretical grounds that the shared variance "ought" to be attributed solely to ideological diversity. Even if this argument is correct, however, it ignores the fact that the polarization covariate could not have survived in the model unless it is still registering some residual effect on government survival that cannot be attributed to the ideological diversity index. How could this be?

One answer would be that stripped of its association with the ideological diversity within governments, polarization records a weaker but still noticeable effect on survival emanating from the complexity of the bargaining environment. Before reopening the door to the bargaining approach, however, let us examine the ideological diversity interpretation more closely. The essence of that interpretation is that the polarization variable shows a positive relationship with the rate of government termination because a strong parliamentary presence for antisystem parties tends to necessitate the formation of ideologically diverse governments. This line of reasoning is based on the assumption that the governments to be formed are *majority* governments; obviously, governments that do not command parliamentary majorities may be much less diverse. Although minority governments may avoid the problem of internal ideological diversity, they must face the problem of mustering parliamentary support from outside their ranks. Thus, the ideological diversity that minority governments must deal with is not fully represented by their own composition: their survival depends on the ideological positions of parties that are neither cabinet members nor declared or formal support parties.[17]

On this reasoning, one would expect polarization's remaining effect on survival to be concentrated in minority governments because only in those cases would the ideological diversity within governments not be sufficient to capture the full diversity on which their fate depends. This hypothesis can be tested very easily by reestimating model 6 of Table 4.4 separately for majority and minority governments. Table 4.5, which contains the results, confirms this expectation unequivocally: although polarization shows a highly significant impact on government survival in both majority and minority situations before ideological diversity is introduced (models 1 and 3), a comparison of models 2 and 4 shows that it survives the introduction of the ideological diversity index only in minority government situations. Correspondingly, the significant effect conveyed by the ideological diversity index is confined to majority governments.

Table 4.5 provides an important additional measure of confirmation for the ideological diversity hypothesis because it sustains an explanation for the residual presence of polarization in the full model that is consistent with the hypothesis. Where the ideological diversity on which a government's survival depends is encompassed within the government's membership, then ideological diversity does indeed replace polarization (as well as effective government size). Where the full ideological diversity relevant for governmental survival extends beyond the government's own membership, however, polarization continues to exercise a residual role by representing relevant aspects of ideological diversity that the index cannot. Thus, the lingering presence of polarization in Table 4.4 is not an anomaly; it is testimony to the problems minority governments face in attracting support in ideologically polarized parliaments.[18]

Table 4.5. *Survival in minority and majority governments*

	Minority governments		Majority governments	
	Model 1	Model 2	Model 3	Model 4
Covariates				
Postelection status	-0.37	-0.36	-0.68	-0.57
	(0.27)	(0.27)	(0.24)	(0.24)
Investiture	0.41	0.33	0.51	0.55
	(0.30)	(0.31)	(0.24)	(0.24)
Returnability	1.26	1.22	1.34	0.48
	(0.83)	(0.84)	(0.68)	(0.70)
Polarization	4.20	3.77	3.86	1.18
	(1.34)	(1.43)	(0.81)	(1.10)
Ideological diversity[a]	—	0.27	—	0.64
		(0.24)		(0.17)
Log-likelihood	-205.0	-204.4	-531.2	-524.6
Number of cases	84	84	200	200

Note: Coefficients are PL estimates (standard errors in parentheses).
[a]Ideological diversity is a linear combination of PMP Left-Right diversity, Dodd clerical-secular diversity, and Dodd regime-support diversity, using the coefficients derived from model 3 of Table 4.4 as weights.

IDEOLOGY AND MINIMAL WINNING STATUS

The evidence of this chapter provides considerable justification for accepting ideological diversity as a contributing factor to government survival. If this is so, why has this factor been so neglected in previous work? Apart from the difficulties of measuring ideological diversity, the explanation is largely to be found in the emphasis early game-theoretic approaches placed on the desire of parties to share in the spoils of office rather than to realize policy goals as such. *Minimal winning* (MW) status[19] became the favorite independent variable for this reason; it suggested that what mattered most was not sharing the rewards of office more widely than was strictly necessary to command a parliamentary majority. When policy concerns were taken up, it was usually done within the context of minimizing bargaining difficulties among coalition members, a condition believed to be favored in "connected" coalitions, that is, coalitions formed of parties adjacent on a Left–Right scale. Combining these two considerations led to the expectation that *minimal connected winning* (MCW) governments – governments that cannot lose a member party without ceasing to be either connected or minimal winning –

would tend to form and, if formed, would be especially durable (Axelrod 1970). Although embodying primarily an office-seeking perspective, the MCW hypothesis became the principal expression of the role of ideological or policy considerations in government survival.[20]

There is clearly an element of plausibility in the assertion that governments would prefer not to have more members than required for a majority (or fewer). Yet if the ability to bargain among coalition members is also an important consideration – which most likely means that parties are policy seekers as well as office seekers – then one can readily imagine a scenario in which even MW coalitions are unable to overcome internal policy or ideological differences. In fact, it may be that the relationship between MW or MCW status and survival is largely or even entirely due to the fact that governments with these properties tend to be less diverse than other majority governments. Does being "minimal" matter, or is it simply a surrogate for being ideologically nondiverse?

This question will be explored in this section using both the C (cabinet only) and the CDS data subsets. The reason for this double test is that the MW hypothesis, although embodying primarily an office-seeking rationale, can also be given a policy-seeking interpretation: parties prefer MW coalitions in order to minimize policy compromises. Under the former, the benefits of MW governments extend only to cabinet members; where policy matters, however, support parties stand to gain by keeping the government in power so as to realize policy goals.

Table 4.6 contains the results of tests of the role of MW status for both the C and CDS definitions of government membership. The results listed under model 1 show that when majority status and MW status are entered together in a PL analysis using either data set, the MW effect dominates, reducing majority status to insignificance. The same basic pattern also appears in the reduced sample (model 2) for which the ideological variables are available. To determine the extent to which this effect is due to a tendency for MW governments to be less ideologically diverse than other majority governments, the ideological diversity index is added in model 3. The result is a reversal: majority status now enters the model significantly and with the expected sign, while MW status is reduced to near insignificance. Moreover, with the other fixed covariates in the model (model 4), MW status becomes statistically insignificant in both data subsets. Although the MCW hypothesis is an attempt to inform the minimal winning condition with the necessity of governments to keep bargaining difficulties (i.e., ideological diversity) in check, the application of this testing procedure to MCW status (not shown) produces exactly the same sequence of results.

Further evidence that the minimal winning condition is not the key to longevity in office can be obtained by considering the effect of ideological diversity on government survival *within* minimal winning governments. If MW status were all that was required, then ideological diversity should play no role in the survival of these governments. As Table 4.7 indicates, however, regardless of whether government membership is defined broadly or not, the ideological diversity index has virtually as powerful an effect on survival for MW governments as it does for all governments.[21]

Table 4.6. *Minimal winning status versus ideological diversity*

	Model			
	1	2	3	4
I. C data subset				
Covariates				
Majority status	0.25 (0.16)	0.45 (0.18)	-1.01 (0.29)	-0.77 (0.30)
Minimal winning status	-1.34 (0.17)	-1.49 (0.20)	-0.49 (0.25)	-0.34 (0.27)
Ideological diversity[a]	—	—	0.86 (0.12)	0.40 (0.15)
Postelection status	—	—	—	-0.35 (0.18)
Investiture	—	—	—	0.54 (0.19)
Returnability	—	—	—	1.06 (0.53)
Polarization	—	—	—	2.10 (0.91)
Log-likelihood	-1,174.4	-879.0	-853.9	-834.0
Number of cases	361	281	281	281
II. CDS data subset				
Covariates				
Majority status	0.08 (0.16)	0.25 (0.18)	-1.15 (0.27)	-1.14 (0.28)
Minimal winning status	-1.32 (0.17)	-1.48 (0.19)	-0.57 (0.23)	-0.40 (0.25)
Ideological diversity[a]	—	—	0.85 (0.11)	0.35 (0.14)
Postelection status	—	—	—	-0.47 (0.17)
Investiture	—	—	—	0.50 (0.19)
Returnability	—	—	—	1.46 (0.52)
Polarization	—	—	—	2.20 (0.84)
Log-likelihood	-1,186.8	-890.6	-863.4	-842.0
Number of cases	364	284	284	284

Note: Coefficients are PL estimates (standard errors in parentheses).
[a]Constructed as in Table 4.5, using weights derived from the appropriate data subset.

The state of being minimal winning, whether defined narrowly in terms of the cabinet membership or expanded to incorporate formal and support parties as well, appears not to contribute any noticeable effect on survival once factors such as ideological diversity are taken into account. But could there be an effect related to the degree to which a government approaches MW status? One could argue, for instance, that a government that falls just slightly below majority status may well face no greater risk of termination than a majority government – even a small degree of dissension or absenteeism among opponents on any issue would allow the

Table 4.7. *The effects of ideological diversity in minimal winning governments*

	C data subset		CDS data subset	
	All governments (model 1)	Minimal winning governments (model 2)	All governments (model 3)	Minimal winning governments (model 4)
Covariates				
Majority status	-1.43 (0.19)	—	-1.60 (0.19)	—
Ideological diversity[a]	1.00 (0.10)	0.98 (0.24)	1.00 (0.09)	0.93 (0.22)
Log-likelihood	-855.8	-207.7	-866.4	-224.6
Number of cases	281	110	284	120

Note: Coefficients are PL estimates (standard errors in parentheses).
[a]See Table 4.6.

government to survive. Similarly, the division of spoils in a government that is just slightly above MW status may not be sufficiently suboptimal to provoke a government collapse.

Dodd (1976:117–19), who saw this conceptualization as crucial to government survival, proposed three variants of what he termed *cabinet coalitional status* to measure deviation from MW status. The first assesses the degree of deviation as a product of (1) the number of parties that would have to be added or removed to achieve MW status and (2) the weight or percentage of parliamentary seats held by these parties. Since more than one set of parties can often be chosen, this measure selects the set whose weight is minimal for undersized governments and maximal for oversized ones. The second measure is identical to the first except that it chooses among competing sets of parties on the basis of their products rather than their weights alone. The third version differs from the first in that it ignores party numbers and bases deviancy from MW status solely in terms of parliamentary weights.

The present data set contains the most strongly differentiated of the three measures of cabinet coalitional status (CCS), the first and third variants. Testing of these variants against majority status indicated that the first or main version of the variable is in fact the more closely related to government survival in both the C and CDS data subsets. This version of CCS was therefore subjected to precisely the same sequence of analyses as were MW status and MCW status. The results, presented in Table 4.8, show that its significant impact on government survival is eliminated by the ideological diversity index alone in both data sets. Interestingly, when the other covariates are added to the model, CCS becomes significant in the

Table 4.8. *Cabinet coalitional status versus ideological diversity*

	Model			
	1	2	3	4
I. C data subset				
Covariates				
Majority status	-0.37 (0.14)	-0.27 (0.16)	-1.33 (0.20)	-0.86 (0.25)
Cabinet coalitional status	1.56 (0.28)	2.05 (0.36)	0.66 (0.42)	1.04 (0.43)
Ideological diversity[a]	—	—	0.93 (0.11)	0.38 (0.13)
Postelection status	—	—	—	-0.38 (0.18)
Investiture	—	—	—	0.58 (0.19)
Returnability	—	—	—	0.97 (0.52)
Polarization	—	—	—	2.40 (0.87)
Log-likelihood	-1,191.1	-893.2	-854.6	-832.3
Number of cases	361	281	281	281
II. CDS data subset				
Covariates				
Majority status	-0.53 (0.14)	-0.45 (0.16)	-1.57 (0.21)	-1.36 (0.24)
Cabinet coalitional status	1.60 (0.27)	1.77 (0.32)	0.16 (0.39)	0.25 (0.39)
Ideological diversity[a]	—	—	0.98 (0.11)	0.40 (0.14)
Postelection status	—	—	—	-0.49 (0.17)
Investiture	—	—	—	0.51 (0.19)
Returnability	—	—	—	1.31 (0.51)
Polarization	—	—	—	2.46 (0.82)
Log-likelihood	-1,205.7	-909.0	-866.3	-843.1
Number of cases	364	284	284	284

Note: Coefficients are PL estimates (standard errors in parentheses).
[a]See Table 4.6.

C data subset only. Further analyses reveal that this result is confined entirely to minority situations, suggesting that the effect of counting only cabinet members is to overestimate the degree to which minority governments fall short of majority status, while underestimating other factors such as the degree of ideological diversity they must deal with.

The issue of the differences in results across different definitions of government membership will be discussed more fully in Chapter 7. All in all, however, the results of this section suggest that the minimal winning approach, whether treated as a dichotomy, a continuum, or qualified by a connectedness criterion, is a false track: apparently, it is not whether a government represents or approaches a minimum of bargaining complexity and spoils sharing that matters, but rather how ideologically complex it actually is.

CONCLUDING REMARKS

Most of the work that has been done on governing coalitions in parliamentary contexts allocates a central role to the minimal winning criterion, defined in terms of cabinet membership. As Laver and Schofield (1990:68–9) point out, however, this focus makes sense only if policy or ideology matters relatively little to political parties. To the extent that policy does matter, formal cabinet membership becomes less important, since policy outputs are public goods available to all. Where policy concerns predominate, therefore, MW cabinets lose their privileged status in both formation and survival theory.

The evidence presented in this book indicates that West European parties are indeed policy oriented. Not only do measures of the ideological range of governments along Left–Right, clerical–secular, and regime-support dimensions relate significantly to rates of termination, but they eliminate the association of minimal winning cabinets with stability that has guided so much previous research. Majority governments, in control of their own parliamentary destinies, do last longer than minority ones, but beyond that, no survival advantage derives from achieving or approaching the minimal winning condition. Nor does modifying MW status to incorporate ideological diversity, whether by adding the connectedness criterion or by expanding the government to include formal and declared support parties, improve its performance; ideology must be reckoned with in its own right.

The bargaining-complexity interpretation advanced by Laver and Schofield and seconded by King et al. seeks to avoid the limitations of earlier approaches by taking account of the ideological or policy positions of parties and jettisoning any binding linkage to minimal winning status. Its basic argument is that governmental instability is characteristic of complex bargaining environments because they allow greater scope for small changes in party positions or strengths to alter the distribution of bargaining power, thereby encouraging attempts to unravel coalitions. Three variables that showed significant effects in the KABL model are interpreted as indicators of bargaining-system complexity: the fractionalization and polarization of the parliamentary party system and the number of failed formation attempts. Of the three, the party system's fractionalization or effective size is undoubtedly the most central. The data analysis undertaken here indicates, however, that its role in the explanation of government stability does not survive the introduction of the government's effective size; this latter variable, moreover, turns out to be a surrogate for its ideological diversity. As for formation attempts, this effect, weak in the King et al. analysis, is insignificant in the data set used here. This leaves polarization as the only indicator of bargaining-environment complexity that survives when ideological diversity and the other significant covariates (majority status, investiture, postelection status, and returnability) are included in the analysis. Nevertheless, it is difficult to interpret the role of this variable in a fashion supportive of the bargaining-complexity thesis.

Laver and Schofield (1990:162) suggest that stability in a bargaining system may be assessed by the number of alternative governing coalitions that appear to be viable at any given time – the greater this number, the more unstable the system. Yet the evidence presented here indicates that polarization's effect on government survival is tied to its operationalization in terms of the proportion of parliamentary seats controlled by extremist parties. Since these parties are usually noncoalitionable (Laver and Schofield 1990:200–1), one would expect high polarization values to be associated with a reduction in coalitional alternatives and hence a greater stability for bargaining environments and for governments. In fact, the relationship of polarization to survival runs in the opposite direction: higher polarization values are associated with greater instability.

To understand this result, we need to approach the role of the polarization variable from a different angle. We begin by assuming that the variable measures exactly what it appears to measure, the size of the noncoalitionable part of the parliament. If this is the case, then it should be positively associated with returnability: a larger noncoalitionable presence implies a greater likelihood that a given coalitionable party will have to be included in any majority government. The correlation between the two variables is in fact .38 ($p < .01$). More important, the widespread involvement of coalitionable or prosystem parties in government should translate, other things being equal, into greater levels of governmental ideological diversity (assuming majority governments can be formed at all). Taking both features into account leads to the hypothesis that governments terminate sooner in polarized systems because policy disagreements among government members are more likely to arise and because members know their chances of returning to power in the next government are high – in other words, the costs of defecting are relatively small. The relationships of returnability and ideological diversity with the rate of government termination, as well as their roles in reducing the effect of polarization, are consistent with this reasoning.

The final piece of evidence that polarization is a surrogate for ideological diversity derives from its role in minority governments. By definition, minority governments depend on support from outside their membership; given the definition of government membership used here, this means outside the ranks of their formal and declared support parties as well. To obtain this support, they must deal in some fashion with the policy or ideological preferences of one or more nongovernment parties. Thus, unlike majority governments, the ideological diversity with which minority governments contend extends beyond that represented within their ranks. On the assumptions (1) that the measures developed in this chapter adequately measure ideological diversity within governments and (2) that the residual presence of polarization in the model stands in for unmeasured ideological diversity that governments face, one would expect its effect to be confined to these minority situations. We have seen that this is indeed the case.

The analysis of the past two chapters has resulted in an explanation of government survival markedly different from its predecessors. Nevertheless, it bears one striking similarity: it comprises only variables that are fixed or constant throughout a government's period of office. If the events theorists' critique of attribute approaches has any validity, however, then the explanation must be deemed incomplete since it ignores developments taking place during the lifetimes of governments. These developments may be systematic in nature, such as trends in economic indicators, or they may be the random occurrences that so preoccupied the events theorists. In the next two chapters, we look for both types of effect, beginning with the systematic.

5

Economic conditions and government survival

The tendency to seek the causes of government survival in the attributes of governments or their parliamentary environments, which characterizes the past two chapters as well as most previous empirical work, implies a static perspective on the topic. Changes in these kinds of attributes affect the survival of governments only in a comparative static sense – by altering the predicted survival rate for a government as a whole. What is excluded is the possibility that the hazard rate of any one government may vary over time in accordance with changes in other factors.

A prime candidate for a dynamic influence on government survival is the evolving state of the economy. In the period since 1945, citizens of West European polities have come to expect their governments to manage economic affairs so as to assure high levels of employment and reasonable price stability; most elections, in consequence, have the state of the economy as their main issue. Although government survival in parliamentary regimes depends more often on parliamentarians than voters, it may be expected that parliamentary support for governments also varies with the economic conditions that seem to matter so much to the public – after all, parliamentarians are responsible to their electorates in the final analysis.

Despite the very considerable attention devoted to associating economic conditions with government standings in opinion polls or with electoral outcomes (Paldam 1981; Lewis-Beck 1988), the related question of how the economy affects government survival has only rarely been tackled. A standard property of these investigations, moreover, is the characterization of economic conditions during each government by means of average economic indicator values (e.g., Robertson 1983b, 1983c; Budge and Keman 1990:176–82), thereby confining the analysis to a static format.[1] There is no need to adopt this tactic: one of the principal advantages of event history analysis over techniques such as regression is that it can incorporate variables whose values change over the duration of individual cases directly into the analysis. The intent of this chapter is to exploit this capacity to determine whether, and under what conditions, rates of inflation, unemployment, and economic growth convey significant independent effects on government survival in West European parliamentary democracies.

METHODS AND DATA

As one might expect, the introduction of time-varying covariates complicates the analysis considerably: instead of associating one value of a given covariate with each government, each government must now be linked to the variety of different covariate values that crop up over the course of its existence. An added complication follows from the fact that this linkage is achieved in partial likelihood analysis by a procedure that differs fundamentally from that employed in maximum likelihood analysis. In this section, I briefly introduce the PL approach to time-varying covariates, discuss the manner in which it will be implemented in the present investigation, and outline the sources of the economic data that will be utilized. The method of handling time-varying covariates in maximum likelihood (ML) estimation will be taken up in the next chapter, where attention turns to the development of a full ML model.

We saw in Chapter 2 that the PL method, in essence, determines whether a given covariate x affects the hazard rate by comparing each case's x-value with the x-values for all cases that survived at least as long as it did; if the x-values for the surviving cases are generally lower (or higher), then the covariate is assumed to increase (decrease) the hazard. With time-varying covariates, the principle is the same: the PL technique compares, for the case that terminated at duration t, its x-value at that time with the x-values at the same point in the durations of all surviving cases. The implication is that a government's x-value must be known not just for the time it terminates, but for each of its duration values at which other governments have terminated as well.

Given that durations are recorded in days, the amount of data involved in these comparisons is potentially very large. This is less of a problem where an economic covariate is calculated as annual rates – growth rates in gross domestic product, for example – since the task of linking values to governments simply involves attributing an annual value to each day of the year in question. For inflation and unemployment, however, this may not be enough. Although these indicators are calculated in terms of annual rates, parliamentarians know that they are reported for monthly intervals and in fact are changing all the time. This suggests that it might be appropriate to derive daily estimates for these indicators from monthly data. This strategy can be implemented by recording the monthly indicator values for a limited number of time points over the course of each government's lifetime and estimating intermediate values by means of linear interpolation. Specifically, if x_1 and x_2 are the values of covariate x at times t_1 and t_2, respectively, the interpolated value of x at a time t that falls between them would be

$$x_T = x_1 + \{(t - t_1)(x_2 - x_1)\}/(t_2 - t_1),$$

where all times are measured from some fixed date such as the date the government was formed.[2]

To implement this strategy, it is necessary to select time points to use as the basis for interpolations. The procedure used here derives daily values for inflation and unemployment from linear interpolations of their December monthly values.

Clearly, the appropriateness of this procedure depends on the answers to two basic questions: (1) do December values represent good measurement points from which to interpolate values, and (2) are interpolated values based on one month per year sufficiently accurate?

Although, in principle, any month could have been chosen as the basis for the interpolations, December values possess the important property of being very close to annual values. The coefficients of 0.92 and 0.97 generated when annual values of inflation and unemployment, respectively, are correlated across all countries with their corresponding December values suggest that the December values are rarely idiosyncratic. In addition, the slope coefficients of 0.93 and 0.92 produced when the annual values are regressed on the December values indicate that December is broadly representative of the year as a whole (a perfect match would be reflected in a coefficient of unity). The effect of interpolating December values is therefore to register the trends in the data at a level that is representative of the entire year, eliminating in the process any distortions due to seasonal fluctuations (which are especially likely to afflict unemployment rates).

The smoothing effect of interpolation also removes a certain degree of month-to-month fluctuation that is normally present in economic data. If these fluctuations represent random "noise," this smoothing confers a significant added benefit (especially as the PL model does not incorporate a random disturbance term). It is possible, however, that the erratic high values that may occur in any month are what induce government collapses; if so, the data would underestimate the phenomenon. To test for this possibility, inflation was coded in two versions: the actual monthly rate and a pseudomonthly rate constructed from the interpolated daily values. When the relationships of the two variables with the rate of government termination were tested by means of the PL method, the pseudomonthly rate proved to have a noticeably stronger effect.[3] This finding suggests that parliamentarians react not to the bad figures of a single month but to underlying trends extending over longer periods of time – trends more clearly evident in the interpolated values.

The economic data collected for this investigation encompass the following indicators of economic performance: unemployment rates, inflation rates, and growth rates in gross domestic product. Information on these indicators was taken from publications of the United Nations (UN), the International Monetary Fund (IMF), and the Organization for Economic Cooperation and Development (OECD). The primary source for the unemployment data is the UN *Monthly Bulletin of Statistics* (1947–90). For earlier years, this source was supplemented, where appropriate, by data from the ILO's *International Labor Review*. Because of gaps and inconsistencies in the UN data for Spain and the Netherlands (in the 1980s), data from OECD's *Historical Statistics, 1969–88* (1990) were substituted in those cases.

Concerning inflation, annual values were taken from the IMF's *International Financial Statistics Yearbook* (1979, 1983, 1989). The December inflation values for the periods 1946–63, 1964–9, and 1970–89 derive from consumer price data listed in *International Labor Review* (1946–63), the ILO *Bulletin of Labor Statis-*

tics (1964–70), and the IMF *International Financial Statistics* (1970–90), respectively. For years in which only consumer price index values are given, the inflation rate was calculated from annual percentage changes in these values.

Data on the final type of economic indicator, gross domestic product, derive from two somewhat inconsistent sources: the OECD and the IMF. The first set of data are from the *OECD Economic Outlook* (1990a) for the period from 1970 and the *OECD National Accounts II: Main Aggregates, 1950–78* and *1960–88* (1980, 1990c) for the earlier years. The second series was taken from the IMF *International Financial Statistics Yearbook* (1983–9). To calculate growth rates in gross domestic product (GDP) per capita, population data were taken from the IMF yearbooks, updated by the *UN Monthly Bulletin of Statistics* (1989).

Despite the variety of sources consulted, the economic data for the sixteen countries of this study over the relevant time frames are far from complete. Concerning unemployment, rates are not available for the French Fourth Republic or Iceland and are scanty at best in the early years for most other countries. In addition, in several countries the method of calculating rates or index numbers is not consistent across the entire postwar period, producing values that are noncomparable. When changes in rates are the object of investigation, the loss of cases is not great (since only values spanning a transition in method have to be excluded), but when the rates themselves are being examined, the entire earlier series must be excluded, reducing the number of cases appreciably. The situation with respect to the other two indicators is not nearly so severe, but the consumer price data are less precise before 1964, when index values were given in whole numbers only. Following the IMF practice, rates for this period were calculated to the nearest whole number only. Fortunately, the lack of precision affects relationships only slightly.[4] Table 5.1 summarizes the availability of economic data for the countries of the sample.

The organization of the investigation into the interrelationship of economic conditions and government survival is as follows. In the next section, the basic time trends in the economic indicators over the postwar era will be examined and the various indicators will be tested for their connection to rates of government termination, using the PL method. The analysis will then be broadened to incorporate the causal factors identified in previous chapters. The final data analysis section examines the possibility that the impact of inflation and unemployment on government survival has varied over time and, in particular, that economic trends have had a greater impact on government stability in the more troubled economic climate prevalent in Europe since 1973. That section also considers the success that governments of different ideological complexions – specifically, socialist and nonsocialist – have had in coping with inflation and unemployment and relates these records to their survival in office.

TESTING ECONOMIC INDICATORS

Before beginning the data analysis proper, it is useful to have in mind a general impression of the behavior over time of the three economic indicators, the consumer

Table 5.1. *The availability of economic data*

	Economic indicator			
	Unemployment, annual		Unemployment, December	
	Recent series	Earlier series	Recent series	Earlier series
Austria	1957-89	1947-56	1957-89	1949-56
Belgium	1945-89	—	1947-89	—
Denmark	1977-89	1944-76	1977-89	1949-76
Finland	1976-89	1958-75	1976-89	1958-75
France	—	—	—	—
Iceland	—	—	—	—
Ireland	1953-89	1947-52	1953-89	1947-52
Italy	1969-89	1948	1969-89	1953-68
		1950-68		
Luxembourg	1955-89	—	1964-89	—
Netherlands	1948-88	—	1954-88	—
Norway	1944-89	—	1945-49	—
			1953-89	
Portugal	1975-89	—	1985-88	—
Spain	1978-89	—	1978-88	—
Sweden	1956-89	1947-55	1956-89	1947-55
United Kingdom	1944-89	—	1947-89	—
West Germany	1948-89	—	1948-89	—

	Economic indicator			
	Consumer prices		Gross domestic product	
	Annual series	December series	OECD series	IMF series
Austria	1944-89	1960-89	1951-89	1953-89
Belgium	1945-89	1948-89	1954-89	1954-89
Denmark	1944-89	1944-89	1951-89	1953-89
Finland	1946-89	1946-89	1951-89	1953-89
France	1949-58	—	1951-58	1953-58
Iceland	1950-89	1970-89	1951-89	1957-89
Ireland	1947-89	1947-89	1951-89	1953-89
Italy	1947-89	1948-89	1952-89	1953-89
Luxembourg	1946-89	1945-89	1961-89	1953-89
Netherlands	1945-89	1946-89	1951-89	1953-89
Norway	1944-89	1944-89	1951-89	1953-89

Table 5.1 (*continued*)

| | Economic indicator | | | |
| | Consumer prices | | Gross domestic product | |
	Annual series	December series	OECD series	IMF series
Portugal	1975-89	1975-89	1975-89	1975-89
Spain	1978-89	1978-89	1978-89	1978-89
Sweden	1947-89	1947-89	1951-89	1953-89
United Kingdom	1944-46	1944-46	1953-89	1953-89
	1948-89	1948-89		
West Germany	1950-89	1950-89	1951-89	1953-89

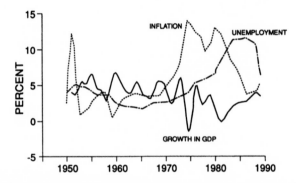

Figure 5.1. Average annual inflation, unemployment, and GDP growth rates, sixteen European countries, 1950–89. Sources: Consumer prices, International Monetary Fund; unemployment, United Nations; GDP, Organization for Economic Cooperation and Development.

price inflation rate, the unemployment rate, and the rate of growth in the GDP (OECD version). In Figure 5.1, the time trends of these indicators are presented for the period 1950–89. These trend lines are based on weighted averages of annual values of the indicators for the sixteen countries of the sample, with the populations of the countries comprising the weights. The year 1950 was chosen as the starting point because of the paucity of data before that time.

The trend lines pictured in Figure 5.1 indicate that after an initial bout of high inflation, both inflation and unemployment established and maintained relatively low levels throughout the 1950s and 1960s. In the 1970s, inflation rose to much higher levels and experienced two peaks, corresponding to the oil "shocks" of 1973–4 and 1979; it then declined dramatically in the 1980s. The rise in unem-

Table 5.2. *Economic covariates and survival*

	Annual values			Interpolated daily values		
	Coeff.	SE	*N*	Coeff.	SE	*N*
1. Inflation						
Rate of increase in consumer prices (%)	0.011	(0.006)	348	0.014	(0.008)	305
Change in rate over preceding year	0.017	(0.009)	345	0.024	(0.018)	292
2. Unemployment						
Unemployment rate (%), recent series	0.044	(0.017)	224	0.060	(0.018)	193
Change in rate over preceding year, all series	0.083	(0.072)	269	0.226	(0.057)	224
3. Gross domestic product						
(a) IMF series						
Rate of growth in GDP (%)	-0.013	(0.028)	292			
Change in rate over preceding year	-0.020	(0.024)	280			
Per capita growth rate (%)	-1.725	(2.837)	292			
Change in rate over preceding year	-2.199	(2.443)	277			
(b) OECD series						
Rate of growth in GDP (%)	-0.021	(0.028)	305			
Change in rate over preceding year	-0.036	(0.024)	296			
Per capita growth rate (%)	-2.503	(2.855)	305			
Change in rate over preceding year	-3.207	(2.419)	293			

Note: All coefficients are derived from PL analyses that include majority status as a control variable. Interpolated daily values for the inflation and unemployment covariates are derived from December monthly data.

ployment in the 1970s was much more gradual, reaching an apex only in the mid-1980s before beginning a substantial decline. As for economic growth as measured by the OECD's estimates of real increases in GDP, it oscillates much more frequently and regularly than do either of these indicators, but nonetheless reveals an overall tendency to decline over the period covered.

Although these trends contain few surprises, they do suggest that there is no simple trade-off between inflation and unemployment: both may be high or low at the same time. It is possible, therefore, that the two indicators have effects on government survival that are independent of each other. Conversely, there appears to be a tendency for higher levels of inflation and unemployment to be associated with lower GDP growth rates and vice versa, suggesting that the latter may not convey new information about economic performance.

The hypothesis that economic conditions are related to government survival receives a preliminary PL examination in Table 5.2. The table reports the effects on the hazard of a variety of economic covariates. For each economic indicator, the effect of the rate itself and the change in the rate over the preceding year (365 days) are recorded. In addition, the table shows the effects of inflation and unemployment calculated on the basis of both annual values and daily values interpolated from December data. It should be noted that each of these procedures was performed with majority status included as a control. This was done to prevent the possession of a parliamentary majority, or the lack of it, from masking the roles of economic covariates.[5]

The impact on government survival of the four inflation-based measures comprises the first part of the table. The direction of these relationships is as one would expect: high or increasing inflation rates are associated with higher hazard rates and thus a greater probability of government termination. A comparison of the two columns, one reporting the results for the covariates derived from annual consumer price data and the other the corresponding results for daily interpolations from December data, indicates that the coefficients are larger for the interpolated versions. Moreover, for the latter, it is clear that the inflation rate itself is more closely related to the hazard ($t = 1.76$) than is the change in the inflation rate over the preceding year ($t = 1.30$), even allowing for the slightly greater number of cases on which it is based. The t-value in question is, however, not particularly large, achieving statistical significance at the .05 level in a one-tailed test only.

The second part of the table presents the corresponding relationships for unemployment. For reasons of noncomparability of data series noted previously, the unemployment rate itself is taken only from the most recent data series. The measures involving changes in unemployment rates may appropriately include earlier series based on different counting methods, provided appropriate transitional situations are removed; this inclusion has the effect of increasing the number of cases modestly. The results again indicate that the covariates based on interpolated values provide the stronger relationships, although in this case it is the change in the unemployment rate over the preceding twelve months that figures more prominently in this regard. As the standard errors indicate, these relationships are noticeably stronger than were the corresponding relationships for the inflation covariates.

The final section of Table 5.2 shows the relationships with government termination of the growth in GDP. Eight versions of the hypothesis linking economic growth with government survival were tested, based on (1) whether the source of the GDP data is the IMF or the OECD, (2) whether the measurement utilizes simple growth rates or growth rates per capita, and (3) whether the growth rate itself or the change in the growth rate from the preceding year constitutes the independent variable. Although all relationships show that economic growth or increasing economic growth is associated with enhanced survival rates (lower hazard rates), none of the relationships is significant at the .05 level (one-tailed or two-tailed tests).

The results reported in Table 5.2 provide some indication that economic trends, especially unemployment, are indeed associated with government survival in West European parliamentary democracies. This assessment accords with Robertson's (1983b, 1983c) earlier findings that the duration of governments is significantly related to average levels of unemployment, but not inflation, in a more limited set of countries. The conclusion is, of course, ceteris paribus; we cannot place confidence in it until the linkages have been shown to persist even after other relevant causal factors have been taken into account. The next section is devoted to this task.

The analyses in the next section will utilize the two indicators that showed the most promising results in Table 5.2, the interpolated versions of the inflation rate and the change in the unemployment rate. Not only is each of these covariates more significantly related to government survival than is the other version of the same economic trait (as indicated by a comparison of *t*-values), but further analysis reveals that the presence of either of these measures in a PL model precludes a significant role for its alternative. This suggests that the alternative indicators have relatively little to add to the statistical explanation of government survival. This selection criterion is not foolproof, but in the absense of any theory linking specific indicators to government survival, it is probably the most appropriate way to proceed at this stage.[6]

BARGAINING COMPLEXITY, IDEOLOGICAL DIVERSITY, AND THE ECONOMY

We have seen that explanations of government survival in parliamentary contexts have tended to bifurcate along two very different interpretative lines: the bargaining-environment thesis and the ideological diversity thesis. The bargaining-environment interpretation associates government instability with changes in party positions or strengths that create incentives for parties to seek alternative coalitions. A complex bargaining environment – one with more parties aligned along a greater number of ideological dimensions – increases the likelihood that small changes will generate these alternatives. The ideological diversity interpretation, in contrast, sees government terminations as emanating principally from ideological or policy differences within governments, regardless of the availability of alternatives. Thus far in the analysis, the evidence has favored the ideological diversity hypothesis, but the model specification may be incomplete; the issue now is: Do economic trends play a significant independent role in the explanation of government survival and does this alter our understanding of the roles assigned previously to fixed attributes?

The analysis of the role of economic trends in the overall explanation of government survival begins with the model as it appeared in Chapter 4. That model is reproduced as model 1 of Table 5.3. Since the two economic covariates to be considered here, the inflation rate and the change in the unemployment rate, are not available for the full set of cases, model 2 of the table reestimates the model for the smaller set of cases for which complete data can be obtained.[7] Although the coefficient values are affected to some extent by the reduction in cases, the key finding is that all covariates but one – postelection status – remain significantly related to the hazard rate in model 2. Given that postelection status is not a theoretically important covariate from the perspective of either interpretation explored here, the similarity

Table 5.3. *Bargaining complexity, ideological diversity, and the economy*

	Model			
	1	2	3	4
Covariates				
Majority status	-1.39	-1.52	-1.69	-1.97
	(0.23)	(0.32)	(0.33)	(0.29)
Postelection status	-0.49	-0.29	-0.32	-0.36
	(0.17)	(0.21)	(0.21)	(0.21)
Investiture	0.49	0.52	0.62	0.75
	(0.19)	(0.22)	(0.22)	(0.21)
Returnability	1.30	1.35	1.63	1.79
	(0.50)	(0.60)	(0.62)	(0.60)
Polarization	2.50	2.33	1.31	—
	(0.82)	(0.95)	(1.08)	
Ideological diversity index	0.43	0.43^a	0.55^a	—
	(0.13)	(0.18)	(0.19)	
Left-Right diversity	—	—	—	0.39
				(0.12)
Clerical-secular diversity	—	—	—	0.20
				(0.07)
Regime-support diversity	—	—	—	0.14
				(0.08)
Change in unemployment rate	—	—	0.287	0.283
			(0.073)	(0.073)
Inflation rate	—	—	0.024	0.043
			(0.021)	(0.021)
Log-likelihood	-843.3	-516.2	-507.0	-506.5
Number of cases	284	202	202	202

Note: Entries are PL coefficients (standard errors in parentheses).
[a]The weights used to construct the ideological diversity index used here are based on 202 cases.

between the two models in other respects means that we shall be able to assess the contributions of the economic covariates to what is essentially the same model.

That assessment is undertaken in model 3 of the table, which adds the inflation rate and the change in the unemployment rate to model 2. The principal result engendered by the inclusion of the economic covariates is the reduction in the coefficient associated with polarization, which is now statistically insignificant. It is also notable that the inflation rate coefficient is larger than was reported in Table 5.2, yet highly insignificant. These findings suggest that the two covariates overlap to some extent in their effects on government survival; in other words, systems with a large antisystem presence also tend to have higher inflation rates, and both features correlate with government survival. Clearly, one of these covariates must be removed.

In the preceding chapter, we saw that polarization's continuing presence in the model is attributable to minority situations, apparently because the ideological diversity that minority governments must accommodate is (necessarily) underestimated by the ideological diversity measures in the model. Model 3 raises the possibility, however, that the real reason may be that minority governments are more vulnerable to high levels of inflation. Is inflation more destructive to minority than to majority governments? In fact, the very opposite appears to be the case. When model 3 was reestimated separately for minority and majority governments, the change in unemployment plays approximately the same role in both situations, but the inflation rate shows an effect only in *majority* situations.[8] This means that the overlap between the explanatory roles of polarization and inflation must result from the ability of inflation to account for aspects of survival rates among majority governments that were formerly attributed to polarization.[9] Thus, the supposition that polarization's role in the model has been confined to registering unmeasured ideological diversity affecting minority governments remains intact; the difference is that this role, stripped of other associations, is no longer statistically significant.

This evidence helps us to simplify the model. Because inflation's role is largely confined to majority governments, it cannot be a substitute for unmeasured ideological diversity within minority governments; as far as we know, the nature of the inflation effect is precisely what it appears to be. Polarization, in contrast, continues to play a surrogate role, most probably as an indirect measure of extragovernmental ideological diversity affecting minority governments. For these reasons, the more preferable step is to remove polarization from the model. This does not mean that the phenomenon that polarization inadvertently measures is no longer present but simply that when the other, more directly relevant factors are taken into account, it is no longer strong enough to be statistically significant in this sample.

The effect of removing polarization from the specification is given in model 4 of Table 5.3. The three ideological diversity measures are entered separately in model 4 to demonstrate that each is related significantly to government survival; note, however, that regime-support diversity achieves statistical significance only in a one-tailed test. Also significant only in a one-tailed test is postelection status. As a comparison of models 1 and 2 reveals, the weakness of this covariate is largely the result of the sample reduction. More relevant to our immediate concerns are the time-varying covariates. With respect to the change in unemployment, model 4 shows a noticeably larger coefficient associated with the covariate than was evident previously (see Table 5.2), indicating that controlling for other relevant factors actually enhances its role in accounting for government survival.

Table 5.4. *Economic influences on survival, before and after 1973*

	Terminations before November 1973 (model 1)	Terminations after October 1973 (model 2)
Covariates		
Change in unemployment rate from preceding year	0.206 (0.101)	0.463 (0.118)
Inflation rate	0.187 (0.075)	0.036 (0.029)
Number of cases	100	102

Note: Entries are PL coefficients derived from reestimations of the full model (model 4 of Table 5.3) for the appropriate period (standard errors in parentheses).

As for inflation, its coefficient has tripled in magnitude and is now statistically significant (two-tailed test).

Model 4 establishes that two economic covariates, the inflation rate and the change in the unemployment rate, have significant roles to play in the explanation of government survival in West European parliamentary regimes. Apparently, the fate of governments is determined not just by certain attributes that they or their parliamentary systems display, nor merely by these attributes together with the impingement of random events: systematic developments in one area of the environment surrounding the political area – the economy – are also involved. But in demonstrating this point, we have opened the door to a number of further questions. For instance, have unemployment and inflation affected government survival in a uniform fashion across the postwar period? Do they influence all types of governments equally? Finally, can governments do anything to affect them, and thus indirectly to influence their own fate? These matters are considered in the next section, which explores more fully the nature of the economy–survival connection.

ERAS AND IDEOLOGIES

An important dimension along which the impact of economic factors on government survival may vary relates to the period during which governments held office. Few would dispute that the oil crisis of 1973 marked a critical watershed in Western economic history, the end of the long postwar economic boom. Certainly, both inflation and unemployment became much worse in the 1970s and 1980s, as Figure 5.1 indicates. This naturally raises the question of whether economic conditions came to assume a more pronounced role in government survival in the period after October 1973.

This issue is explored in Table 5.4, which presents the effects of the economic covariates when the full model was estimated separately for the two eras defined by the 1973 oil embargo. A comparison of the pre–oil crisis and post–oil crisis models provides scant support for the hypothesis of a general increase in the impact of the economy on government survival: while the role of changes in unemployment is much stronger after 1973, that of inflation shows a corresponding decrease. Apparently, economic conditions played a significant role in government survival in both eras, but the relative importance of the two economic indicators shifted dramatically.

A notable feature of the results reported in Table 5.4 is that changes in unemployment have a more powerful effect on government survival in the period when unemployment showed its major increases, that is to say, after October 1973. This suggests that the importance of economic covariates for survival may vary according to how salient they are at the time. In Figure 5.1, it is possible to identify three distinct periods of varying saliencies without too much difficulty: an initial period to 1965 when both indicators remained at relatively benign levels (with the small exception of an early and short-lived spike in inflation); a middle period of about ten years when the principal change was a very large rise in the inflation rate; and finally a period in which the large increases belong to the unemployment rate. Do the impacts of the two economic covariates vary according to this periodization?

Table 5.5, which presents the relevant results, confirms this expectation surprisingly well. In the 1945–64 period, both covariates sport coefficients roughly similar to their coefficients in the overall model (model 4 of Table 5.3), although neither is statistically significant – a reflection of the relatively small number of cases involved. In the 1965–75 period, however, the inflation coefficient increases more than fivefold and is highly significant even though the number of cases has increased only slightly; the change in unemployment shows a noticeable drop in importance. This pattern is reversed in the 1976–89 period, when the coefficient associated with unemployment changes triples in size, while that of inflation falls to near zero.[10] These results need to be taken with a grain of salt since they depend on a periodization that is (inevitably) somewhat arbitrary, but they do support the hypothesis that economic indicators matter according to how salient they have become in the popular consciousness.[11]

The analysis presented to this point has implicitly assumed that economic conditions are external or exogenous to governments, but this is clearly a simplification: a great deal of government activity involves attempts to influence the economic conditions that matter for their survival. These efforts, moreover, may not be ideologically neutral. It is a commonplace of political observers that left-wing governments typically concern themselves more with unemployment than inflation, whereas right-wing governments reverse that order of priorities. These preferences are often explained in terms of the perceived economic interests of their supporters. High unemployment tends to be seen by the Left as a "human" cost of capitalism that disproportionately affects the less well off and requires government intervention to rectify or at least alleviate; concerns expressed over inflation may appear, however, as a pretext for beating back union wage demands. The Right takes a less zero-sum view of the workings of capitalism, but it does

Table 5.5. *Economic influences on survival, by period*

	1945-64 (model 1)	1965-75 (model 2)	1976-89 (model 3)
Covariates			
Change in unemployment	0.228	0.139	0.422
rate from preceding year	(0.157)	(0.100)	(0.151)
Inflation rate	0.052	0.294	0.014
	(0.110)	(0.056)	(0.031)
Number of cases	56	58	88

Note: Entries are PL coefficients derived from reestimations of the full model (model 4 of Table 5.3) for the appropriate period (standard errors in parentheses).

find economic virtue in the creation and maintenance of a favorable business climate, which typically involves price stability as well as moderation in tax and social spending levels. Thus, the expectation has been, at least until the rightward drift in economic policy of the 1980s, that left-wing governments will cater to their working-class base by pursuing high employment policies even if it stimulates inflation, whereas right-wing governments will focus on their middle-class constituency's concern for price stability even if it risks jobs.

To what extent are these expectations justified? Table 5.6 addresses this question by presenting the records of socialist and nonsocialist governments on the two economic indicators most closely related to government survival, the inflation rate and the change in the unemployment rate. The two government types were created by defining a Left–Right ordering of parties for each system, dividing these orderings into socialist and nonsocialist components, and coding each government on whether it is composed wholly from the socialist component or wholly from the nonsocialist component ("mixed" governments, that is, governments composed of both socialist and nonsocialist parties, were excluded). To assess the performance of the two types of government, mean values of the economic covariates were estimated for each government from interpolated daily values; these means were then averaged across governments of each type.[12]

Table 5.6 does, in fact, reveal broad tendencies that conform to the expectations just outlined. Although inflation and changes in unemployment show considerable fluctuation over the lifespans of all types of governments (as indicated by the standard deviations), socialist governments clearly do experience higher mean levels of inflation than do nonsocialist governments; conversely, nonsocialist governments typically experience a greater tendency for unemployment rates to increase than do socialist governments.

Table 5.6. *Unemployment and inflation in different types of governments*

	Type of government	
Economic indicator	Nonsocialist	Socialist
Change in unemployment		
Average monthly value	0.24	0.02
	(92)	(42)
Standard deviation in monthly values	0.49	0.55
	(86)	(42)
Final month value	0.26	0.15
	(92)	(42)
Inflation		
Average monthly value	5.29	7.28
	(92)	(42)
Standard deviation in monthly values	0.94	1.10
	(86)	(42)
Final month value	5.23	7.55
	(92)	(42)

Note: Main entries are mean values for each type of government, with the number of governments given in parentheses. Only governments with valid data for both economic covariates are included. Values for individual governments were derived by dividing government durations into thirty-day intervals ("months") and estimating the annual rates of inflation and change in unemployment at the beginning of each interval (using December figures). Means and standard deviations were then calculated over the intervals and the values in the final interval noted.

This conclusion is reinforced by the results obtained when the full model was estimated separately for socialist and nonsocialist governments. The estimated coefficients for the economic covariates in these analyses are given in Table 5.7. The two models present a pattern of findings that, at first glance, may appear surprising: changes in unemployment are significantly related to government survival among nonsocialist governments (one-tailed test only), while inflation shows a significant effect solely among socialist governments. These relationships cannot be due to the tendency for nonsocialist governments to outperform socialist ones on inflation, or to be outperformed by them on unemployment, because the models relate each government's economic record only to those of other governments of the same type. Thus, model 1 associates higher termination rates with nonsocialist governments that undergo greater increases in unemployment relative to other nonsocialist governments, and similarly for socialist governments with re-

Table 5.7. *Economic influences on survival, by type of government*

	Nonsocialist governments (model 1)	Socialist governments (model 2)
Covariates		
Inflation rate	-0.001	0.171
	(0.037)	(0.058)
Change in unemployment	0.229	0.159
rate over preceding year	(0.122)	(0.191)
Number of cases	88	40

Note: Entries are PL coefficients derived from reestimations of the full model (model 4 of Table 5.3) for the appropriate subset of cases (standard errors are given in parentheses).

spect to inflation (model 2). Nor do these results appear to be due to any tendency for socialist governments to be concentrated in the 1965–75 period, when inflation was the prime concern, or for nonsocialist governments to predominate in the 1976–89 period, when unemployment came to the forefront.[13] The most likely interpretation of these results is that nonsocialist and socialist governments are perceived as being uniquely equipped to handle inflation and unemployment, respectively – a perception borne out by the evidence in Table 5.6 – and are therefore vulnerable only to adverse developments in the other indicator.

The evidence presented thus far seems to point to the conclusion that governments of different ideological types are, to some extent at least, in control of their destinies: each type shows a superior record on the economic indicator that is of greater concern to it and is "punished" when it falls behind the pace on the indicator with which it is less closely associated. There is one piece of evidence in Table 5.6, however, that obliges us to question that conclusion. That evidence consists of average values of the economic covariates for the two types of government in the last month of their existence. A comparison of these final month averages with the average values spanning the lifetimes of governments shows a very substantial degree of similarity. This finding suggests that both socialist and nonsocialist governments are rather ineffective at improving these basic economic indicators – on average the economic covariates remain at the end of a government very much as they were throughout its lifetime.[14] But if governments of both types are relatively ineffective at improving the economic indicator that is salient to them, how is it that each type shows a superior average performance on that indicator?

One answer might be that each government type tends to assume office during periods when its favored indicator is doing relatively well. Not only does this make very little sense in terms of voter behavior but, as noted earlier, it lacks empirical support as well: socialist governments are not concentrated in the 1965–75 period, nor are nonsocialist governments concentrated in the post–1975 era. A better answer may lie in the idea of continuity. It may be that the economic covariates show so little tendency to improve over the lifetimes of individual governments because economic trends span longer time frames than do governments. Policies initiated by a nonsocialist government to reduce inflation, for example, may not bear fruit until after that government has terminated.

For this interpretation to work, another tendency must be present as well: a tendency for governments of the same type to succeed one another. To pursue the example, socialist governments would show superior records on unemployment in the face of a slowly changing economy only if the fruits of one socialist government's employment policies were reaped by a socialist government that succeeded it. Do governments of the same type tend to succeed one another? In fact, socialist and nonsocialist governments follow governments of the same type in just over 60% of cases. The majority of the remaining cases concern changes involving mixed (part socialist, part nonsocialist) governments. In only 11.5% of government changes did a socialist government follow a nonsocialist one or vice versa. Discontinuity thus appears to be the exception rather than the rule.

Thus, the picture that emerges is one in which the ideological orientations of governments have an effect on economic performance, but not in any immediate sense. Socialist governments have superior records in checking unemployment increases apparently because socialist or partly socialist governments tend to follow one another, thus permitting the policies of one government to produce results that accrue to the benefit of its like-minded successors – not because individual socialist governments are able to effect substantial improvements while in office. Similarly, the effect of nonsocialist policies on inflation appears to involve a longer term than the lifetimes of individual nonsocialist governments. A note of caution must be struck here, however. The analysis has been based upon categorizations of periods and ideological types that inevitably distort reality to some extent: for one thing, any periodization is arbitrary since time and economic trends are continuous; for another, the ideological orientations of governments are more a matter of degree than of types.[15] Compounding these problems is the fact that dividing governments according to period and ideological type reduces dramatically the number of cases upon which conclusions are based. The results must therefore be taken as suggestive, a subject for further investigation rather than a convincing demonstration in themselves.

CONCLUDING REMARKS

The introduction of economic indicators into the explanation of government survival involves a degree of causal ellipsis: economic conditions do not cause governments to collapse prematurely, politicians do. While we cannot measure the intermediary stages of parliamentary disapproval or internal government dissension that poor economic figures may engender, the evidence presented here strongly indicates that these intermediary stages may be inferred. The principal piece of evidence consists of the finding that, net of the fixed attributes identified in the previous two chapters, two time-varying economic covariates play significant roles in government termination rates: the inflation rate and the change in the unemployment rate over the preceding year.

Somewhat more direct evidence for these processes can be gleaned from the economic records associated with different types of termination. In particular, it is notable that governments that terminated prematurely and under political pressure had significantly higher mean levels of the two economic covariates than did other governments.[16] This suggests that impatience with government economic strategy or a desire not to be associated with economic failure encourages parties or individual parliamentarians to withhold support from incumbent governments. A firmer verdict must await more detailed investigations.

The independence of the roles played by the two economic covariates in the model also merits emphasis. Not only does the addition of these covariates significantly increase the log-likelihood of the model, but further testing shows that their impact is independent of the level of ideological diversity present in the government.[17] Governments at all levels of ideological complexity, including the minimally diverse single-party majority governments, are at risk to adverse economic developments.

Independence with respect to the other covariates in the model need not mean constancy over all circumstances. One of the more interesting findings of the analysis is that the relative weight of the two economic covariates varies in suggestive ways over the periods and types of governments covered by the sample. Although there is no evidence to support the contention that economic factors became important only in the more troubled economic circumstances of the post–oil crisis period, there is evidence that the impact of the economic indicators on government survival varies with their relative saliency. Specifically, the inflation rate, weaker than the change in the unemployment rate as a factor in government survival over the entire postwar period, turns out to display by far the larger role during the period of its dramatic growth between the mid-1960s and the mid-1970s. The change in unemployment, by contrast, dominates after 1975 when inflation leveled, then declined, while unemployment rose to levels unheard of for nearly half a century.

The impact of these factors also varies according to the ideological orientation of the government in question. In general, the evidence presented here supports the contention that, within ideological types, governments are vulnerable only on the economic indicator they are generally less adept at handling. Thus, socialist governments do not terminate when their unemployment records fall behind the norm for governments of that type – presumably because of the favorable reputation they share on the issue – but they are at greater risk if their inflation performance is off the mark. For nonsocialist governments, the immunity pertains to inflation and the vulnerability to unemployment.

Governments are not merely the victims of economic trends – there are indications that they can influence them as well. Socialist governments, for example, appear to outperform nonsocialist governments with respect to changes in the unemployment rate and to underperform them on inflation. This conclusion needs to be tempered, however: it is not individual governments of a given ideological type that experience improvements on the relevant indicator but – as far as one can tell – series of such governments. Economic results thus appear to be long-term, or at least longer-term than the lifespan of individual governments; those concerned with democratic accountability may be comforted by the thought that given the clustering of governmental types, the credit or blame is not entirely misplaced. Temperance is also warranted by the indirect nature of some of the evidence supporting this interpretation.[18]

There is another reason to be especially cautious about these findings. Although we have introduced time into the picture in two different ways – through the variation of economic indicators over government lifetimes and through the variation in the impact of these indicators by economic era – there is a third way in which time could affect the connection between the economy and government survival: through variations in the impact of these indicators according to how long a government has occupied office. It is possible, in other words, that the impact of inflation or changes in unemployment depends to some degree on whether the government under consideration is a relative newcomer or a time-tested survivor. In the next chapter, where our attention turns to the nature of the underlying trend in rates of government survival, we shall see that there are indeed effects of this sort. The linkages between economic conditions and government survival identified here turn out to be only a part of a considerably more complex – and intriguing – story.

6

The underlying trend in government survival

Dynamic effects on government survival can come in a variety of forms. The form that first drew serious scholarly attention is the incidence of outside "events" – foreign crises, political assassinations, and the like – that occasionally challenge and topple governments. As the analyses reported in Chapter 5 demonstrate, developments of a more systematic sort, such as the changing state of the economy, also have a role to play in government survival. A third type of dynamic effect is autocorrelative: the potential influence of past government durations on present and future ones.[1] Finally, there is the possibility that governments face a changing risk of termination the longer they remain in power, quite apart from any idiosyncratic events or systematic developments occurring in the outside environment. This change could take the form of a reduction in risk over time, indicating a process of consolidation of power; a rising risk over time, suggestive of an unravelling of the reins of power; or even some more complex, nonmonotonic pattern.

This chapter is concerned primarily with the last type of effect, about which almost nothing is known. The "events" assumption that the underlying rate of termination is constant throughout the lifetimes of governments represents the simplest treatment of the issue, but it is also the most optimistic: it assumes that there are not systematic trends apart from those measured by the covariates in the model. Given some evidence that this optimism may not be warranted, at least with respect to the KABL model (Warwick and Easton 1992), it is appropriate that we subject the underlying rate of termination to scrutiny. In simplest terms, the question to be addressed is: Is there some time trend to government survival rates that exists independently of the factors identified thus far?

THE DURATION DEPENDENCE EFFECT

In Chapter 2, the overall hazard rates implicit in a set of duration data were attributed to two sources, a vector of (possibly time-varying) covariates $\mathbf{x}(t)$, representing various causal factors, and an underlying or baseline hazard, $\lambda_0(t)$, common to all cases:

$$\lambda(t) = \exp(\boldsymbol{\beta}'\mathbf{x}(t))\lambda_0(t). \tag{6.1}$$

The analyses of Chapters 3 through 5 were concerned exclusively with the task of identifying an optimal set of covariates; by employing the PL method in this task, we precluded any consideration of the $\lambda_0(t)$ term. This term, nevertheless, is important for a complete understanding of government survival because it captures the underlying trend in the hazard once the effects of all measured covariates, both fixed and time-varying, have been taken into account. Situations where the baseline hazard changes with the length of time the case has survived are said to represent instances of duration dependence. The duration dependence is positive when the underlying rate of termination increases with duration time; negative duration dependence, conversely, characterizes a process of consolidation or "momentum" in which longevity appears to breed upon itself. The presence of either type of effect – not to mention a more complex pattern – would clearly have major implications for our understanding of government survival in parliamentary regimes.

One of the more striking features of event history analysis is that duration dependence can be assessed empirically even though its causes are unknown and therefore unmeasured. A simple illustration can clarify this capacity of the technique. Suppose a researcher has good reason to believe that the baseline hazard present in some phenomenon is changing monotonically with duration time. (It is not necessary to know in advance whether it is rising or falling.) The researcher might then specify the following Gompertz model:

$$\lambda(t) = \exp(\beta'\mathbf{x}(t))\exp(\gamma t). \tag{6.2}$$

The baseline hazard in this model is expressed in terms of the product of a parameter γ and duration time. With suitable data, this parameter can be estimated along with the other parameters in the model by means of maximum likelihood estimation. The sign attached to the estimated parameter would indicate whether the duration dependence is positive or negative; the size of the parameter would express the strength of the effect. The important point to note is that this duration dependence parameter is estimated even though its sources are not specified in the model.[2]

The key element that makes this estimation possible is the knowledge that the hazard is monotonic over duration time; a Gompertz model would not have been an appropriate choice for a hazard that rises over part of the range of duration values and falls elsewhere. Our first task, therefore, is to assess the nature of the underlying trend in government termination rates. The standard starting point for this assessment is to calculate hazard estimates and plot them against duration time. The hazard rate in any interval of duration time can be estimated from the ratio of the number of terminations that occur in the interval to the number of cases still available for termination (i.e., still surviving) at the beginning of the interval. Because these hazard estimates tend to fluctuate considerably across intervals, a smoothing procedure is often applied to the estimates to assess more readily the underlying trend that characterizes them.[3]

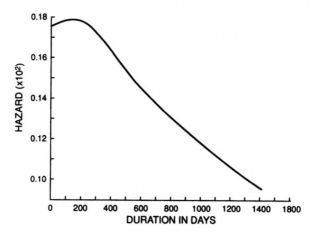

Figure 6.1. Smoothed Nelson–Aalen hazard rates by duration, sixteen West European parliamentary democracies.

A plot of the smoothed hazard estimates based upon 374 postwar governments in the sixteen West European parliamentary democracies is given in Figure 6.1. The predominant feature of the graph is unmistakable: the hazard function appears to fall with duration time, suggesting a declining risk of collapse the longer a government remains in power. One must be cautious in embracing such a conclusion, however, for negative duration dependence may be a statistical artifact of pooling data characterized by different rates of termination. Consider two systems, one highly unstable, the other more stable, that are combined in a sample. At low duration values, the hazard estimates for the sample will reflect both the high rate of termination of the unstable system and the lower rate of the stable system. As duration values increase, this overall hazard rate will appear to decline simply because the proportion of cases from the unstable system will have decreased (due to its higher rate of termination). The declining hazard, in other words, is generated by the changing relative proportions of cases from the two systems that result from their different rates of termination, not by any inherent tendency toward "momentum" within either system. Since parliamentary systems with highly distinct records of governmental stability have been grouped together to produce Figure 6.1, it is possible that a heterogeneity effect of this sort is at work.

A simple expedient to control for the presence of country-based heterogeneity is to prepare separate hazard plots for the individual countries. Since these plots would each involve a relatively small number of cases, a great deal of reliance should not be placed on the outcome for any one system; what matters more is whether a pattern emerges across the fifteen systems.[4] In fact, the most common pattern revealed by smoothed hazard plots for the individual countries is not the declining hazard of the entire sample but rather the opposite: eight systems show a continuously rising hazard over duration time, while a ninth reveals a hazard that

Table 6.1. *A summary of country plots of the raw hazard*

Country	Number of cases	Hazard plots	
		All cases	Majority or minority only
Austria	19	Rising	
Belgium	32	Rising, then declining	Rising, then declining (maj.)
Denmark	27	Rising, then declining	Rising (min.)
Finland	45	Rising, then declining	Rising, then declining (maj.)
France	28	Declining	Rising (maj.)
Iceland	19	Rising	—
Ireland	16	Rising	—
Italy	53	Declining	Mostly rising (maj.)
Luxembourg	14	Declining	Declining (maj.)
Netherlands	22	Mostly rising	—
Norway	21	Rising	—
Portugal	14	Rising	—
Sweden	20	Rising	—
United Kingdom	19	Rising	—
West Germany	21	Rising	—
All	374	Mostly declining	Rising, then declining (maj.)

Note: Spain is not given a separate analysis because of its small number of cases, but it is included in the analysis of the total sample.

mostly rises. Figure 6.2 illustrates these findings with the plot for Austria, which clearly shows a rising hazard, and for France, which does not. The patterns for all fifteen countries are summarized in the third column of Table 6.1.

The possible existence of a general pattern of rising hazards can be assessed more readily if a second obvious source of heterogeneity is controlled as well: the distinction between majority and minority governments. Minority governments, generally speaking, do not survive in office as long as majority ones; in systems where minority governments are common, therefore, the hazard rate may appear to decline simply because of the increasing concentration of majority cases at higher duration values. To control for this source of heterogeneity, smoothed hazard plots were calculated for the more common type of government – majority or minority – in each of the six countries that did not show a rising hazard. These plots, whose patterns are also summarized in Table 6.1, reveal continuously or predominantly rising hazards in three of the six systems. The plot for one such system – France (majority cases) – is also shown in Figure 6.2.

Although country differences or differences between majority and minority governments may not be the only confounding factors in these data, controlling

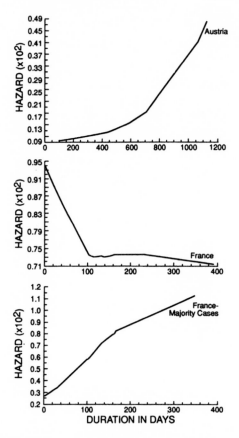

Figure 6.2. Smoothed Nelson–Aalen hazard rates by duration, Austria and France (Fourth Republic).

for them has been sufficient to reveal evidence of positive duration dependence in twelve of the fifteen countries tested. Given the approximations involved in estimating hazard rates for a limited number of discrete intervals and then smoothing those estimates, this is probably as much as can be profitably concluded from this form of analysis. The results to this point are suggestive only, but what they suggest is remarkable: a rate of termination that increases in most systems with the length of time a government is in power.

   On the assumption that the country plots are correct in portraying the hazards in most systems as basically monotonic, the need to resort to discrete approximations and data smoothing can be avoided with a second test. This test consists of fitting a Gompertz model of the form

$$\lambda(t) = \exp(c)\exp(\gamma t). \qquad (6.3)$$

In this model, $\exp(c)$ is a constant denoting the value of the hazard at the time of government formation ($t = 0$), and γ, as before, is a parameter recording the di-

Table 6.2. *Hazard estimates, by country*

Country	No covariates (model 1)			Including majority status (model 2)		
	N	γ	SE	N	γ	SE
Austria	19	0.00080	(0.00075)	19	0.00099	(0.00077)
Belgium	32	-0.00031	(0.00057)	32	0.00001	(0.00058)
Denmark	27	0.00138	(0.00068)	27	0.00241	(0.00085)
Finland	45	-0.00125	(0.00079)	38	-0.00084	(0.00081)
France	28	0.00163	(0.00178)	28	0.00121	(0.00177)
Iceland	19	0.00113	(0.00095)	19	0.00179	(0.00106)
Ireland	16	0.00207	(0.00080)	16	0.00273	(0.00097)
Italy	53	0.00039	(0.00079)	53	0.00086	(0.00080)
Luxembourg	14	-0.00006	(0.00086)	14	-0.00006	(0.00086)
Netherlands	22	0.00105	(0.00074)	22	0.00137	(0.00077)
Norway	21	0.00028	(0.00091)	21	0.00056	(0.00096)
Portugal	14	0.00131	(0.00143)	11	0.00175	(0.00152)
Sweden	20	0.00068	(0.00114)	20	0.00068	(0.00114)
United Kingdom	19	-0.00060	(0.00086)	19	0.00026	(0.00094)
West Germany	21	-0.00013	(0.00083)	21	-0.00013	(0.00083)
All	374	-0.00055	(0.00019)	364	-0.00042	(0.00019)

Note: Model 1 reports estimated values for the constant term γ in the Gompertz model $\lambda(t)$ = $\exp(c)\exp(\gamma(t))$. Model 2 reports γ values for the model $\lambda(t) = \exp(c + \beta x)\exp(\gamma(t))$, where x is majority status. Spain is not given a separate analysis but is included in the analysis of the total sample.

rection and strength of any duration dependence effect. When the model is fitted to the entire sample using MLE, the result is an estimated γ coefficient of -0.00055 ($t = 2.94$), consistent with the declining hazard plotted in Figure 6.1.[5] The individual country fits, however, reveal a different pattern: ten of the fifteen γ coefficients are positive, indicating rising hazards. These coefficients and their associated standard errors are listed under model 1 in Table 6.2. Only two of the coefficients are statistically significant at the .05 level, but this is to be expected given the small numbers of cases available for each analysis; the important point remains the overall pattern. That pattern again appears to be one of positive duration dependence.

This test can be adapted very easily to control for any heterogeneity introduced by the presence of both majority and minority governments. Instead of examining only the more common type of government in each country, the modification consists of replacing the $\exp(c)$ term in equation 6.3 with the term $\exp(\beta_0 + \beta_1 x)$, where x is the majority status covariate. The results of estimating this modified model for each country are reported under model 2 in Table 6.2. Two of the five countries (West Germany and Luxembourg) that showed negative γ coefficients in the first test have no variability in majority status (they had no minority governments), and their γ coefficients, accordingly, do not change. But of the remaining three countries, two now show positive γ coefficients, while the third (Finland) has become noticeably less negative. As was the case with the hazard plots, controlling for majority status results in twelve of the fifteen countries displaying a hazard that appears to rise with duration time.

ISOLATING THE BASELINE HAZARD

The two tests reported in the preceding section suggest the possibility that the risk of government termination in West European parliamentary systems increases with the length of time a government remains in power. This effect is not apparent in every system, but it must be borne in mind that the model specification is incomplete. Although country differences and differences between majority and minority governments have been controlled, this may not have eliminated all of the effects denoted by the vector of covariates x in equation 6.1. The next step in the analysis, therefore, is to elaborate the model by introducing the full set of covariates.

A regrettable feature of the introduction of the nine covariates identified in earlier chapters is that it entails a sizable loss of cases. Largely due to limitations in the Party Manifestos Project data and gaps (particularly in the earlier years) for the economic indicators, the available data are reduced from 374 cases to 202. Although this loss of cases appears not to misrepresent the effects of the covariates (see Tables 4.4 and 5.3), it may be that it skews the analysis of the baseline hazard.

This possibility can be assessed by reestimating the country γ coefficients listed under model 1 of Table 6.2 on the basis of the reduced sample. These results are reported under model 1 of Table 6.3. A comparison of the two sets of γ coefficients shows that every negative γ coefficient in the larger sample persists in the reduced sample; as before, no significant distortion appears to follow from the loss of cases.[6] This puts us in a good position to ascertain whether the inclusion of the covariates clarifies the existence of a general pattern of positive duration dependence.

Before we can proceed, however, we must deal with a second potential complication implicit in introducing the full set of covariates. This complication has to do with the fact that the method by which time-varying covariates are handled in ML estimation differs significantly from that employed in PL estimation. Whereas the PL technique utilizes covariate values at various points of the case's lifetime, ML estimation requires the ability to integrate covariate values over intervals of time.[7] The standard procedure for facilitating this integration is to split government durations into intervals and attribute covariate values for the beginning of each interval to the entire interval. In the present application, thirty-day intervals and interpolated covariate values for the first day of each interval were used. Does this change make any difference to the results? In fact, a reestimation of

Table 6.3. *Country analyses of the baseline hazard*

Country	N	No covariates (model 1)		Covariates (model 2)	
		γ	SE	γ	SE
Austria	11	-0.00032	(0.00107)	0.00146	(0.00166)
Belgium	26	-0.00001	(0.00062)	0.00063	(0.00065)
Denmark	20	0.00080	(0.00087)	0.00371	(0.00141)
Ireland	13	0.00147	(0.00090)	0.00324	(0.00142)
Italy	40	0.00055	(0.00088)	0.00204	(0.00101)
Luxembourg	5	-0.00076	(0.00201)	—	
Netherlands	16	0.00002	(0.00087)	0.00119	(0.00109)
Norway	17	0.00011	(0.00107)	0.00145	(0.00129)
Sweden	16	0.00121	(0.00178)	—	
United Kingdom	18	-0.00045	(0.00087)	0.00125	(0.00111)
West Germany	20	-0.00010	(0.00085)	0.00076	(0.00101)
All	202	-0.00048	(0.00025)	0.00072	(0.00028)

Note: Model 1 reports estimated values for the constant term γ in the Gompertz model $\lambda(t) = \exp(c)\exp(\gamma(t))$. Model 2 reports γ values for the model $\lambda(t) = \exp(\beta'x)\exp(\gamma(t))$, where x is the vector of nine covariates identified in earlier chapters and β is the vector of associated coefficients. Full-model estimates for Sweden and Luxembourg could not be produced, because of either the small number of cases (Luxembourg) or the small number of noncensored cases (Sweden).

the model developed thus far (model 4 of Table 5.3) using the event-splitting procedure produces virtually identical covariate parameter estimates.[8] Any change in coefficient estimates that follows from the specification of a duration dependence effect may therefore be attributed to that source, rather than to the method of encoding the time-varying covariates.

The effects on the baseline hazard (γ) coefficients of including the full set of covariates into the Gompertz specification are shown in model 2 of Table 6.3. The results support the rising-hazard hypothesis across the board. Not only is there a reversal of signs in the systems that had previously shown negative γ coefficients, but the positive γ coefficients of the other systems have all increased in magnitude. Although most of these covariates remain statistically insignificant (reflecting the small numbers of cases involved), it is the consistency of the results across the ten countries that impresses.

This section has produced evidence that (1) the loss of cases entailed by missing data for some of the covariates does not affect the initial estimates of that baseline hazard very much, and (2) the introduction of the full set of covariates into the

Table 6.4. *Proportionality tests of country baseline hazards*

Country	Interaction term	SE	*t*-value
Austria	0.058	0.440	0.131
Belgium	0.028	0.186	0.150
Denmark	0.305	0.357	0.857
Ireland	1.125	0.652	1.725
Italy	-0.305	0.177	-1.725
Netherlands	-0.013	0.275	-0.046
Norway	-0.161	0.346	-0.465
Sweden	1.025	0.580	1.767
United Kingdom	-0.213	0.304	-0.699
West Germany	-0.146	0.242	-0.605

Note: The interaction terms were defined as $Z_n = D_n\{\ln(t) - \ln(c)\}$, where D_n is the country dummy for country n, t is duration time, and c is the mean duration of the sample as a whole (620.96 days). The coefficients for the interaction terms were derived from models that also included all relevant covariates. Luxembourg is excluded because of its small number of available cases.

model leads to the appearance of a rising baseline hazard in all countries for which full data are available. What we do not yet know is whether the rate of increase in the risk of termination is comparable in all systems. This issue is important because the application of a Gompertz or PL model that conforms to equation 6.1 rests on an assumption of a common baseline hazard for all cases, and in the present context, intercountry differences constitute the most likely basis for divergence in baseline hazards.

The presence of country differences in the rate of increase in the baseline hazard can be readily assessed through the estimation of a series of PL models, each incorporating the covariates plus an interaction term between a given country dummy and duration time. A significant coefficient attached to any of these interaction terms would indicate that the difference between the baseline hazards of the country in question and the rest of the sample increases or decreases with duration time, suggesting a duration dependence effect stronger or weaker in that country than elsewhere.[9]

The estimated coefficients for the interaction term for each country are listed in Table 6.4, along with the associated standard errors and *t*-values. The signs of the coefficients indicate that in some countries the baseline hazard rises more rapidly, in other countries less rapidly, than the rest of the sample, but in no country does the extent of this deviation reach statistical significance at the .05 level. Although the duration dependence may be less pronounced in Italy and more pronounced in

Ireland and Sweden than it is elsewhere, the overall pattern of the evidence suggests that it is of comparable strength in all systems.[10]

The findings presented in Table 6.4 reinforce the conclusion that a similar process of positive duration dependence is present in all countries that can be tested and support the fitting of a single Gompertz model to the entire sample.[11] The results of this fit are given as model 1 of Table 6.5. For purposes of comparison, the table also presents a PL estimation of the model based on the same event-splitting methodology (model 2). This comparison shows the models to be virtually identical except for the appearance of a significant γ coefficient in the Gompertz model, reflecting the presence of positive duration dependence in the sample as a whole.

One should not be misled by the apparently meager size of the duration dependence effect in model 1. The estimated coefficient may seem small ($\gamma = .00072$), but it indicates that each hundred days in office increases a government's risk of termination by 7.5%; after two years, the risk has increased by a substantial 69.1%. On this reckoning, the impact of the increasing risk of collapse on government survival in West European parliamentary democracies must be judged to be very substantial indeed.

ACCOUNTING FOR THE BASELINE HAZARD

The data analysis of the previous sections has proceeded in an inductive fashion because so little was known a priori about the underlying risks affecting West European parliamentary governments. The constant hazard adopted in previous work was based on the assumption that the sole source of termination, apart from known explanatory factors, is the random occurrence of outside events. This would be a reasonable assumption if the model specification were complete, but there is no reason to believe that this is the case. The clear indication of the present analysis is that there are one or more factors at work that have caused the underlying risk of termination to rise with the length of time a government stayed in power. Unless we are willing simply to assume that the effect is identical in all governments in the sample – an assumption implicit in the models of Table 6.5 – the task before us now is to identify the factors that are responsible and introduce them into the model.

The first point to be made in this regard concerns what is not involved: the arrival or anticipation of regular elections. All terminations brought on by regular elections were censored in the preceding analyses, as were unprovoked terminations occurring within twelve months of regularly scheduled elections. This means that unless anticipatory terminations occur before one year of the end of the mandate or involve contrived collapses, they cannot have affected the results presented here. The irrelevancy of elections is also suggested by the very ubiquity of the rising hazard, for it is present both in systems where anticipatory terminations are customary (Britain) and in systems where they are absent (Norway).

Table 6.5. *A Comparison of Gompertz and partial likelihood models*

	Gompertz (model 1)	Partial likelihood (model 2)
Constant	-7.88 (0.46)	—
Covariates		
Majority status	-1.96 (0.29)	-1.97 (0.29)
Postelection status	-0.38 (0.21)	-0.35 (0.21)
Investiture	0.76 (0.21)	0.75 (0.21)
Returnability	1.80 (0.60)	1.79 (0.60)
Left-Right diversity	0.41 (0.12)	0.39 (0.12)
Clerical-secular diversity	0.19 (0.07)	0.20 (0.07)
Regime-support diversity	0.15 (0.08)	0.14 (0.08)
Change in unemployment	0.30 (0.07)	0.29 (0.07)
Inflation	0.04 (0.02)	0.04 (0.02)
Duration dependence	0.00072 (0.00028)	—
Log-likelihood	-895.8	-506.6
Number of cases	202	202

Note: Entries are estimated covariate coefficients (standard errors in parentheses).

The elimination of anticipatory elections as a cause still leaves the field wide open. Indeed, it may be that the sources of the rising hazard lie with factors that are unmeasured, perhaps inherently unmeasurable: a gradual disillusionment among government ranks that comes with policy errors or failures, a general tendency for the popularity of governments to decline over time, and the like. Before we abandon the goal of ascertaining the root causes empirically, however, it would be appropriate to examine the factors that we have already identified as causal influences of government survival rates, the nine covariates in the model.

It may seem odd to consider the covariates already in the model as potential causes of the rising baseline hazard, since we have found evidence that the latter phenomenon exists independently of these factors. Nevertheless, it is still possible that government survival is linked not just to these covariates but also to interactions between one or more of them and duration time. In other words, the effect of any given covariate on the hazard may increase or decrease with the length of time a government has held office. Some covariates may have effects that are strong early in a government's life but diminish as it becomes more firmly established; others may become even more powerful in governments that have already survived a relatively long period of time. Since the types of effects have not been allowed for in the model, they may have found expression in the persistent appearance of a rising baseline hazard.

Although we are operating on totally uncharted ground, we can be reasonably sure that the rising hazard is not caused by covariates that take on values of zero for entire countries – as before, the very ubiquity of the phenomenon rules this out. This consideration eliminates three of the nine covariates: investiture, clerical–secular diversity, and regime-support diversity. As for the other covariates, the most appropriate way to proceed is simply to introduce interactive terms for each of them. The model implied by this exercise is a Gompertz model of the form[12]

$$\lambda(t) = \exp\{\boldsymbol{\beta}'\mathbf{x}(t)\}\exp\{\boldsymbol{\gamma}'[\mathbf{y}(t)t]\}. \tag{6.4}$$

In this model, two vectors of covariates are involved, the original set of nine covariates ($\mathbf{x}$) and a subset of six covariates ($\mathbf{y}$) that are entered in multiplicative relationships with duration time. This means that two sets of coefficients will be estimated. Henceforth, the β coefficients associated with the simple or noninteractive entry of the covariates will be referred to as the *first vector* of coefficients; the *second vector* will comprise the γ coefficients attached to the interactive terms.

The coefficients produced by estimating this fifteen-covariate model are given as model 1 of Table 6.6.[13] Most of the first-vector coefficients in model 1 are significant, or close to significant, at the .05 level; moreover, three of the interactive terms – those formed with returnability and the two economic covariates – also approach statistical significance.[14] This provides some indication that interactive effects may be involved, but the key issue is the effect of their presence on the constant term in the second vector, which would convey any unexplained duration dependence. Model 1 shows that this term has become much larger in magnitude and statistically insignificant, which suggests that a great deal of overdetermination is present in the model.

The first step in eliminating this overdetermination and producing a more parsimonious model is to eliminate the three highly insignificant interactive terms from the model.[15] The results of estimating this simplified model are shown as model 2 of Table 6.6. This model is noteworthy in two respects: (1) all first-vector coefficients are statistically significant (at least in one-tailed tests) with the

Table 6.6. *Accounting for the baseline hazard*

	Model					
	1		2		3	
First vector						
Constant	-8.46	(0.80)	-8.56	(0.78)	-7.79	(0.45)
Majority status	-2.34	(0.37)	-2.08	(0.29)	-2.08	(0.29)
Postelection status	-0.42	(0.31)	-0.40	(0.21)	-0.42	(0.21)
Investiture	0.64	(0.22)	0.72	(0.22)	0.76	(0.22)
Returnability	3.27	(1.03)	3.07	(1.04)	2.03	(0.62)
Left-Right diversity	0.25	(0.20)	0.44	(0.13)	0.43	(0.13)
Clerical-secular diversity	0.21	(0.07)	0.20	(0.07)	0.20	(0.07)
Regime-support diversity	0.17	(0.08)	0.15	(0.08)	0.16	(0.07)
Change in unemployment	0.44	(0.10)	0.44	(0.10)	0.44	(0.09)
Inflation	0.01	(0.03)	0.01	(0.03)	—	
Second vector						
Constant	1.48	(1.29)	1.53	(1.15)	0.05	(0.38)
Majority status	0.76	(0.68)	—		—	
Postelection status	-0.03	(0.64)	—		—	
Returnability	-2.67	(1.42)	-1.86	(1.38)	—	
Left-Right diversity	0.39	(0.31)	—		—	
Change in unemployment	-0.42	(0.22)	-0.43	(0.22)	-0.47	(0.22)
Inflation	0.10	(0.05)	0.10	(0.05)	0.14	(0.04)
Log-likelihood		-889.0		-891.0		-891.9
Number of cases		202		202		202

Note: Entries are estimated β and γ coefficients from the model $\lambda(t) = \exp\{x(t)'\beta\} \times \exp\{[y(t)t]'\gamma\}$, where $x(t)$ is denoted the first vector and $[y(t)t]$ the second vector of covariates. For ease of presentation, all γ (second-vector) coefficients have been multiplied by 1,000 (standard errors in parentheses).

one exception of the inflation rate, and (2) among interactive terms, returnability is now clearly insignificant ($t = -1.35$), whereas the interactive terms involving the economic covariates remain very close to statistical significance. The second-vector constant term, representing any residual duration dependence, is still large but insignificant. Moreover, a reestimation of the model (not shown) excluding the highly insignificant inflation covariate from the first vector substantially strengthens these trends: the returnability interactive term becomes even less significant, while both economic interactive terms become statistically significant at the .05 level.

The removal of the insignificant returnability interactive covariate further clarifies the picture, as model 3 of Table 6.6 shows. In this model, not only are all covariates statistically significant, but the second-vector constant has collapsed in magnitude and become even more insignificant (its *t*-value is just 0.12). The implication of these results is startling: it would appear that the interaction of the two economic covariates with duration time totally accounts for the cross-system phenomenon of a rising hazard.[16]

Model 3 substantially revises our understanding of the role of the economic covariates in government survival in the postwar era. It indicates, first of all, that the appearance of a rising baseline hazard is the result of an overly simplified view of the operation of these covariates. Not only do the values of these variables fluctuate over the lifetimes of individual governments, but the effect of any one value varies with the length of time the government experiencing it has been in office. Specifically, the change in unemployment covariate, so powerful a factor in previous model specifications, now appears as one whose importance for government survival declines with the length of time in office. Conversely, the inflation rate covariate, which barely achieves statistical significance in previous models, now shows a highly significant effect – but only in an interaction with duration time. Inflation, on this evidence, has been especially damaging to long-lived governments.

The fact that the effect of changes in unemployment on government survival declines with duration time bears a curious implication: at some duration value, its overall effect will be reversed. According to model 3, this reversal occurs at about 947 days.[17] Since it is highly unlikely that governments surviving beyond 947 days are actually helped by rising unemployment, it is possible that the inflation interactive term is so powerful because it must counteract this expectation. In other words, the strong impact attributed to inflation among long-lived governments may be due, largely or even entirely, to the fact that it must offset the boost in survival rates the model associates with rising joblessness among these governments.

To what extent is this true? This question may be addressed with the aid of Table 6.7, which presents two reestimations of the model, each excluding one of the interactive terms. Model 1 shows very clearly that without the unemployment interactive term, the inflation interactive term exhibits an effect that is marginally diminished but still quite strong and highly significant. With the inflation interactive term omitted, however, model 2 reveals the effect of the unemployment interactive covariate to be noticeably weaker and its statistical significance, which was just barely above the .05 cutoff point in the full model (two-tailed test), now falls considerably below that level.[18] These results suggest that there may be a tendency for the effects of these two covariates to be inflated so as to balance each other off, but it is only a fairly minor one at best. The inflation interactive effect, in particular, appears to be quite legitimate. The models also underscore something that the signs of their coefficients in the full model implied: that the rising hazard is exclusively the result of the greater impact of inflation among long-lived governments.

Why should inflation have had its greatest impact among long-lived governments and changes in unemployment among short-lived governments? One possible explanation is that governments tended to last longer in the 1965–75 period,

Table 6.7. *Examining the effects of the interactive terms*

	Model			
	1		2	
First vector				
Constant	-7.68	(0.44)	-7.95	(0.47)
Majority status	-2.05	(0.29)	-1.97	(0.29)
Postelection status	-0.38	(0.21)	-0.41	(0.21)
Investiture	0.77	(0.22)	0.75	(0.21)
Returnability	1.93	(0.61)	1.84	(0.60)
Left-Right diversity	0.43	(0.13)	0.40	(0.12)
Clerical-secular diversity	0.19	(0.07)	0.19	(0.07)
Regime-support diversity	0.17	(0.07)	0.15	(0.08)
Change in unemployment	0.29	(0.07)	0.40	(0.10)
Inflation	—		0.04	(0.02)
Second vector				
Constant	0.01	(0.39)	0.82	(0.29)
Change in unemployment	—		-0.33	(0.23)
Inflation	0.12	(0.04)	—	
Log-likelihood	-893.9		-894.8	
Number of cases	202		202	

Note: Entries are estimated β and γ coefficients from the model $\lambda(t) = \exp\{x(t)'\beta\} \times \exp\{[y(t)t]'\gamma\}$, where $x(t)$ is denoted the first vector and $[y(t)t]$ the second vector of covariates. For ease of presentation, all γ (second-vector) coefficients have been multiplied by 1,000 (standard errors in parentheses).

when inflation became the main economic concern. This possibility is difficult to address in a definitive manner because it is not the actual durations that are at issue, but those durations that would (presumably) have occurred in the absense of nonrelevant terminations. Nevertheless, what evidence there is does not support this contention. As Table 6.8 shows, the mean duration of governments in the 1965–75 period is slightly higher than the means for the periods before and after it, but its proportion of censored cases is correspondingly lower. Thus, the middle period may show longer durations, on average, simply because it had fewer durations that needed to be adjusted for premature termination.

Although "true" durations may not have been longer in the 1965–75 period, we saw in Chapter 5 that the effects of the economic covariates do differ substantially across periods. It is possible, therefore, that a reexamination of these differences may help us understand the more complex relationships that have emerged in the present analysis. In Table 6.9, two models are presented for each of the three

Table 6.8. *Government duration in three periods*

Period	Number of cases	Mean duration (days)	Censored cases (percent)
1945-64	56	549.9	50.0
1965-75	58	663.3	32.8
1976-89	88	638.3	39.8

periods defined earlier. The first model shows the estimates obtained for the economic covariates and the baseline hazard under the original Gompertz specification; the second shows the results when the interactive covariates are added to the specification. Both model specifications clearly reveal substantial variation across periods. In the first period (1945–64), the two models display very weak effects from the economic covariates, as well as a rising hazard, although the latter falls just below statistical significance in the expanded model (model 2). The picture changes markedly in the second period (1965–75), when inflation became the prime economic concern. Although the original specification (model 3) reveals a strong effect for inflation and a weaker but still significant effect from changes in unemployment, the more complete specification (model 4) shows the effects of both covariates falling just below statistical significance in the first vector, but inflation contributing a strong effect in the second or interactive vector. It appears that the inflation effect in model 3 has been partitioned between main and interactive effects in model 4. For the 1976–89 period, the strong effect from changes in unemployment is also partitioned, but in this instance the partitioning yields an even stronger positive coefficient in the first vector and a negative second-vector coefficient that falls just slightly below statistical significance. As for inflation, it now displays a second-vector effect that is just barely significant.

The findings reported in Table 6.9 reinforce our conclusions concerning periods in Chapter 5: neither the inflation nor the change in unemployment covariate seems to have played very much of a role in government survival in the pre-1965 period; inflation then comes to the fore in 1965–75, followed in the 1976–89 period by the predominance of changes in the unemployment rate. While the strengths of the inflation and unemployment effects vary across periods, it is notable that the signs of the coefficients remain consistent with the overall model in both the high-inflation and high-unemployment periods. In both cases, changes in unemployment show a strong positive impact on the hazard in the first vector, offset by a negative interactive effect, whereas inflation has a weaker first-vector impact than was originally found but a positive second-vector effect that reduces the baseline hazard coefficient to statistical insignificance. This consistency across two very different periods of high economic saliency provides some measure of confirmation that the interactive effects uncovered in this section are indeed valid.[19]

Table 6.9. *Economic influences on survival, by period*
(revised estimates)

	1945-64		1965-75		1976-89	
	Model 1	Model 2	Model 3	Model 4	Model 5	Model 6
First vector						
Change in	0 .140	0 .017	0 .217	0 .332	0 .400	0 .690
unemployment	(0.143)	(0.255)	(0.102)	(0.171)	(0.149)	(0.223)
Inflation	0.053	0.118	0.249	0.124	0.014	-0.022
	(0.106)	(0.136)	(0.052)	(0.065)	(0.031)	(0.039)
Second vector						
Constant	1.520	2.320	1.422	-1.508	0 .961	0.437
	(0.759)	(1.223)	(.512)	(1.127)	(0.473)	(0.749)
Change in	—	0.460	—	-0.338	—	-0.710
unemployment		(0.614)		(0.421)		(0.369)
Inflation	—	-0.309	—	0.514	—	0.131
		(0.417)		(0.159)		(0.067)
Log-likelihood	-203.5	-203.0	-276.8	-271.5	-392.8	-389.8
Number of cases	56	56	58	58	88	88

Note: Entries are estimated coefficients derived from Gompertz models that also included the seven fixed covariates. Second-vector coefficients have been multiplied by 1,000 (standard errors in parentheses).

Another possible interpretation of the interactive effects relates to the ideological orientations of governments. Chapter 5 reported tendencies for nonsocialist governments to have suffered primarily from rising levels of unemployment and for socialist governments to have been especially vulnerable to inflation (see Table 5.7). We have now seen that changes in unemployment have their strongest effect at short-duration values and inflation at high-duration values. Could these interactive effects be the result of a tendency for socialist governments to survive longer than nonsocialist ones? In this instance, mean duration values do provide some evidence in support of this contention. As Table 6.10 shows, socialist governments did tend to survive longer, on average, than nonsocialist ones. Moreover, a higher proportion of them were censored, suggesting that their true durations are likely to have been longer still.

A more direct test of the hypothesis is to look at the effects of these covariates within the two types of governments; if the hypothesis is true, the interactive effects should be substantially reduced, or even disappear, when the model is tested

Table 6.10. *Duration of nonsocialist and socialist governments*

Government	Number of cases	Mean duration (days)	Censored cases (percent)
Nonsocialist	88	636.9	45.5
Socialist	40	766.0	60.0

separately on nonsocialist and socialist governments. Table 6.11 contains the relevant findings. In models 1 and 3 of the table, the analyses conducted in Chapter 5 are repeated using the first or original Gompertz specification, which merely adds a baseline hazard to the covariates of the PL model. As can be seen, the results are roughly equivalent to the earlier findings. The addition of the unemployment and inflation interactive covariates to the model changes the picture noticeably, however. For nonsocialist governments (model 2), the unemployment effect is partitioned into a strong positive effect in the first or main vector and a negative impact in the second or interactive vector. As for inflation, it shows the opposite pattern: the negligible impact in model 1 is now split into a negative first-vector effect and a positive second-vector effect, both of them statistically significant. Thus, for nonsocialist governments, changing rates of unemployment have a strong impact, albeit one that diminishes with duration time, while inflation's very weak net effect appears to be composed of a counterintuitive negative impact in the first vector (governments with higher inflation rates are less likely to collapse) that, within a year (327 days), is counteracted by a positive second-vector effect. Apparently, inflation is not irrelevant for nonsocialist governments, although its total impact, at least in these eighty-eight governments, is close to zero.

Turning to the relatively small sample ($n = 40$) of socialist governments, the addition of the two economic interactive terms (model 4) also appears to make matters much more complex. As was true of the overall model, the impact of inflation on government survival turns out to belong entirely to the interactive term. However, the insignificant unemployment effect has been partitioned into a large but insignificant first-vector effect counterbalanced by a similarly large, insignificant second-vector effect. Clearly, there are too many covariates in the model. The evidence of model 5, which excludes both the inflation covariate and the unemployment interactive term, clarifies the picture: it shows that only the inflation interactive term is statistically significant. Thus, inflation was the prime economic concern for socialist governments, but its impact was felt most strongly at higher duration values.

From the viewpoint of the hypothesis under consideration, the important feature of the results reported in Table 6.11 is that the patterns of economic covariate effects within both nonsocialist and socialist governments are broadly consistent with the overall model. In particular, the negative unemployment interactive term

Table 6.11. *Economic influences on survival, by type of government*
(revised estimates)

| | Government | | | | |
| | Nonsocialist | | Socialist | | |
	Model 1	Model 2	Model 3	Model 4	Model 5
First vector					
Change in unemployment	0.220	0.423	0.223	0.807	0.235
	(0.122)	(0.150)	(0.204)	(0.460)	(0.186)
Inflation	-0.008	-0.118	0.144	0.021	—
	(0.037)	(0.055)	(0.053)	(0.091)	
Second vector					
Constant	0.983	-0.922	0.626	-1.633	-2.178
	(0.458)	(0.871)	(0.781)	(1.968)	(1.206)
Change in unemployment	—	-0.690	—	-1.448	—
		(0.310)		(0.997)	
Inflation	—	0.360	—	0.310	0.338
		(0.125)		(0.206)	(0.113)
Log-likelihood	-362.8	-358.1	-127.6	-125.8	-126.9
Number of cases	88	88	40	40	40

Note: Entries are estimated coefficients derived from Gompertz models that also included the seven fixed covariates. Second-vector coefficients have been multiplied by 1,000 (standard errors in parentheses).

appears significantly within nonsocialist governments, as does the positive inflation interactive term within socialist governments (as well as within nonsocialist governments). The appearance of these effects within the two types of government means that their presence in the overall model cannot be attributed to differences in durations between the two. Although socialist governments do outlive nonsocialist ones in the present sample, this fact does not account for the weakening of the unemployment effect over duration time or the corresponding strengthening of the inflation effect.

To sum up, our reexamination of eras and ideologies in this section has found that the interactive effects isolated earlier in the chapter hold up within periods of both high inflation and high unemployment, as well as for both nonsocialist and socialist governments. It is also significant that the interactive covariates account for a rising hazard that appears to have been present in most or all of the systems under examination. These findings suggest that the interactive effects are not confined to any particular country, type of economic challenge, or type of government – although somewhat surprising, they appear to be systematic.

To say that the interactive effects are systematic need not imply that they are not "conjunctural." Indeed, the fact that they are largely absent in the period before 1965 implies that they have more to do with the economic circumstances of the 1970s and 1980s than with any generalizable phenomenon. One is tempted to suggest, for example, that there may have been a "Thatcher effect" at play: the more durable governments may have succeeded in changing the criterion for economic success from controlling unemployment to controlling inflation. The evidence at our disposal can neither confirm nor disprove this speculation, but it does demonstrate the complexity that may characterize economic conditions and their effects on government survival. Evidently, governments may be subject not only to changing economic conditions over their lifetimes, but also to changes in the strength of the impact of these conditions on their chances of survival. By elaborating the model to allow for this possibility, we have found that economic conditions played a greater role in the survival of postwar governments than originally appeared to be the case.

CONCLUDING REMARKS

Very early in the chapter, I alluded to the notion that a flat baseline hazard implies, or at least is consistent with, a high degree of explanatory success. The logic behind this claim is straightforward: if every systematic source of government termination has been determined, then all that would remain would be the random pattern of collapses anticipated by the events theorists. The KABL model assumed this situation, but further analysis showed that the assumption was overly optimistic. So, too, with the model developed in Chapters 3 through 5; although incorporating a more powerful set of explanatory factors, it still left in its wake a baseline hazard that rises consistently in all of the systems in the sample.

The transition from a PL to an ML approach enabled us to estimate the direction and strength of this underlying effect without requiring an identification and measurement of its sources. This is a very valuable facility of MLE, given that those sources could, very plausibly, have been unmeasurable. As it happened, however, there was no need to draw a curtain on the analysis at that stage. By expanding the baseline hazard term to incorporate the effects of covariates as well as a constant, the source of the rising hazard was very quickly revealed: it lay in a tendency for the impact of economic conditions, in this case inflation, to change with the length of time governments have occupied office.

By answering one question, of course, we simply open the way for others. Why should the inflation effect, negligible at first, grow with duration time while the opposite is true of the unemployment effect? Because the result was unanticipated theoretically and offers no readily testable explanation, there is a natural temptation to dismiss it – even though it holds up for both nonsocialist and socialist governments and in periods of both high inflation and high unemployment. Yet a little reflection reveals that a similar skepticism can be applied to the other elements of the model. Just as the fractionalization and polarization effects were shown not to be the signposts of a bargaining-environment scenario, so the various covariates of the present model could turn out not to represent what they seem. One can go further still. Just because the constant term in the baseline hazard is now statistically indistinguishable from zero need not imply that all causal factors, much less all correct causal factors, have been identified. It is possible, for instance, that two or more omitted time-varying factors affect the rate of termination in opposite ways and therefore tend to cancel each other out, producing a constant residual baseline hazard.

These questions are unanswerable in any ultimate sense since no model specification can be proved correct and complete. Nevertheless, there are a number of tests that can be devised to check the assumptions of the model, the validity of the covariates it contains, and its robustness under different conditions, definitions, and so forth. These tests will be explored in the next chapter, which concentrates on the adequacy of the model developed in this investigation. The results of these tests will inform the conclusions concerning government survival in parliamentary regimes that I offer – at least tentatively – in Chapter 8.

7

Model adequacy

The preceding chapters have elaborated a model of government survival in West European parliamentary democracies that is at odds with much previous theorizing and empirical work on the topic. In Chapter 8, I shall have much to say about these differences and their import for the development of our understanding of government functioning and survival. Before we can turn to that matter, however, it is necessary to deal with a prior issue: how much confidence can we have in the model advanced here?

The question of confidence involves several issues. First, the model was developed on the basis of certain definitional decisions concerning what constitutes a government termination, which terminations are artificial and merit censoring, and what degree of commitment to a government can be taken to constitute membership in it. Given the central and potentially controversial nature of these choices, the extent to which the results reported in Chapters 3 to 6 depend on them needs to be explored.

Apart from the model's robustness with respect to definitions, we must also consider the adequacy of the model's specification. In Chapter 2, I noted that the absense of a measure of explained variance in event history methodology is both a frustration and a blessing: although we cannot know how much of the dependent variable has been explained by the covariates, we avoid the pitfall of assuming that a high R^2 reflects a correctly specified model. Nevertheless, one cannot help but wonder how far the model takes us in the direction of explaining government survival. We shall be concerned in this chapter with three aspects of the specification: (1) can the model account for the sizable intercountry differences in overall rates of government termination, (2) can it account for any intercountry variations in the rate of increase in the underlying or baseline rate of termination, and (3) do the covariates in the model really measure what they are meant to measure?

The final area to be addressed concerns the assumptions of the likelihood analyses undertaken in this study. We saw in Chapter 6 that the PL assumption of a common baseline hazard turns out not to have been justified – hence, the introduction of a second vector of covariates to the ML model.[1] But there remains a very important assumption of both the PL and ML analyses that has yet to be subjected to any sort of examination: the assumption that cases are independent of one another.

It is this assumption that warranted the multiplication of likelihoods associated with individual cases (or, more precisely, the addition of their log-likelihoods) to generate overall likelihoods for the various estimated models. Since there is a temporal ordering to cases within each country, it is plausible that this assumption is not met with these data. We therefore must address the question: Is there any evidence of autocorrelation or the dependence of one government's duration on those of its predecessors? An affirmative answer would suggest another kind of time-based effect that would have to be incorporated into the model.

VARYING THE DEFINITIONS

The decision adopted here has been to register a termination not only when a government resigns or is defeated in its parliament, but also when it undergoes a change in leader or party composition or when an election has intervened, changing its parliamentary context to some extent at least. Situations where a termination, so defined, seems artificial were then adjusted by means of censoring. This raises questions regarding both the categories of termination and the censoring categories; indirectly, it also implicates the way in which government membership itself has been defined.

Concerning the first issue, the definition of terminations, this study follows the definition developed by Browne, Gleiber, and Mashoba (1984) in all respects but one: the treatment of government resignations that are offered but not accepted by a head of state. The rationale for treating these resignations as terminal – the choice adopted here – is that they mark a government breakdown; the subsequent inability of the system to produce a replacement government is not germane. Browne, Gleiber, and Mashoba took the opposite position, presumably because the government in fact continued on in office. Does it make any substantial difference to the empirical results if the second version of the definition is adopted?

The data set developed for this investigation was designed in such a way that either definition of government termination can be utilized. Because the use of one definition rather than the other affects not only the durations of some governments, but also the total number of governments involved and the calculation of returnability rates, the data subsets generated by the alternative definitions have the potential of producing very dissimilar results. As it turns out, however, unaccepted resignations are relatively rare in West European parliamentary democracies (confined largely to Italy and Finland). This accounts for the overall similarity of the results when the model was reestimated on the data set embodying the BGM definition, shown in Table 7.1. The treatment of unaccepted resignations appears, in the West European context at least, not to matter very much.[2]

The same is much less likely to be true with respect to censoring schemes, since censoring can easily affect a very large number of cases. For example, some 40.6% of cases were censored in the full model developed in Chapter 6. How crucial, then, is the censoring scheme? This issue is explored in Table 7.2, which presents model estimates using a variety of censoring schemes. Model 1 shows the effect

Table 7.1. *The effects of alternative definitions of government termination*

	All resignations counted (model 1)		Nonaccepted resignations ignored (model 2)	
First vector				
Constant	-7.79	(0.45)	-7.82	(0.46)
Majority status	-2.08	(0.29)	-2.10	(0.29)
Postelection status	-0.42	(0.21)	-0.42	(0.22)
Investiture	0.76	(0.22)	0.75	(0.22)
Returnability	2.03	(0.62)	1.92	(0.63)
Left-Right diversity	0.43	(0.13)	0.43	(0.13)
Clerical-secular diversity	0.20	(0.07)	0.22	(0.07)
Regime-support diversity	0.16	(0.07)	0.16	(0.08)
Change in unemployment rate	0.44	(0.09)	0.43	(0.10)
Second vector				
Constant	0.05	(0.38)	0.12	(0.37)
Change in unemployment rate	-0.47	(0.22)	-0.49	(0.23)
Inflation rate	0.14	(0.04)	0.14	(0.04)
Log-likelihood		-891.9		-848.2
Number of cases		202		188

Note: Entries are ML (Gompertz) coefficients (standard errors in parentheses).

of treating every termination as valid, that is, of invoking no censoring at all. If model 1 is compared with model 3, which utilizes the censoring scheme of the previous chapters, it is clear that the principal result of not censoring any cases is to weaken most of the covariate coefficients. This result makes sense once we recall that treating every termination as valid has the consequence of introducing a great deal of random variation into government terminations. To take one illustration, if a government that has attribute values associated with longevity is formed shortly before regularly scheduled elections, the no-censoring model would treat its subsequent early demise as a real collapse, contradicting the contributions of its attributes and thereby weakening their roles in the model. It is noteworthy, therefore, that even under this extreme assumption that all terminations, even those occasioned by statutory elections, are equally meaningful, model 1 still shows that attributes play a significant role in government survival: only one covariate – clerical–secular diversity – is clearly eliminated as a causal factor.

Model 2 of Table 7.2 embodies a restrained interpretation of artificial terminations, censoring only those governments that lasted beyond the observation period (end type 14) or that terminated because of the arrival or approach (within one

Table 7.2. *The effects of alternative censoring regimes*

	End types censored				
	None	1, 14	1, 4, 5, 14, 15	1, 4-7, 14, 15	0, 1, 3-5, 14, 15
	(model 1)	(model 2)	(model 3)	(model 4)	(model 5)
First vector					
Constant	-7.20 (0.31)	-7.45 (0.40)	-7.79 (0.45)	-7.81 (0.47)	-8.06 (0.50)
Majority status	-1.44 (0.21)	-1.70 (0.26)	-2.08 (0.29)	-1.92 (0.30)	-2.40 (0.31)
Postelection status	-0.92 (0.17)	-0.46 (0.20)	-0.42 (0.21)	-0.48 (0.22)	-0.45 (0.22)
Investiture	0.41 (0.16)	0.55 (0.20)	0.76 (0.22)	0.74 (0.22)	0.85 (0.23)
Returnability	1.77 (0.42)	1.96 (0.56)	2.03 (0.62)	1.91 (0.64)	2.36 (0.69)
Left-Right diversity	0.25 (0.10)	0.28 (0.12)	0.43 (0.13)	0.45 (0.13)	0.48 (0.14)
Clerical-secular diversity	0.01 (0.05)	0.13 (0.06)	0.20 (0.07)	0.19 (0.07)	0.26 (0.08)
Regime-support diversity	0.17 (0.07)	0.14 (0.07)	0.16 (0.07)	0.17 (0.07)	0.17 (0.07)
Change in unemployment rate	0.39 (0.08)	0.42 (0.08)	0.44 (0.09)	0.44 (0.10)	0.48 (0.10)
Second vector					
Constant	1.48 (0.24)	0.02 (0.35)	0.05 (0.38)	0.11 (0.38)	0.03 (0.42)
Change in unemployment rate	-0.56 (0.15)	-0.58 (0.20)	-0.47 (0.22)	-0.47 (0.22)	-0.48 (0.25)
Inflation rate	0.06 (0.03)	0.11 (0.04)	0.14 (0.04)	0.13 (0.04)	0.13 (0.05)
Log-likelihood	-1,429.2	-1,032.3	-891.9	-861.8	-807.1
Number of cases	202	202	202	202	202

Note: Entries are ML (Gompertz) coefficients (standard errors in parentheses).

year) of regular elections (end type 1). This censoring scheme may be thought of as a revised operationalization of the King et al. criterion; the difference is that, instead of censoring all long-lived governments on the assumption that they must have encountered elections or dissolved themselves in anticipation of them, the censoring scheme is based on an examination of the individual cases and a determination of which ones actually ended in this fashion. The results obtained with this censoring scheme show a much greater resemblance to model 3 than did model 1: all covariate coefficients are now statistically significant, and most re-semble their counterparts in model 3 very closely. It appears, then, that the cen-soring of cases terminated by regular elections (there are only a few cases censored because of the end of the observation period) is a major step in generating the model developed in this study.

A noteworthy characteristic of models 1 to 3 is that, while most estimated co-efficients increase with the expansion of the censoring regime, the coefficients at-tributed to the baseline hazard (the second-vector constant) and the postelection status covariate decline markedly, especially between models 1 and 2. The reasons for this countertendency have to do with regular elections. If terminations brought on by regular elections are not censored, then the longer a government remains in power the more likely it is to encounter a regular election – hence, the rising haz-ard. Once the interference of these elections is controlled for by means of censor-ing, this tendency disappears. As for governments formed immediately after elections, the noncensoring of elections gives them a built-in advantage in terms of survival: they simply have more time available to them. The censoring of reg-ular elections, of course, eliminates this technical advantage. Models 2 and 3 do show, nonetheless, that there still remains some advantage to being the first. Ap-parently, governments that spring from the electorate's verdict are less prone to falling apart or succumbing to their parliaments early on than governments formed later on in the parliamentary term, quite apart from the greater amount of time available to them.[3]

Models 4 and 5 in Table 7.2 take the opposite approach to models 1 and 2: they expand the censoring scheme beyond that utilized throughout this investigation. The first expansion, in model 4, involves cases in which one or more parties were added to a government (end types 6 and 7). As noted in Chapter 2, terminations occasioned by the addition of parties could be regarded as artificial because these additions typically occur before the point at which a government is faced with im-mediate collapse or defeat. Since censoring merely involves treating the true du-ration of a case as being at least as long as its recorded duration, no distortion is likely to come from censoring these cases. As model 4 makes clear, however, not much good comes from it, either. Some coefficients increase from model 3 to model 4, but others decrease, and it is not evident that any net gain in terms of sta-tistical power accrues from this expansion of the censoring regime.[4]

The final expansion of the censoring regime involves two categories of termi-nation that appear to be voluntary: resignations without any indication of political troubles (end type 0) and early elections (before one year of the scheduled date) without any such indication (end type 3). It goes without saying that political dif-ficulties not reported in the sources consulted may have been involved in these cases; the true nature of these terminations is thus uncertain. Nevertheless, the ef-fect of adding these categories to the censoring scheme is to preserve or enhance the size of all covariate coefficients save one (postelection status). This result is consistent with the conclusion that these terminations truly were voluntary and that by removing them from the set of real or necessary terminations, we have further clarified the role of the explanatory variables. This is merely an inference, however, and the matter remains open to interpretation.

Models 4 and 5 of Table 7.2 provide no compelling evidence against extending the censoring regime to incorporate these other types of termination, but neither do they provide compelling grounds for doing so. The censoring of terminations created by the addition of parties to the government can be justified reasonably well in the abstract, but it is clear that little is to be gained empirically by this course of action. A definite enhancement of the covariate effects is produced by the expansion to include apparently voluntary terminations; the obstacle here is that we cannot be sure what the nature of these terminations really is. All in all, it seems most appropriate to continue with the censoring scheme that has been used throughout this study. Future researchers would do well, however, to take cognizance of the importance of this matter and be prepared to explore a variety of censoring options.[5]

The final, and perhaps most controversial, definitional issue to be considered in this section concerns government membership. In many parliamentary systems, varying degrees of affiliation or association with a government can be identified, from actual membership (involving the assumption of one or more cabinet portfolios), to formal alliance, to a willingness to support the government in parliamentary votes challenging its survival – whether openly declared or not – to a willingness to abstain in such circumstances (again, whether openly indicated or not). Although membership is generally understood to involve only the first circumstance, it is possible that one or more of the other forms of association may be functionally equivalent, at least with regard to the issue of government survival. As noted in Chapter 2, data subsets were created to incorporate a variety of alternative conceptualizations of government membership, ranging from the most narrow – cabinet parties only (C) – to the most expansive – cabinet parties plus all declared or known support or abstention parties (CASA). These alternatives involve not merely differences in government majority status, but also differences in the number of governments and in their ideological diversity and returnability values; the effect of choosing one of these definitions over the others could therefore be quite substantial.

Table 7.3 presents the results obtained when the full model was estimated under each of these alternative conceptualizations. Perhaps the most outstanding feature of the six models is their similarity: although covariate coefficients fluctuate from one data subset to another, they generally stay within a fairly tight range. A comparison of the results listed under the C and CDS data subsets, for example, shows that virtually all of the covariates significant in the CDS model are also significant (in a one-tailed test, at least) under the more standard cabinet-only definition of government membership. The only exception is postelection status, which, as noted in Chapter 5, saw its effect on the rate of termination sharply diminished in the two sample reductions imposed by the limited availability of some of the other covariates.

Table 7.3. *The effects of alternative definitions of government membership*

	Data subset					
	C	CFS	CDS	CDSA	CAS	CASA
First vector						
Constant	-8.21	-8.14	-7.79	-7.98	-7.48	-7.69
	(0.51)	(0.49)	(0.45)	(0.47)	(0.45)	(0.46)
Majority status	-1.38	-1.64	-2.08	-2.08	-2.18	-2.10
	(0.25)	(0.28)	(0.29)	(0.30)	(0.28)	(0.29)
Postelection status	-0.32	-0.28	-0.42	-0.32	-0.52	-.040
	(0.21)	(0.21)	(0.21)	(0.21)	(0.22)	(0.22)
Investiture	0.82	0.80	0.76	0.84	0.65	0.77
	(0.22)	(0.22)	(0.22)	(0.22)	(0.22)	(0.22)
Returnability	1.84	1.96	2.03	2.35	2.05	2.41
	(0.64)	(0.66)	(0.62)	(0.65)	(0.62)	(0.65)
Left-Right diversity	0.39	0.46	0.43	0.39	0.37	0.32
	(0.14)	(0.13)	(0.13)	(0.13)	(0.12)	(0.12)
Clerical-secular diversity	0.13	0.17	0.20	0.18	0.18	0.14
	(0.07)	(0.07)	(0.07)	(0.07)	(0.07)	(0.07)
Regime-support diversity	0.20	0.16	0.16	0.15	0.17	0.15
	(0.08)	(0.08)	(0.07)	(0.07)	(0.06)	(0.06)
Change in unemployment rate	0.41	0.42	0.44	0.43	0.45	0.43
	(0.09)	(0.09)	(0.09)	(0.09)	(0.09)	(0.09)
Second vector						
Constant	-0.02	-0.04	0.05	-0.16	0.19	-0.07
	(0.38)	(0.38)	(0.38)	(0.38)	(0.38)	(0.38)
Change in unemployment rate	-0.39	-0.41	-0.47	-0.46	-0.50	-0.47
	(0.21)	(0.22)	(0.22)	(0.22)	(0.22)	(0.21)
Inflation rate	0.13	0.14	0.14	0.15	0.13	0.14
	(0.04)	(0.04)	(0.04)	(0.04)	(0.04)	(0.04)
Log-likelihood	-879.9	-877.5	-891.9	-894.6	-879.3	-895.2
Number of cases	199	199	202	202	201	201

Note: Entries are ML (Gompertz) estimates (standard errors in parentheses).
Abbreviations: C, cabinet parties; FS, formal support parties; DS, declared support parties; AS, all support parties; A, abstention parties.

The definition of government membership is not irrelevant, however. One of the more striking consequences of expanding the definition to include noncabinet parties is to increase the size of the coefficient associated with majority status. Clearly, the advantages for survival of commanding a parliamentary majority become increasingly more evident to the extent that we count as part of the government those parties willing to side with it in parliament. The only exceptions to this tendency occur in the two data subsets that incorporate parties willing to abstain for the government; the evidence of Table 7.3 indicates that this type of definitional expansion is not appropriate. But across the four main conceptualizations – C, CFS, CDS, and CAS – there is strong evidence that the inclusion of allied parties outside the cabinet conveys a better picture of the true government majority. In addition, the fact that the coefficients associated with the ideological diversity covariates show no tendency to diminish with these expansions suggests that the inclusion of the ideological positions of allied parties entails little distortion of the ideological diversity at play in these situations.

Should we, then, have used the most inclusive of the four major definitions, the CAS definition? Again, the evidence of Table 7.3 affords no basis for resisting such a course of action; moreover, we shall encounter further evidence in the next section that would favor it. Nevertheless, since the expansion from the CDS to the CAS definition is rooted in subjectivity – it involves the inclusion of "known" but apparently undeclared support parties – I am reluctant to take the extra step. Table 7.3 does make it very clear, however, that there is no empirical evidence for the belief that confining the definition of government membership to cabinet parties alone reflects the underlying situation; to do so, arguably, is to elevate a formal or legal criterion over empirical reality.

ASSESSING THE MODEL

The model development undertaken in the three preceding chapters was guided by two statistical criteria: (1) t-tests of the statistical significance of individual covariate coefficients, and (2) χ^2-tests of improvement in model log-likelihoods resulting from the addition of one or more covariates. King et al. utilized another test to develop a more substantively oriented standard for models based on cross-system data: the ability of the set of explanatory variables to account for significant differences in survival rates across the various systems. Their test consists of adding a set of dummy variables representing individual countries to the explanatory variables in the model to determine whether they contribute anything additional to the explanation; a failure to do so would imply that all significant intercountry differences in survival rates have already been accounted for by the explanatory variables.

In principle, the test is a simple one to implement. Dummy variables representing each country in the sample but one (to avoid multicollinearity) are added to the model specification, and the resultant improvement in the log-likelihood of the model is noted. This improvement, multiplied by 2, is distributed as χ^2 with de-

Table 7.4. *Tests of the contributions of country differences*

	Data subset			
	C (model 1)	CFS (model 2)	CDS (model 3)	CAS (model 4)
First vector				
Log-likelihood of original model	-879.9	-877.5	-891.9	-879.3
Log-likelihood with country dummies	-873.7	-870.5	-884.8	-874.6
χ^2 (8 d.f.)	12.2	14.1	14.2	9.3
Second vector				
Log-likelihood of original model	-879.9	-877.5	-891.9	-879.3
Log-likelihood with country dummies	-872.6	-868.3	-881.2	-871.4
χ^2 (10 d.f.)	14.4	18.3	21.4	15..8
Both vectors				
Log-likelihood of original model	-879.9	-877.5	-891.9	-879.3
Log-likelihood with country dummies	-870.3	-865.7	-877.7	-868.3
χ^2 (18 d.f.)	19.2	23.5	28.4	21.9

grees of freedom equal to the number of extra covariates (country dummies) added to the model. If this value exceeds the critical χ^2-value for some generally accepted level of significance (say, the .05 level), it would support the inference that the country dummies as a group contribute to the explanation of government survival beyond that achieved by the explanatory factors or, in other words, that the latter do not account for all significant differences among countries in rates of government termination.

The test, although possessing a persuasive rationale, is somewhat less valuable in the present context because two of the explanatory covariates – returnability and investiture – are constant within systems and thus collinear with the set of country dummies.[6] Three country dummies therefore must be excluded in order to perform the test. The consequence is that each of the country dummies entered in the model will assess a country's deviation in survival rates from the combined record of the three excluded countries – clearly a less than perfect test, given that the latter will inevitably differ among themselves in survival rates. To minimize this problem, the countries whose dummies are to be left out were selected on the basis of the similarity in mean rates of government duration: Norway (733.5 days), Sweden (734.4 days), and Britain (804.5 days).[7]

The χ^2-value generated by the addition of a set of eight country dummy covariates to the first vector of the final model is presented in the first part of Table 7.4 for each of the four main data subsets. At 8 degrees of freedom, the critical χ^2-

value indicating a significant improvement at the .05 level is 15.5. This critical value is not met or exceeded in any of the four models. Thus, although the set of explanatory covariates was derived on the basis of the CDS data subset, these tests provide some indication that these covariates are capable of accounting for inter-country differences in termination or survival rates, no matter which definition of government membership is used.

Since these tests are (inevitably) somewhat compromised, we may explore the possible existence of significant country differences in termination rates through another method. This method consists of estimating a series of models, in each of which a single country dummy is added to the first-vector specification. The value of this procedure is that it allows us to test all of the countries individually and to determine which ones have termination rates that differ significantly from the rest of the sample, controlling for the explanatory covariates. We begin with our prime focus of concern, the CDS data subset.

When performed on the CDS data, this series of tests isolated three systems as significantly deviant: Sweden, Italy, and Britain. Given the CAS model's impressive capacity to account for intercountry differences (as indicated by the very small log-likelihood change in Table 7.4), it may be suspected that situations of undeclared support may be involved. In Sweden, for example, the Communists have sometimes openly declared their support for Social Democratic governments and at other times apparently not (according to *Keesing's*); either way, these Social Democratic "minority" governments were typically very durable. Undeclared support parties are also common in Italy. The importance of undeclared support to the deviant status of Sweden and Italy can be assessed by redoing the individual country dummy tests using the CAS data subset, which counts undeclared support as government membership. The results of these tests were both in the expected direction: in the case of Italy, the country dummy becomes insignificant, and for Sweden, it approaches insignificance.[8] It appears, then, that the deviations of Sweden and Italy discovered in the CDS data set relate principally to the problematic status of parties that are known to be support parties but that are not recorded as having declared this support.

The deviation of Britain can be traced to a more idiosyncratic source: the support offered the Callaghan government of 1976–9 (for a time) by the Liberals. This is indicated by a test of the role of the U.K. dummy variable using the C data subset, which treats the Callaghan government as one government; the test shows the U.K. dummy not to be significant.[9] The reason this dummy played a significant role in the CDS data is that the counting of support parties as government members has the effect of breaking the Callaghan government into three governments, thus making Britain appear more unstable than its covariate values would indicate. Needless to say, the Liberal–Labor alliance of 1977–8 is not typical of party politics in postwar Britain.

There is another way in which country differences may affect the model: through variations in the rate at which the baseline hazard changes with duration time. That the baseline hazard generally rises with duration time was established in the preceding chapter; this phenomenon turned out to be attributable to the changing impacts of the economic covariates, particularly inflation. But can this explanation account for the rate of increase in the baseline hazard in all countries, or do some countries reveal significant residual differences? The evidence presented in Table 6.4 suggests that intercountry differences in the rate of increase are not extreme, although a few countries do show deviations from proportionality that approach statistical significance. Now that we have a model that accounts for the rising baseline hazard, it is appropriate that we test whether this account is sufficient for all countries.

This can be achieved very simply by adding the country dummies to the second vector of the full model. Since any covariates included in the second vector are multiplied by duration time, these additional covariates are approximately equivalent to the interactive covariates used in the proportionality tests in Chapter 6; the test differs mainly in that the set of interactive country dummies will be entered simultaneously so as to assess the total effect of country differences in proportionality.

The improvements in the log-likelihoods generated by adding ten country dummies to the second or interactive vector of the model are listed in the second part of Table 7.4 for the four main data subsets.[10] For two of the data subsets, C and CAS, the interactive country dummy covariates do not generate a significant improvement in the overall log-likelihood; under these definitions of government membership, the baseline hazard appears to be roughly the same across different countries, suggesting a common process. For the CFS data subset, however, the χ^2 value of 18.3 that denotes significance at the .05 level at 10 degrees of freedom is just reached, whereas for the CDS data subset it is clearly exceeded. Under the latter definition especially, it would appear that significant intercountry differences exist in duration dependence that cannot be attributed to the economic covariates.

Let us explore the presence of nonproportionality in the CDS data subset a little further by a parallel method to that used earlier: the estimation of a series of models in each of which one country dummy is entered in the second vector. Significantly, the countries that showed the strongest deviations in these tests were Italy, Sweden, and Britain – the same countries that were deviant when country dummies were tested in the first vector. This finding suggests that there may be some redundancy or "spillover" in these tests; in other words, the deviance of these three countries may appear in whichever vector the dummies are placed. The explanation so far presented for the deviation of these countries relies heavily on the manner in which the CDS definition of government membership affects the majority status of governments; this implies that the deviations of these countries are not a consequence of nonproportionality. To determine if this is indeed the case, a third series of individual country dummy tests were performed, this time with the country dummy in question entered in both vectors. The results confirm our expectations: for all three countries, it is the dummy entered in the first vector whose coefficient achieves or approaches statistical significance; the second-vector coefficients are all highly insignificant.[11] In fact, only one country – Denmark –

reveals a significant second-vector country dummy in these tests, and that effect is largely offset by a near-significant first-vector dummy of the opposite sign.[12] Thus, apart from Denmark, which appears to have a lower but more rapidly rising hazard rate, the economic covariates account for an underlying rate of termination that rises in a roughly uniform fashion in all systems tested.

The final test of the importance of country differences in government survival rates consists of entering the full set of country dummies in both vectors of the model simultaneously. Since eight dummies can be entered in the first vector and ten in the second, there are 18 degrees of freedom associated with this test. The increase in the log-likelihoods generated by the addition of these covariates is given in the third part of Table 7.4 for each of the four main data subsets. In no instance does the increase achieve the χ^2 value of 28.9 required for statistical significance at the .05 level. The χ^2 increase produced with the CDS data subset does come very close to this criterion, however, reflecting the impact of the deviant cases of Italy, Sweden, and Britain.

The evidence amassed here thus points to the conclusion that the CDS definition of government membership may be too inclusive in one context (Britain) and too limited in others (Sweden and Italy). These findings, however, should not be interpreted as fatal blows to the CDS definition because they imply that no definition can capture the reality in all countries equally well. Indeed, it seems very likely that the improvements in log-likelihoods registered in Table 7.3 by the country dummies for all data subsets derive largely from the fact that no one definition of government membership is optimal for all systems. If this is so, then the set of explanatory covariates identified here must be deemed very powerful in their capacity to account for intercountry differences in government survival.

EVALUATING THE COVARIATES

The fact that the ten covariates in the model possess statistically significant coefficients and are capable, collectively, of accounting for intersystem differences in rates of government termination does not establish that they are the true causes or determinants of survival. In a strict sense, of course, no amount of evidence can establish causality definitively, but it should be possible to explore whether any of the covariates stand in for unmeasured factors or play some other type of artificial or spurious role. In this section, we shall consider the roles of the ideological diversity covariates and investiture in this light.

A notable limitation of the measurement of ideological diversity undertaken in this study is that it is confined to interparty diversity. This follows from the fact that none of the available ideological scales registers diversity within parties; they all locate each party at a single point. This limitation undoubtedly introduces inaccuracy into the assessment of the ideological diversity within governments, especially in the case of single-party governments, which are assumed to have no ideological diversity at all. Since single-party majority (SPM) governments, in particular, tend to be long-lived, could it be that the role of the ideological diver-

Table 7.5. *The contribution of single-party majority governments*

	All governments counted (model 1)		Single-party majority governments excluded (model 2)	
First vector				
Constant	-7.79	(0.45)	-7.86	(0.49)
Majority status	-2.08	(0.29)	-2.23	(0.34)
Postelection status	-0.42	(0.21)	-0.45	(0.22)
Investiture	0.76	(0.22)	0.77	(0.23)
Returnability	2.03	(0.62)	2.21	(0.69)
Left-Right diversity	0.43	(0.13)	0.46	(0.14)
Clerical-secular diversity	0.20	(0.07)	0.22	(0.08)
Regime-support diversity	0.16	(0.07)	.017	(0.07)
Change in unemployment rate	0.44	(0.09)	0.45	(0.10)
Second vector				
Constant	0.05	(0.38)	0.32	(0.41)
Change in unemployment rate	-.047	(0.22)	-0.41	(0.26)
Inflation rate	.14	(0.04)	0.09	(0.05)
Log-likelihood		-891.9		-822.1
Number of cases		202		171

Note: Entries are ML (Gompertz) coefficients (standard errors in parentheses).

sity covariates is inflated by the erroneous attribution of minimal ideological diversity to these types of governments?

This question can be easily answered by reestimating the model with the SPM governments left out. The results of this test for the CDS data subset are given in Table 7.5 (the other data subsets produce equivalent results). A comparison of the results with those produced on the basis of the full set of available cases, also given in the table, indicates that the exclusion of the SPM governments has no material effect on the magnitude of the coefficients associated with the ideological diversity covariates. In fact, the coefficients become slightly larger once the SPM governments are removed.[13] Clearly, the roles of the ideological diversity covariates are not artificially enhanced by our inability to assess ideological diversity within SPM governments.

Although the effects shown by the ideological diversity covariates are not artifacts of the measurement procedure for SPM governments, it is still possible that they are not what they seem. In fact, it is rather easy to imagine how we might have been misled into attributing to one or more of those covariates an effect that, in reality, does not involve ideological diversity at all. Suppose that a certain type of

Table 7.6. *The role of regime-support diversity outside Italy*

	All available cases (model 1)		Italy excluded (model 2)	
Covariates				
Majority status	-1.76	(0.21)	-1.56	(0.24)
Postelection status	-0.60	(0.17)	-0.61	(0.20)
Investiture	0.68	(0.18)	0.55	(0.19)
Returnability	1.63	(0.49)	1.08	(0.52)
Left-Right diversity	0.25	(0.08)	0.32	(0.09)
Clerical-secular diversity	0.15	(0.06)	0.16	(0.06)
Regime-support diversity	0.17	(0.06)	0.17	(0.08)
Log-likelihood		-846.7		-601.8
Number of cases		284		231

Note: Entries are PL coefficients (standard errors in parentheses).

ideological dimension exists only or primarily in one system. Suppose, further, that it affects most or all governments in that system and that the system has, on average, either higher or lower rates of government termination than the rest of the sample. If that system possesses some other factor unique to it that determines the distinctiveness of its rates of termination, an ideological diversity covariate based on the ideological dimension it alone possesses would necessarily be correlated with it. A failure to enter this other factor – the true cause – would result in its role being attributed to the ideological diversity covariate.

In the present situation, the covariate most likely to fit this role is regime-support diversity. This dimension is present in two countries, France (Fourth Republic) and Italy, but since the inclusion of the economic covariates eliminates France from the sample, it is confined to just Italy in the full model. Moreover, the addition of the country dummy for Italy to the full model renders this covariate insignificant. Therefore, in principle, it could be anything unique to the Italian system that is contributing to the relatively short durations of Italian governments; regime-support diversity need not be involved. Is there any way that we can assess this possibility?

There is no sure method of demonstrating that it is indeed regime-support diversity that is the driving force behind the relationship, but we can determine whether it could be something unique to the Italian situation by reestimating the model without Italy. This procedure must be performed without the economic covariates in order to allow the other system with a regime-support dimension, France, to remain in the analysis. When this fixed-covariate model is reestimated using the PL method, the results, shown in Table 7.6, show no change at all in the magnitude of the coefficient associated with regime-support diversity when Italy

Table 7.7. *The effect of the investiture covariate on country deviations*

Country dummy	Investiture required?	Investiture covariate included		Investiture covariate excluded	
Austria	No	0.23	(0.47)	-0.30	(0.45)
Belgium	Yes	-0.09	(0.32)	0.42	(0.29)
Denmark	No	-0.05	(0.40)	-0.43	(0.38)
Ireland	Yes	-0.22	(0.71)	1.00	(0.61)
Italy	Yes	0.93	(0.39)	1.30	(0.37)
Luxembourg	No	-1.59	(1.03)	-1.95	(1.02)
Netherlands	No	0.08	(0.43)	-0.46	(0.39)
Norway	No	0.63	(0.52)	0.21	(0.54)
Sweden	Yes (from 1975)	-2.19	(0.73)	-2.13	(0.73)
United Kingdom	No	1.24	(0.43)	0.60	(0.40)
West Germany	Yes	0.13	(0.36)	0.51	(0.34)

Note: Entries are country dummy ML (Gompertz) coefficients estimated when each of the listed country dummies was entered separately into the full model (standard errors in parentheses).

is excluded. Whatever this covariate represents, therefore, it must be something characteristic of both the French and Italian situations; it cannot be a unique "Italian" attribute.

Another covariate whose causal role may be questioned is investiture. We saw in Chapter 3 that the rationale for this role cannot be that an investiture requirement brings about some very early terminations because the effect remains present even when the governments that collapse on investiture votes are excluded from the analysis; this remains the case when the full model specification is used. Could it be, then, that the investiture covariate is a surrogate, standing in for some other factor present, say, in one or perhaps two systems?

One way to test for this possibility is to perform a series of analyses in each of which a country dummy is substituted for the investiture covariate. If investiture is standing in for some idiosyncratic attribute of a particular system that leads to government terminations, one would expect the country dummy for that system to receive a markedly positive coefficient once investiture is no longer in the model. The relevant results of these tests are listed in Table 7.7. The striking finding portrayed in the table is that with the investiture covariate excluded, the country dummy effect becomes (more) positive not in one or even two systems but in each of the four systems that had an investiture requirement throughout the observation period, indicating that these systems appear especially unstable if the investiture requirement is not taken into account.[14] The implication of this pattern of results clearly is that whatever the investiture effect amounts to, it is present in each of the four main investiture systems. This strongly suggests that the investiture effect is not totally accidental; there must be something associated with the investiture requirement, apart from the possibility of failing an investiture vote itself, that entails higher rates of government termination.

The tests undertaken in this section do not establish that regime-support diversity and investiture are valid measures. What they do indicate is (1) that the effect attributed to regime-support diversity must have something to do with both France and Italy, and (2) that the investiture effect is common to all four systems that required investiture votes throughout the postwar period. These findings are, nevertheless, quite important for interpretative purposes. At various points in this study, we have come upon indications that the most striking trait of both Fourth Republic France and Italy with respect to government survival is that they are both polarized pluralist systems. The pivotal characteristic of such systems is the presence of significantly sized antisystem parties at both extremes of the Left–Right spectrum. If regime-support diversity is not the true cause of the effect attributed to it, therefore, it seems likely that the true cause will turn out to be something very closely related to it. As for investiture, we have less theoretical guidance to go by, but the very difficulty in finding any other attributes shared by such diverse systems as Belgium, Ireland, Italy, and West Germany suggests that some feature of, or associated with, the investiture rule must be involved.

TESTING THE INDEPENDENCE ASSUMPTION

Like the classical linear regression model, event history models are based on an assumption of independence in the phenomenon under scrutiny: the duration of any one case is assumed to be independent of the durations of any other cases. As noted earlier, this assumption warrants the multiplication of the likelihoods of individual cases to form the overall likelihood for a sample. In the present application, one can readily imagine scenarios that would violate this assumption. It may be, for example, that the early demise of a government tends to be followed by a reluctance to attack or defect from its successor for fear of appearing unwilling to allow the country to be governed. Alternatively, a tradition of short governments may tend to feed on itself, producing early terminations even in cases where the attributes of the incumbent government would not in themselves warrant it. This raises the question: Should we incorporate some sort of serial dependency – a dependency of one government on its predecessor(s) – into the model?

The simplest kind of dependency that might be proposed would be the situation in which the duration of a government is influenced by that of its immediate predecessor, sometimes called first-order autocorrelation. This kind of dependency may be evaluated by using the duration of the preceding government in each system as an explanatory factor. As model 1 in Table 7.8 indicates, a government's rate of termination does appear to be related to its predecessor's duration or *duration-lagged*, as it is labeled in the table.[15] We must be cautious in interpreting this result as indicative of a case of dependency, however, because the relationship may

Table 7.8. *Tests for first-order autocorrelation*

	Model			
	1		2	
First vector				
Constant	-6.40	(0.17)	-7.88	(0.49)
Duration-lagged[a]	-0.61	(0.20)	0.13	(0.22)
Majority status	—		-2.10	(0.29)
Postelection status	—		-0. 46	(0.22)
Investiture	—		0 .78	(0.22)
Returnability	—		2.09	(0.63)
Left-Right diversity	—		0.43	(0.13)
Clerical-secular diversity	—		0.21	(0.07)
Regime-support diversity	—		0.16	(0.07)
Change in unemployment rate	—		0.45	(0.10)
Second vector				
Constant	-0.36	(0.26)	0.03	(0.38)
Change in unemployment rate	—		-0.47	(0.22)
Inflation rate	—		0.14	(0.04)
Log-likelihood	-947.2		-891.7	
Number of cases	202		202	

Note: Entries are ML (Gompertz) coefficients (standard errors in parentheses).
[a]Duration-lagged was divided by 1,000 for presentational purposes.

be due to a sharing of common attributes between consecutive governments. In other words, the survival of two consecutive governments may be associated not because the earlier one affects the later one but because both governments possess a similar combination of relevant attributes.

To test for this possibility, we must introduce the other covariates into the model. The consequence, as model 2 demonstrates, is dramatic: the effect attributed to duration-lagged is sharply reduced in magnitude and rendered statistically significant. It appears, then, that any linkage in the survival records of consecutive governments is due to their possession of similar values on the explanatory covariates.

Dependency between consecutive cases need not be the only type of dependency, however. It is possible that the duration of any one case depends not on its immediate predecessor but on the general experience of previous governments. This possibility may be assessed with another covariate, *past instability*, that registers for each government the mean duration value of all previous governments

Table 7.9. *A test of the overall effect of past instability*

	Model			
	1		2	
First vector				
Constant	-5.33	(0.25)	-7.90	(0.79)
Past instability	-0.87	(0.15)	0.04	(0.22)
Majority status	—		-2.09	(0.30)
Postelection status	—		-0. 42	(0.21)
Investiture	—		0 .77	(0.23)
Returnability	—		2.10	(0.72)
Left-Right diversity	—		0.43	(0.13)
Clerical-secular diversity	—		0.20	(0.07)
Regime-support diversity	—		0.17	(0.08)
Change in unemployment rate	—		0.45	(0.10)
Second vector				
Constant	-0.13	(0.26)	0.05	(0.38)
Change in unemployment rate	—		-0.47	(0.22)
Inflation rate	—		0.14	(0.04)
Log-likelihood	-934.9		-891.9	
Number of cases	202		202	

Note: Entries are ML (Gompertz) coefficients (standard errors in parentheses).

in its particular system. As Table 7.9 shows, the fate of this covariate corresponds very closely to that of duration-lagged: past instability is significant in a bivariate relationship with the hazard rate (model 1), but its role is eliminated with the addition of the explanatory covariates to the specification (model 2). Although any number of alternative conceptualizations of dependency could be proposed, the failure of both duration-lagged and past instability to show any significant independent effect strongly suggests that the survival of governments does not depend in general on the experiences of their predecessors. For the purposes of statistical analysis, the assumption of a random dependent variable appears to be met.

There is, nevertheless, a more limited possibility that may be suggested: the possibility that a situation of dependency occurs only when governments of the same composition follow one another. This phenomenon could take either of the following two forms: (1) governments with the same composition (the same party membership and the same leader) as their predecessors tend to be short-lived, other things being equal; or (2) governments of the same composition as their predecessors tend to be more short-lived, provided those identical predecessors were relatively long-lived (again, ceteris paribus). Both versions embody what is essentially a "weariness" hypothesis.

This hypothesis can be addressed with the assistance of two covariates, the first indicating whether a government has the same composition as its immediate predecessor, the second registering the total uninterrupted duration of preceding governments of the same composition. The results produced by including either of these covariates in the full model may be stated succinctly: neither showed any significant net effect on the hazard rate.[16] It appears, then, that each government starts its period in office with a clean slate – a reassuring conclusion not only for the model developed here but for democratic theory as well.

CONCLUDING REMARKS

The purpose of this chapter has been to show that the covariates of the full Gompertz model represent a good selection from a variety of perspectives: (1) they survive variations in the way nonaccepted resignations are handled and government membership is defined; (2) they are capable of accounting for differences in survival rates across systems as well as for the temporal correlation of durations within systems; and (3) the more questionable of them appear to represent what they are intended to represent. A subsidiary purpose has been to show that the choices made here concerning the treatment of government terminations (including the censoring regime) and government membership are reasonable, given the available evidence.

The task to which we shall now turn is to evaluate the theoretical import of this model and its implications for future research. The theoretical debate that has been engaged to this point has involved the relative merits of the bargaining environment and ideological diversity interpretations; that debate aside, the approach pursued here has been predominantly inductive and data-based rather than deductive or theory-driven. The import of the findings presented in this study goes far beyond a critique of the bargaining-environment thesis, however. As I shall argue in the final chapter, they involve a significant reorientation in the standard way of conceptualizing behavior in parliamentary contexts.

8

Conclusion: an alternative perspective on government survival

The importance of the issue of government survival in parliamentary regimes relates primarily to the central place it occupies in any assessment of the viability of parliamentarism as a system of government: a parliamentary system that does not produce durable governments is unlikely to provide effective policy making, to attract widespread popular allegiance, or perhaps even to survive over the longer run. Major issues tend to provoke plethoras of different explanations, and government survival is no exception. Nevertheless, much of the debate hinges on the answers to the following two questions: (1) do government terminations originate in differences in political belief or ideology, and (2) if so, why should differences of this sort have that effect?

A negative answer to the first question points to an interpretation of coalition government instability in terms of the opportunistic or careerist motivations of politicians whose alleged ideological differences, often trumpeted for public consumption, mask strong bonds of collegiality. The cynicism of this interpretation is captured nicely in Jouvenel's (1914:17) well-known pronouncement on politics in the French Third Republic: "There is less difference between two deputies of whom one is a revolutionary and the other isn't, than between two revolutionaries of whom one is a deputy and the other isn't." In the model developed here, support for the view of parliamentary politics as an unprincipled game of musical cabinet chairs rests primarily with the role attributed to the returnability variable, which indicates that, other things being equal, government termination rates increase with the likelihood of the same parties returning to office. Nevertheless, it need not follow that the underlying motivation is self-centered; it could be that political leaders exploit situations of high returnability less to jockey for personal advantage than to pursue policy goals.

A policy interpretation of the returnability relationship would be much more consistent with the causal roles attributed in the model to the ideological diversity within governments, as measured along Left–Right, clerical–secular, and regime-support dimensions. These relationships strongly indicate that ideology does matter for government survival, notwithstanding the anecdotal evidence of pervasive pragmatism and careerism in certain ideologically polarized systems. Indeed, it is tempting to speculate that the inevitability of highly diverse governments in such systems encourages these types of behavior; in a policy stalemate, there may be little else to pursue but pragmatic compromise on the less charged issues and perhaps personal advantage as well. The important point, in any case, is the larger context: notwithstanding the collegiality, adaptability, and ambition of party leaders, governments that are seriously polarized on major issues tend to be relatively short-lived.

This conclusion brings us to the second question: Why should ideological diversity be inimical to government survival? The question is not as easily answered as it may seem. Consider the situation of a party that is considering whether to join, or to remain in, an ideologically divided coalition government. Regardless of the extent of the ideological differences, any party that assumes cabinet portfolios in the government, or even agrees to provide necessary support for it in the parliament, can expect to have at least as much influence on the policies of that government as if it did neither – and perhaps a good deal more. In addition, cabinet membership means that party leaders enjoy the power and prestige of occupying senior government positions, which often also confers the ability to dispense patronage and other types of favors to supporters. These considerations suggest that parties will prefer to enter and stay in governments, even highly divided ones, unless alternative coalitions that are likely to provide superior benefits in these areas can be identified. The implication of this line of reasoning is that we must consider not just the state of affairs in the government but the state of the larger parliamentary environment as well.

Game-theoretic models of government formation and survival, which dominate theoretical work on these topics, adhere closely to this guiding rationale. The result has been some fascinating insights into the logic of parliamentary politics and some very plausible explanations for why coalition governments are or are not able to maintain themselves – which makes it all the more surprising that the evidence of this study is not especially consistent with the rationale itself. This chapter addresses the discrepancy by developing briefly the main thrust of the game-theoretic approach and examining evidence that has been presented in support of it. The conclusions reached in that examination as well as other, less systematic evidence will then be used to fashion an alternative view of coalition behavior, one that can make better sense of the results presented in the preceding chapters. The discussion concludes with some observations on what has been achieved and what remains to be learned about government survival in parliamentary regimes.

THE CORE AND CHAOS

Unlike earlier game-theoretic work that took office seeking to be the dominant (or only) motivation, most of the recent models of government formation and duration explicitly incorporate the idea that policy matters in the parliamentary game. This focus finds expression in the representation of parliamentary parties in an ideological or policy space. The dimensionality of the policy space is an empirical issue, reflecting the number of salient issues or policy dimensions in the political system under examination. The locations of the parties in the space indicate their preferred or ideal positions on the salient dimensions that have been identified; parties are taken to be internally cohesive or disciplined, so that each party can be located at just one point, known as its "ideal point." It is assumed that the degree to which a party favors any given policy is inversely proportional to the distance between that policy's location and the party's ideal point, although the form of this relationship can vary.[1] Since any (cohesive) party that possesses a majority in parliament is in a position to form and maintain a government by itself, theorists concentrate their efforts on situations in which no majority party exists. The following discussion adopts that focus.

The simplest parliamentary setting, and the one most amenable to stable governmental outcomes, is the one-dimensional policy space. In this setting, the ideal points of all parties, and hence of all legislators, are aligned along a single straight line. It will usually be the case that one party contains the median legislator in this array, and by the median voter theorem (Black 1958), the ideal point of this party dominates the policy space. No parliamentary majority can form around any other point because the median party can always rally a majority that prefers its ideal point from among its own ranks plus the ranks of all parties that lie on its other side. For this reason, the median ideal point is said to constitute the *core* of the policy space, and the party located at that point can expect to form coalitions whose policies will coincide with its own.

Things become considerably more complex when we move to two-dimensional policy spaces. A median line in a two-dimensional space is a line that divides the space such that at least half the legislators lie on or to one side of the line and at least half lie on or to the other side. By an extension of the logic of the median voter theorem, a core can exist in two dimensions only if all median lines intersect at a single point, known as the "median in all directions" (Plott 1967). If there is such a point, there generally will be a party that occupies it and dominates government formation and policy making (Schofield 1993:6). Unlike the one-dimensional situation, however, there is no reason to believe that a median in all directions and thus a core will normally exist; it depends entirely on the configuration of parties and their respective parliamentary weights (numbers of seats). The existence of a core is thus quite problematic in two-dimensional spaces; in three or more dimensions, it becomes virtually impossible.

In the absence of a core, the assumptions of the approach lead to an expectation of extreme instability or chaos. Because there is no undominated policy point in the space, any majority coalition that forms around a given point can be upset by another majority coalition whose members all prefer some other policy point. Since parties are assumed to be policy maximizers, a process of outbidding should follow as each coalition or proposed coalition is defeated in turn by some other, generating a "voting cycle" that will continue indefinitely, in principle (McKelvey 1976). Even where a core does exist, it may be "weak" in the sense that it can be destroyed by small changes in either the locations of parties in the policy space or their weights; some parties, of course, may find it in their interest to adjust their policy positions so as to effect this result, thereby setting off a voting cycle.

One account of government survival in West European parliamentary regimes that appears to rely on the concept of the core is the bargaining-environment interpretation developed by Laver and Schofield (1990:156–7), which provides the theoretical foundation for the KABL model. The Laver–Schofield explanation rests on a trichotomous division of West European party systems into unipolar, bipolar, and multipolar types. Unipolar systems such as Ireland and Luxembourg are systems whose bargaining processes are dominated by a single party located in the center of the policy space; here the likelihood of chaos is remote. If the single dominant party is located significantly far away from the center of the array, as in Norway and Sweden, there may be an alternation in power between that party and an opposing bloc of parties, but government stability need not be seriously impaired. Nor would it be impaired in the case of bipolar systems such as Austria and Germany, where, as with unipolar systems, a fundamental change in party strengths or policy positions would be needed to upset the relatively simple bargaining situation. It is only in multipolar systems with large (effective) numbers of parties – Finland, Belgium, the Netherlands, Italy, Denmark after 1970 – that small changes in party sizes or positions can change the bargaining logic "and thereby create incentives for politicians to unpick a particular deal even after a coalition has taken office" (Laver and Schofield 1990:157).

Although the core is not mentioned in this interpretation, there are several reasons to believe that it is implied. The dominance of a centrally located party in unipolar systems certainly suggests that it occupies a core position; similarly, the discussion of multipolar systems bears an affinity with the weak-core situation mentioned earlier. In addition, the typology has been developed further by Schofield (1993:22–9) in a way that explicitly incorporates the presence of weak or strong cores, albeit not in the context of accounting for government stability or survival. Most significant, however, is the fact that government stability cannot be explained unless the core or some other stability-inducing mechanism is added. Laver and Schofield structure their discussion in terms of the danger of voting cycles, but the manifestation of cycles depends solely on the array of party positions and weights. If this array is not configured so as to contain a core, then cycling should occur even if the configuration is highly stable. In other words, a stable bargaining environment is not sufficient to ensure durable governments; a core (or something else) must exist as well.

If we add the theory of the core to the bargaining-environment hypothesis, we might come up with an explanation that runs something like this. A stable bargaining environment does not guarantee the existence of a core, but if a core does exist in a stable bargaining environment, it will be a strong core – small changes in the positions (or sizes) of the parties cannot destroy it.[2] In such a situation, which is more likely to characterize relatively simple party arrays, the party that occupies the core position can expect to participate in governments that implement its own policy preferences. Although government survival may be undermined if the

Table 8.1. *The Laver-Schofield analysis of durability and cores in West European parliamentary systems (1946-87)*

Country	Mean duration (months)	Party system	Unidimensional median	Multidimensional core
Luxembourg	45	Unipolar (center)	Typically CSV	
Ireland	39	Unipolar (center)		No core
Austria	38	Bipolar	Typically OVP	
Germany	37	Bipolar	Typically FDP	
Iceland	34	Unipolar (off-center)		No core
Norway	32	Unipolar (off-center)	Labor or Liberal	
Denmark (1945-71)	31	Unipolar (off-center)		SD (1960s) None (otherwise)
Sweden	28	Unipolar (off-center)	SD or Center	
Belgium (1946-71)	28	Multipolar		None (1946-61) PSC (1961-71)
Netherlands	27	Multipolar		KVP or CDA
Denmark (1971-87)	21	Multipolar		No core
Belgium (1971-87)	16	Multipolar	PSC (1981-87)	PSC (1971-81)
Finland	15	Multipolar	SD or Center	
Italy	13	Multipolar		DC

Abbreviations: CSV, Christian Socials (Austria); OVP, Austrian People's Party; FDP, Free Democrats; SD, Social Democrats; PSC, Christian Socials (Belgium); KVP, Catholic People's Party; CDA, Christian Democratic Appeal; DC, Christian Democrats.
Source: Derived from Laver and Schofield (1990:136, 159).

coalition partners of this core party chafe under its control over policy and either defect from the coalition or motivate the core party to seek more subservient allies, the very unbeatability of core policies plus the nonpolicy benefits of government membership should discourage them from reacting in this way. If so, the core party will have little reason to change coalition partners and governments will be relatively long-lived.[3]

The ultimate test of any line of reasoning is whether it accurately describes the real world. Laver and Schofield (1990:136, 159) provide two tables that summarize their own evaluations of twelve West European systems on the relevant factors; these evaluations are combined and reproduced in Table 8.1. On the left of the table are their assessments of the bargaining systems together with the mean durations of postwar governments.[4] If one accepts that unipolar (off-center) systems have more potential for change than do bipolar systems, the typology orders the systems consistently in terms of their mean government durations. The inclusion in the table of their evaluations of the presence of cores in these systems muddies the picture rather seriously, however. The categorization divides systems according to whether they are unidimensional or multidimensional. Although multipolar systems tend to be multidimensional and therefore much less likely to have a core, there appears to be no tendency for cores to be concentrated among the unipolar and bipolar systems that display greater government longevity. Indeed, of the five systems they consider to be multipolar, only Denmark (1971–87) and Belgium in the period 1946–61 are categorized as lacking a core;[5] moreover, cores are not attributed to two unipolar systems with very impressive rates of government survival (Ireland and Iceland).

The Laver–Schofield identification of cores in West European party systems makes no mention of their degrees of stability or strength. The issue is important because a party occupying a weak core, that is, one easily destroyed by small changes in party positions or sizes, would presumably not be able to dominate a bargaining system in the way that a strong core party can. Nevertheless, it seems reasonable to infer from the long periods in which Laver and Schofield record cores in existence and occupied by the same parties in multipolar systems that they could not have been easy to destroy; moreover, in almost all cases, the party occupying the core is the largest party in the parliament, as required by theory (Laver and Schofield 1990:133). Nevertheless, the existence of stable core positions occupied by large parties was apparently not enough to inhibit government instability in most complex, multipolar systems.

The conclusion that would seem to follow from the Laver–Schofield analysis of cores in West European parliamentary systems is that the concept is largely irrelevant to the issue of government survival. The matter is less straightforward than it would seem, however, because there is considerable uncertainty concerning the attribution of cores. A more recent study by Laver and Hunt (1992:101), for example, argues that the policy spaces of many of these systems could be considered either as one-dimensional or as two-dimensional. Under the two-dimensional assumption, they are able to attribute cores only to Sweden and (possibly) Belgium. If some systems are indeed one-dimensional, they believe that cores can be identified in just four systems: Denmark, Iceland, the Netherlands, and Sweden. In addition, the assumption that the cores identified by Laver and Schofield are strong cores is undermined by a subsequent assessment by Schofield (1993:22–9), which identifies five systems – Sweden, Norway, Denmark, Luxembourg, and Belgium – as having only weak cores.

A quick perusal of Table 8.1 shows that these adjustments do not significantly improve the fit between (strong) cores and government stability. On the one-dimensional assumption proposed by Laver and Hunt, the systems with cores appear to be concentrated more in the middle range of duration values than at the top of the list. If two dimensions are assumed, then cores appear too rarely to explain the high levels of government stability enjoyed by several West European systems. As for the weak-core systems identified by Schofield, they are spread across the ranking from top to bottom; nor does combining them with the no-core systems, as identified by either Laver and Schofield or Laver and Hunt, produce a discernible linkage with mean duration.

To those familiar with West European parliamentary systems, the finding that the concept of the core works poorly as an explanans for government stability will come as no surprise. The expectations engendered by the absense of a strong core are both unambiguous and extreme: governmental hyperinstability or chaos. Yet instances of chaos are very difficult to come by in these systems, even though most investigations of their policy spaces, including those based on the Party Manifestos Project (Budge et al., 1987), have found them to be multidimensional, and none has alleged that strong cores are ubiquitous. What does survive the analysis, however, is the idea that complex, multipolar bargaining environments undermine rates of government survival.

The strategy often adopted by formal theorists to cope with the lack of empirical examples of chaos is to propose some kind of constraint to check or limit the availability of alternative coalitions that can defeat the status quo in no-core systems, thereby limiting the risk of cycling. One recent proposal for restricting these alternatives, for example, involves the addition of rules concerning the order in which parties are invited by the head of state to form governments (Baron and Ferejohn 1989; Baron 1991). For our purposes, the important point about restrictions of this sort is that they are unlikely to eliminate the tendency for bargaining complexity to lead to instability, if only because the information and calculations required to find an equilibrium solution tend to become very onerous as complexity rises.[6] They therefore need not be inconsistent with the finding that multipolarity is associated with government instability.

The ability of the bargaining-environment hypothesis to accommodate this type of solution is one of its most important features. Due to the demanding requirements of game-theoretic approaches, the evidence presented in their favor has tended to be anecdotal rather than systematic. With the finding that multipolar systems have shorter mean government durations, we have systematic, if indirect, evidence that the approach itself may be on the right track – provided, of course, that multipolar systems really do have more complex bargaining environments. The next section examines this key assumption.

THE BARGAINING-COMPLEXITY FACTOR

Do multipolar systems generate more complex environments for coalition bargaining? There can be little doubt that larger numbers of parliamentary parties tend to generate greater numbers of possible winning coalitions. Where large numbers of parties are combined with high levels of ideological polarization, one can readily imagine that the complexities involved in arriving at and maintaining a majority coalition would be considerable. Nevertheless, I shall argue in this section that these conclusions, however plausible they appear, are not consistent with the available empirical evidence.

The empirical difficulties of the bargaining-complexity approach can be seen very clearly in the cases of Luxembourg and Italy, the two countries located at the extremes in terms of rates of government survival in Table 8.1. Given the vast differences in government durability in the two systems, the preceding reasoning would lead one to expect a correspondingly large difference in the complexity of their bargaining environments. For Luxembourg, the bargaining logic of postwar parliaments certainly seems to be simple. On the assumption that the small Communist Party's "antisystem" status made it noncoalitionable – that is, uninterested in (or excluded by other parties from) participating in the government coalitions – coalition formation has typically involved three political parties: the Socialists (LSAP), the Christian Socials (CSV), and the Democrats (DP). In three of the ten postwar elections between 1945 and 1984, the parliamentary sizes of the parties were such that the CSV had to be included in any prosystem majority government. In the remaining seven parliaments, it was possible to form a prosystem majority coalition without the CSV – but only if the LSAP, the DP, plus one or more of the Independents or Independent Socialists were included. Since the LSAP and the DP are generally located at a greater ideological distance from each other than either is from the CSV (and should therefore have found it relatively difficult to coalesce with each other), the CSV certainly appears to have held the whip hand in interparty bargaining.

Italy resembles Luxembourg in possessing a dominant, centrally located Christian Democratic Party, but its party system is much more fragmented and polarized. Is its bargaining environment therefore significantly more complex? In fact, it is difficult to say that it is. Since the Communists, Monarchists and neo-Fascists (plus a few tiny regional parties) were generally considered noncoalitionable, majority coalitions had to take one of two forms in the first two decades of the postwar era: either Christian Democrats (DC) in alliance with the Socialists (PSI) or Christian Democrats in alliance with all (or almost all) of the available non-Socialist parties. Given the ideological antipathy between the DC and the PSI, the outcome was generally a non-Socialist coalition. Although the DC occupied the core position according to Laver and Schofield, their bargaining power was limited by the fact that they were not in a position to play off one potential coalition against the other. Thus, the Social Democrats (PSDI), who were usually necessary for a non-Socialist coalition, could not be threatened with the possibility of being excluded in favor of the PSI if they refused to accept the DC's policy position because the PSI were even less likely to make such a concession. The basic dilemma for the DC was that either the PSDI or the PSI had to be included, yet both are located to the DC's left on the dominant Left–Right dimension.

The options became even more constrained in recent Italian parliaments since the participation of both the PSI and the DC was needed to form a majority coalition.[7] Although actual coalition governments typically included two or three smaller parties as well, these inclusions added very little to their ideological range or complexity; the key fact is that all majority coalitions required the DCI and the PSI as their principal members. This situation actually provided fewer coalitional alternatives than that of Luxembourg, where it has usually been the case that no one party is essential for a majority government. Yet Italy has experienced a much higher rate of government turnover.

What makes options more constrained in the Italian case, despite its greater party-system fragmentation, is clearly the parliamentary weight of its antisystem forces (typically between 30% and 40%, as compared with an average of less than 10% in Luxembourg). Can the bargaining-environment approach be salvaged, then, by replacing multipolarity with an indicator of complexity that takes this property into account? The evidence of this study does not support such an interpretation: we found in Chapter 3 that a party-system fractionalization measure based solely on the prosystem parties does not contribute significantly to the explanation of government survival, once other relevant parliamentary and government attributes are taken into account. The same result is produced when this variable is added to the final model.[8]

What is true for fractionalization, total or prosystem, also holds true for such other measures of bargaining complexity as the number of formation attempts and the number of policy dimensions (which should reflect the existence of cores). These negative findings persist, moreover, when the analyses are confined to coalition situations, which indicates that the lack of a relationship is not due to the autonomy single-party majority governments enjoy from their parliamentary environments. Indeed, the only alleged indicator of bargaining complexity that held out any hope of playing some significant independent role – polarization – was ultimately found to possess that capability because it indirectly reflects the ideological diversity within governments. Notwithstanding its plausibility as a conditioning factor, the complexity of the parliamentary bargaining environment appears, on present evidence, to have very little to do with government survival.

AN ALTERNATIVE PERSPECTIVE

The evidence that government survival is independent of the availability of alternative coalitions is puzzling from a theoretical standpoint since we have no good reason to believe that party leaders would not prefer coalitions offering a better policy deal for their parties. But perhaps the key to the puzzle lies with implementation rather than intention. Consider what is involved for a member of a governing coalition to implement a strictly policy-maximizing strategy. First, it must know the positions of all parties on the salient dimensions; these positions may be misrepresented by the other parties or changed at any time. With this information and taking into consideration any variation in saliency across dimensions, the party would then have to evaluate the payoffs it would receive from each viable alternative that it could enter (discounted, perhaps. by the probability of each being asked to form the next government). Finally, the party must consider the possibility that the coalition to which it defects may itself be upset in short order by another, thereby preventing it from realizing the policy advantages that motivated its defection.

An institutional constraint may yield some kind of stable equilibrium in this process, but it is questionable whether the participants in the coalition game could amass sufficiently precise information and work through the calculations required to find that equilibrium – especially if the party array is complex. Instead, they may conclude that the only sensible course is to stay in their present coalition until an alternative arrangement appears that is both superior in terms of payoff and very likely to be able to occupy office sufficiently long to deliver on that payoff. Alternatives that meet these requirements are not more likely to appear in complex bargaining environments than in simple ones; indeed, the opposite may be true. The slipperiness of complex environments may exist in theory only.

Another reason why it may not be possible for a party to slip easily from one coalition to another involves the effect that this behavior is likely to have on other parties. Parliamentary parties exist in a situation with a very distant time horizon, somewhat like an indefinitely iterated prisoners' dilemma. If they defect from a coalition quickly or frivolously – perhaps to an alternative coalition that is only marginally more attractive to them – they may be punished by their erstwhile coalition partners in future coalition formation situations. It is a reasonable assumption that most parties, if given the option, would prefer to avoid negotiating a coalitional arrangement with a party known to be prone to defect whenever a better deal, however slight the gain, becomes available. Indeed, some degree of precommitment may be required as a condition for coalition membership, forcing a party that spies greener pastures elsewhere to bide its time – or risk costly retaliation in the future.

The difficulties of identifying better coalitional alternatives in a complex bargaining environment, the futility of defecting to alternatives that are themselves likely to be short-lived, and the chance that hasty defection will be punished in future rounds of the coalition game may explain why the greater options of complex environments do not translate into higher rates of government instability, once other factors are taken into account. What they do not explain is why this investigation has revealed the principal "other factor" to be the ideological diversity within governments. After all, if an alternative coalition that is both viable and superior in terms of payoff cannot be identified or if a sudden defection to that coalition would be severely punished, then one would expect member parties to stick with their present coalitions, regardless of the internal divisions they contain. Within the standard game-theoretic framework, the role of ideological diversity represents something of an anomaly.

The framework in question is defined by the locations of parties in the policy space, their parliamentary weights, the majority criterion plus any other rules that may apply, and the motivation of party leaders to see public policies accord as much as possible with those advocated by their own parties. This framework says nothing about whether party leaders are sincerely attached to their party's policies, but if they are, then it is possible to imagine that they would be reluctant to associate themselves with the implementation of policies seriously at variance with them. Of course, in cases where a defection from a governing coalition would be likely to lead to even worse policies (from the standpoint of the defecting party), the leadership may feel obliged to swallow its pride and remain in the coalition to minimize the damage. But where a defection would not significantly worsen the policy situation – if policy making is dominated by a core party, for example – a net benefit may accrue to party leaders from a defection that allows them to reduce the discrepancy between the beliefs that led them to enter political life and their actions as politicians.

This scenario rests on two related and rather contentious assumptions: that politicians are sincere ideologues and that they care relatively little about office holding. Given human capacities for self-delusion, it could always be argued that politicians in ideologically uncomfortable coalition governments would rationalize their participation in order to hang on to office. An objection along these lines is only plausible, however, to the extent that the game in question – apart from the introduction of an office-seeking motivation – is defined completely by the preceding framework. What is left out of that framework is the dependence of the parliamentary game on the larger political environment.

The ability of political leaders to achieve their political goals – be they policies or power – derives largely from their capacity for attracting political support. Supporters may be divided into those who vote for the party in elections and those, usually party members, who also work actively to help the party rally voters to the cause. For voters, the benefits of holding office cannot figure significantly in their motivations; theirs must be primarily a policy-seeking orientation. So, too, with party members: although some may join for career or business purposes or because of the personal appeal of a leader, the most useful and enduring membership is made up of individuals who simply wish to participate in the advancement of certain policies. To maintain the support of these individuals, leaders must be able to demonstrate that their current strategy is optimal for realizing the party's policy objectives.[9] If the party has joined an ideologically diverse governing coalition, this may be a formidable task.

In an ideologically diverse coalition, the coalition's policy point cannot be close to the ideal points of all member parties (by definition). For the leaders of a party whose policies on one or more salient dimensions are relatively distant from the coalition's, the argument for continuing in the coalition must be that there is no other parliamentary strategy that would reap a superior reward. This may be true, either because the coalition's policy point denotes a stable equilibrium in the policy space or because there are no viable coalitional alternatives that are clearly better for the party than the status quo, once the likelihood of future retaliation is taken into account. Nevertheless, there is no reason why options need to be restricted to what can be achieved in the existing party array. Because parliaments reflect the divisions of opinion within the larger political community, there is also the possibility of changing the array itself. For a party whose appeal is based on commitment to a particular ideological position, this tends to mean maximizing the party's parliamentary size or weight by cultivating its popularity with the electorate.

The issue of popularity can cut a number of ways. If a party belongs to a popular coalition government whose policies are remote from its own, its leaders may be tempted to stay with the government so as to profit electorally from that involvement, especially with less ideological voters. Another factor inhibiting defection is the possibility that disrupting a governing coalition may be very damaging at the polls if it appears that the interests of the country have been sacrificed to those of a single party; other things being equal, voters tend to prefer governmental stability to instability. On the other hand, for a party, especially an ideologically motivated party, to stay in such a coalition can be very disheartening to its supporters; in particular, the willingness of members to work for the party may dissipate as the gap widens between what the party program asserts and what the party appears to stand for in government. The party leadership will have to convince these individuals not only that no better deal is possible, but also that voters would more likely be alienated from than attracted to the party if it were to abandon the government; many may come to believe that the leadership is simply more interested in power than principles.

If the coalition government's popularity is low, the case for leaving it becomes much stronger. It would be natural in this situation for those individuals sincerely committed to the party's ideological position to conclude that the government's difficulties stem from its bad choice of policies; by leaving the government, the party can dissociate itself from these policies and highlight its commitment to an alternative course. Since government policy is unlikely to move closer to that of a party that has defected, these individuals are likely to believe that the period following its defection will see a continuing demonstration of the error of the government policies that can only help the party in the next elections. Thus, whether the party has made the most favorable coalition arrangements that the party array allows is only part of the story; if the most favorable is still not very satisfactory, the strategy itself may be undermined by the argument that the party's goals can be better advanced by not participating in government at all.

This argument, moreover, need not apply only to ideological parties or parties that rely heavily on extraparliamentary organizations; even a party that is primarily office seeking and/or weakly organized must concern itself with the effect that participation in an unpopular government will have on its prospects in the next election. This may explain why ideological diversity and the economic indicators enter the model separately: while ideologically diverse coalition governments are more likely to contain member parties whose preferred policies are distant from those implemented by the government itself and therefore face internal pressures to defect, parties not concerned with, or not subject to, such diversity may also be tempted to defect if government policy – here indicated by the state of the economy – appears unsuccessful.

The analysis thus far has suggested that three options are available to parties that belong to a governing coalition: stick with the coalition, defect to a viable alternative that offers a better payoff, or go into opposition in order to enhance electoral appeal and hence future bargaining power. In fact, a fourth option may be proposed as well: defect in order to reenter the same coalition. This option is most likely to be feasible in bargaining environments that afford few alternatives to an existing, ideologically diverse coalition government. Typically, levels of party-system ideological polarization sufficiently high to entail the strong presence of antisystem parties create these environments. Given the lack of alternatives, a member-party's leadership may appease discontent over the compromises necessitated by government participation with the occasional well-timed defection, secure in the knowledge that no matter how annoyed its coalition partners are, they will probably have to invite the party to join the next government – perhaps with some policy or portfolio concession to smooth its ruffled feathers.[10] If the government is not popular, a defection could serve the additional purpose of signaling to the electorate the party's detachment from government policies, while its willingness to reenter the coalition conveys the message that it is prepared to make sacrifices to provide the country with government. Parties would appear to have the best of both worlds in such an environment – reflected, perhaps, in the pejorative Italian term *partitocrazia* (partyocracy) – but a larger cost may be involved: disillusionment with the system as a whole. The introduction of the returnability variable into the model was intended to measure, however imperfectly, the exercise of this fourth strategic option.

The expansion of the environment conditioning decisions to stay in or defect from coalition governments to include the perceptions and (anticipated) reactions of supporters and voters places party behavior in parliamentary contexts in a very different light. It means that however much party leaders may wish to maximize policy advantage – or office holding – within the existing party array, they may not be free to do so. For one thing, the objective of attracting voters, especially uncommitted voters, may oblige parties to rule out any decisions that cannot be justified in terms of broader interests, including the interest of the country as a whole. For another, even supporters who conflate their party's advantage with the public good may prefer to see the party abandon government entirely in order to demonstrate to one and all the bankruptcy of compromising on party policies. Choosing not to participate in government, in other words, becomes a legitimate option. No strong assumption of gratification deferral is required to make sense of this strategic choice: for parties, the future arrives with the very next election.

CONCLUDING REMARKS

The preceding discussion is an attempt to account for the central finding of this study, which is that the empirical connection between the complexity of parliamentary bargaining environments and government survival rates in West European regimes disappears when other factors, most notably the degree of ideological diversity within governments, are brought into the picture. That ideological diversity should matter for survival presents a dilemma for approaches that assume that parties will stick with the best deal the parliamentary arena affords, but the roles played by the economic indicators as well as by postelection status point to the need to incorporate the larger environment of supporters and voters, who ultimately determine the partisan shape of parliaments. This need not mean that the particular formulation outlined here is the correct one, for it clearly outstrips the evidential basis from which it was constructed. But the evidence certainly implies that a different theoretical focus is required.

One strength of the formulation presented here is that it surmounts the bifurcation in interpretations of parliamentary behavior along lines of sincerity. Although ideological diversity plays an important role in the account, it does not require an assumption that politicians are sincere ideologues; the fourth strategic option, in particular, leaves ample room for careerism, collegiality, and hypocrisy. Nevertheless, that option, like the others, is a response to an environment in which ideology and ideological differences matter a great deal; indeed, it is only suitable in the most ideologically constrained situations. It may appear to citizens of regimes with high rates of government turnover that their politicians choose to avoid major societal issues, but the argument advanced here implies that they have little choice.

The key, then, in assessing the Janus-faced nature of parliamentarism is not to confuse the symptoms for the disease. The use of the term *disease*, however, should not be taken to imply that this kind of parliamentary regime – although impaired in certain respects – is necessarily condemned to a short existence. Like governments, regimes may survive for relatively long periods despite their weaknesses. After all, even troubled regimes do bring some benefits, not least to the parties and the politicians that run them; any attempt to dismantle them risks making things worse rather than better. Moreover, it is often well appreciated that the problems afflicting governments do not originate in regime structures but rather in the societal conditions that generate support for extremist parties. The functioning of these systems may reinforce the appeal of antisystem parties, but it is unlikely to have caused their presence. As long as they represent major currents of political opinion, the chances of finding an alternative regime type that can command universal support and thereby facilitate stable and effective governments are not encouraging. Institutional engineering can make a difference, as it undoubtedly did in France (the Fifth Republic), but it would be naive to see it as a cure-all.

This investigation was motivated not only by the importance of explaining parliamentarism's two faces, but also by the expectation that event history analysis could take us much further toward that goal. In my view, this expectation has been largely realized. The ability to decipher the causes of government breakdown was hindered in the past by the presence of terminations that clearly did not constitute breakdowns, most notably those occasioned by statutory limits on the length of parliaments. We have seen that the censoring of these cases powerfully affects our assessment of the causal forces in question. If the events theorists were wrong to suggest that causal mechanisms are weak or nonexistent in this domain, they were right to argue that the explanation of government survival must take account of circumstances that occur after the government formation process. The postformation circumstances that this study has linked to government survival – the inflation rate and the change in the unemployment rate – are not "events" in the events theorists' sense, but at least they postdate government formation. Moreover, unlike the causal factors used in previous studies, they are dynamic, changing frequently over the lifetimes of governments.

The final advantage of event history analysis that was to be exploited in this study concerned the baseline hazard, the underlying trend in government terminations net of all measured factors. The enticing prospect of detecting the effects of factors that are inherently unmeasurable was only partly realized: there did prove to be an underlying tendency for the risk of termination to rise with duration time, but this effect turned out to be attributable to the inflation rate, whose impact appears to be most pronounced on long-lived governments. As a result, the model ultimately produced with the aid of event history methodology is able to account not only for all significant intercountry differences in government termination rates, but for the underlying trend in these rates as well.

Does this mean that all systematic influences on government survival have been accounted for, leaving only a flat baseline hazard generated by the incidence of truly random outside events? It seems to me that this is unlikely to be the case. Although this investigation has involved a wide range of possible causes as well as a variety of alternative definitions of key concepts, there is no reason to suppose that possibilities have been exhausted. As in all empirical disciplines, future work will undoubtedly uncover new influences on government survival, some of which may displace factors included in the model developed here. The very difficulty in finding a plausible explanation for the presence of the investiture covariate, for example, suggests that its role is indirect and may someday be displaced by a more immediate cause. The economic covariates, too, are clearly indirect indicators. With time, a sufficient quantity of reliable survey data should become available to test the inference that government popularity is the root cause and, if results are positive, displace these covariates in the model. Finally, the importance attributed earlier to the views of party members suggests that a good place to begin the search for new causes is the assumption of party unity; successful measurement of the ideological divisions within parties may lead to the finding that they play a significant role in decisions to leave coalition governments.

What I do hope the present investigation has achieved is to raise serious questions about the appropriateness of some of the prevailing assumptions of game-theoretic approaches, which have dominated research on this topic. The interpretation presented here places considerably more weight on the acceptability of present coalition arrangements than on the relative appeal of alternative ones and assumes much less of the capacity of politicians for complex calculations of utilities. It sees parties as highly constrained – by the need to keep faith with supporters as well as by the (possibly conflicting) need to keep faith with actual or potential coalition partners – even when, in principle, coalitional alternatives exist. Most fundamentally, it points to the need to incorporate a much broader spectrum of actors into the dynamics of government formation and maintenance. If this investigation has helped to close one door, it is equally as likely to have opened many others.

Appendix: a codebook of variables used in this study

The following is a list of names and descriptions of variables in the data set that are most relevant to the discussion of the preceding chapters. For many of these variables, it was necessary to create separate versions to accord with the principal alternative definitions of government membership utilized in this study. There are four principal definitions:

1. C: parties actually in the cabinet.
2. CFS: the preceding plus parties that formally agree to support the cabinet.
3. CDS: the preceding plus parties that openly declare that they will support the cabinet.
4. CAS: the preceding plus parties that do not declare themselves supporters but are considered by sources as such.

In addition, variables relating to the majority or minimal winning status of governments have two extra versions to account for parties that abstain in favor of the cabinet. These versions accord with the following definitions of government membership:

5. CDSA: government composition as in definition 3, but parties that openly commit themselves to abstain are subtracted from the total size of the parliament.
6. CASA: government composition as in definition 4, but parties that commit themselves or are considered by sources as committed to abstaining are subtracted from the total size of the parliament.

The variables created in the four main versions are indicated with a single asterisk; those that are available in all six versions have a double asterisk. Because the definition of government membership also affects the number and duration of governments, all analyses must be performed on a data subset that incorporates a particular definition. Distinct data subsets exist for (1) the C definition, (2) the CFS definition, (3) the CDS and CDSA definitions, and (4) the CAS and CASA definitions.

Another consideration that affects the number and duration of governments concerns their terminations. The data set incorporates two definitions of termination, differentiated according to whether resignations not accepted by a head of state are counted as terminal events:

1. Terminations are occasioned by parliamentary defeat, resignation of government or prime minister, death of prime minister, change in party composition of government, elections.

2. Terminations are occasioned by parliamentary defeat (if resignation is not required), government or prime ministerial resignation that is accepted by the head of state, death of prime minister, change in party composition of government, elections.

All four data subsets incorporate both the first, or "all resignations," definition and the second, or "accepted resignations only," definition. Analyses must be performed using one of these definitions. Except where indicated, variables are available for both definitions.

A complete codebook, which includes the variables that define the various data subsets as well as numerous others not included here, is available on request.

CASE-DEFINING VARIABLES

CASENO   Case identification number
            Note: Cases encompass all countries from their first postwar election until June 30, 1989. Constituent assemblies (France, Portugal, Spain, etc.) are excluded.
CASESEQ   Case sequence number
            Note: This variable assigns a unique case number even when cases are entered more than once (because of alternative definitions of government membership and termination).
COUNTRY
    1   Austria
    2   Belgium
    3   Denmark
    4   Finland
    5   France
    6   Iceland
    7   Ireland
    8   Italy
    9   Luxembourg
    10   Netherlands
    11   Norway
    12   Portugal
    13   Spain
    14   Sweden
    15   United Kingdom
    16   West Germany
CASETYPE   Type of government
    1   Regular
    2   Caretaker
    3   Noninvested
ENDTYPE   Type of termination
    0   Resignation/voluntary: no indication of political pressures

1	Electoral/statutory: within twelve months of and (presumably) related to end of CIEP
2	Electoral/political: motivated by internal political difficulties
3	Electoral/voluntary: government under no substantial pressure to resign
4	Death or resignation due to illness of head of government (PM)
5	Constitutional/technical
6	Governmental: addition of coalition members without formal resignation
7	Governmental: addition of coalition members with resignation
8	Governmental: resignation of prime minister cabinet for political reasons
9	Governmental: resignation due to scandal, leaks, and the like
10	Parliamentary: defeat or threatened defeat of government
11	Governmental: resignation for "external" reasons (social crisis, loss of referendum, foreign incident, etc.)
12	Governmental: resignation of caretaker government
13	Electoral: provoked by external circumstances
14	Cases not terminated by December 31, 1989
15	Electoral – caretaker governments only

ELAPSED TIME VARIABLES

DUR	Duration of government: number of days from the time the government is officially appointed until its termination
DURPV	Duration of previous government: duration in days of the government immediately preceding the present government
	Note: Missing for first government in each country; available in "all resignations" version only
CRISIS	Number of days between termination of previous government and formation of the present one
CRIS.INV	Number of days between the termination of previous invested government and formation of the present one

GOVERNMENT ATTRIBUTES

Nonideological attributes

MAJ**	Majority status of government, where a majority government is a government whose member parties together control a majority of parliamentary seats
0	Minority government
1	Majority government

MW**	Minimal winning status of government, where a minimal winning government is a majority government that needs every member party to preserve its parliamentary majority
0	Not minimal winning
1	Minimal winning
MCW**	Minimal connected winning status of government, where a minimal connected winning government is a majority government that needs every member party to remain both majoritarian and connected or closed (see CLOS)
0	Not minimal connected winning
1	Minimal connected winning
CCS1**	Cabinet coalitional status 1 (Dodd 1976): the weighted deviation of each coalition from MW status, calculated as CCS1 = $N(\Sigma\ P)$, where N is the number of parties whose addition/subtraction would make coalition minimal winning and P is the proportion of seats held by those parties
	Note: Where more than one set of parties exists, the set whose $\Sigma\ P$ is smallest is chosen for minority governments, and the set whose $\Sigma\ P$ is largest is chosen for majority governments. In case of ties, the set whose $\Sigma\ N$ is smallest is chosen. Unlike Dodd's version, which is signed to denote minority ($-$) and majority ($+$) situations, only the absolute value of the deviation from MW status is assessed.
CCS3**	Cabinet coalitional status 3 (Dodd 1976): the unweighted deviation of each coalition from MW status, calculated as before except that the number of parties (N) is not taken into consideration
NP*	Number of parties in government
NEFF*	Effective number of parties in government (Laakso & Taagepera 1979): the inverse of the sum of the squared proportions of government-controlled parliamentary seats held by its various member parties (its inverse being 1 minus the Rae [1971] fractionalization index)
POSTEL	Postelection status of government
0	Not the first to be formed after an election
1	The first to be formed after an election
CARETAKE	Caretaker status of government
0	Not a caretaker government
1	Caretaker government
ATTS	Formation attempts: the number of formation attempts that preceded the formation of the government
ATTR	Formation attempts, including refusals: the number of formation attempts plus the number of occasions when individuals refused a request to form a government

ATTS.INV	Formation attempts, invested government only: same as ATTS except that noninvested governments are counted as formation attempts
ATTR.INV	Formation attempts, including refusals, invested governments only: same as ATTR except that noninvested governments are counted as formation attempts
SG1	Same government as predecessor 1, where a government is the same if it has the same prime minister and party composition as its immediate predecessor
	Note: Available for C and CDS data subsets only; available in an "all resignations" version only
0	Not same government
1	Same government
SG2	Same government as predecessor 2, where a government is the same if it has the same party composition as its immediate predecessor
	Note: Available for C and CDS data subsets only; available in an "all resignations" version only
0	Not same government
1	Same government
SG1L	Duration of previous same government: duration of previous same government, as defined by SG1
	Note: Available for C and CDS data subsets only; available in an "all resignations" version only
RG1	Reelected government 1: a postelection government that is the same, as defined by SG1
	Note: Available for C and CDS data subsets only; available in an "all resignations" version only
0	Not a reelected government
1	Reelected government
RG2	Reelected government 2: a postelection government that is the same, as defined by SG2
	Note: Available for C and CDS data subsets only; available in an "all resignations" version only
0	Not a reelected government
1	Reelected government
RG1L	Duration of government that was subsequently reelected, as defined by RG1
	Note: Available for C and CDS data subsets only; available in an "all resignations" version only
POSTOIL	Termination of the government either before or after the oil crisis of October 1973
0	Termination before November 1973

1	Termination after October 1973
PERIOD	The period in which the government terminated
1	1945–64
2	1965–75
3	1976–89

Ideological diversity measures

The following are measures of the ideological diversity of the government. The endings S and R indicate whether the measure is based on the standard deviation or range for the government, respectively. The standard deviation versions are computed according to the formula

$$\sqrt{\sum_{i=1}^{n} p_i(x_i - \bar{x})^2}$$

where p_i is party i's proportion of government-controlled parliamentary seats, x_i is its position on the ideological scale in question, $\bar{x}$ is the weighted mean position of government parties on that scale ($\sum p_i x_i$), and the summations are over the n parties in the government. The range versions simply take the difference between the positions of the government parties that are farthest apart from each other on the scale in question. Note that separate versions of all variables (indicated by the presence of a single asterisk) were created for each of the four main definitions of government composition. The "source" refers to the source of the party scales used in constructing the measures.

PMP1.S*	PMP Left–Right diversity
PMP1.R*	Source: first principal component from a principal components analysis of the Party Manifestos Project data
D1.S*	Source: Dodd's (1976) economic conflict scales
D1.R*	
D1D.S*	Source: discriminant analysis of five-point Dodd economic conflict scales
D1D.R*	
D2.S*	Source: Dodd's (1976) clericalism scales
D2.R*	
D2D.S*	Source: discriminant analysis of five-point Dodd clericalism scales
D2D.R*	
D3.S*	Source: Dodd's (1976) regime-support scales
D3.R*	
D3D.S*	Source: discriminant analysis of five-point Dodd regime-support scales
D3D.R*	
BGM.S*	Source: Dodd's (1976) economic conflict scales as updated by Browne, Gleiber, and Mashoba (1984)
BGM.R*	

| BGMD.S* | Source: discriminant analysis of five-point BGM economic con- |
| BGMD.R* | flict scales |

SB.S*   Source: socialist–bourgeois dichotomy (Warwick 1979)
SB.R*

SBD.S* Source: discriminant analysis of socialist–bourgeois dichotomy
SBD.R*

CS.S*   Source: clerical–secular dichotomy (Warwick 1979)
CS.R*

CSD.S* Source: discriminant analysis of clerical–secular dichotomy
CSD.R*

AS.S*   Source: antisystem–prosystem dichotomy (Warwick 1979)
AS.R*

CM.S*   Source: Castles and Mair (1984) Left–Right scales
CM.R*

VS.S*   Source: mean Left–Right self-placements (ten-point scale) of
VS.R*   party supporters, taken from Eurobarometer 6, Eurobarometer 24, and Political Action surveys

MA1.S* Source: mean scores of party supporters on (three-point) post-
MA1.R* materialism index, taken from Eurobarometer 6 and Political Action surveys

MA2.S* Source: means scores of party supporters on (three-point) postma-
MA2.R* terialism index, taken from Eurobarometer 24 and Political Action surveys

The following are variables derived from the first principal components of various subsets of the preceding measures. The first two or three letters (LR or LRD) indicate whether the Left–Right scales on which the source measure are based are discriminant function versions or not; the final letter (S or R) indicates whether the variable utilizes the standard deviation or range versions of the source variables.

LRS*   Expert Left–Right diversity – standard deviation version
        Source: first principal component of CM.S, BGM.S, SB.S, and D1.S
LRR*   Expert Left–Right diversity – range version
        Source: first principal component of CM.R, BGM.R, SB.R, and D1R
LRDS*   PMP Left–Right diversity – standard deviation version
        Source: first principal component of PMP1.S, BGMD.S, SBD.S, and D1D.S
LRDR*   PMP Left–Right diversity – range version
        Source: first principal component of PMP1.R, BGMD.R, SBD.R, and D1D.R

The following are combined indexes measuring total ideological diversity:

LD.S*   Source: Sum of D1.S, D2.S, and D3.S
LD.R*   Source: Sum of D1.R, D2.R, and D3.R

LDD.S*	Source: Sum of D1D.S, D2D.S, and D3D.S
LDD.R*	Source: Sum of D1D.R, D2D.R, and D3D.R
PW.S*	Source: Sum of SB.S, CS.S, and AS.S
PW.R*	Source: Sum of SB.R, CS.R, and AS.R

CLOS*   "Closed" or connected status of government, where a government
           is closed if its member parties are contiguous on a Left–Right scale
           Note: Scales used are based mainly on Castles and Mair (1984),
           supplemented by Browne/Dodd and occasionally by party names
           or coalitional tendencies; parties with less than 2.5% of seats are
           excluded, following De Swaan (1973).

0	Not closed
1	Closed

IDT*   Ideological type of government, as given by the positions of
           member parties on the socialist–bourgeois cleavage defined
           by SB.R

1	Socialist
2	Mixed
3	Nonsocialist

The following are weighted mean ideological positions of governments as defined by various ideological scales, with party sizes used as weights. As before, separate versions of all variables (indicated by the presence of an asterisk) were created for each of the four main definitions of government composition.

PMP1.P*	Source: first principal component of Party Manifestos Project data
D1.P*	Source: Dodd's (1976) economic conflict scales
D1D.P*	Source: discriminant analysis of five-point Dodd economic conflict scales
BGM.P*	Source: Dodd's (1976) economic conflict scales as updated by Browne, Gleiber, and Mashoba (1984)
BGMD.P*	Source: discriminant analysis of five-point BGM economic conflict scales
SB.P*	Source: socialist–bourgeois dichotomy (Warwick 1979)
SBD.P*	Source: discriminant analysis of socialist–bourgeois dichotomy
CM.P*	Source: Castles and Mair (1984) Left–Right scales

The following are first principal components of various subsets of the preceding ideological position measures:

POS*	Expert Left–Right position
	Source: first principal component of BGM.P, SB.P, D1.P, CM.P
POSD*	PMP Left–Right position
	Source: first principal component of PMP1.P, BGMD.P, SBD.P, and D1D.P

PARLIAMENTARY AND PARTY-SYSTEM ATTRIBUTES

N1 to N22	Parliamentary strengths of up to twenty-two parties
NPREV1– NPREV22	Parliamentary strengths of up to twenty-two parties in the preceding parliament
INVEST	Parliamentary approval or investiture requirements for head of government, government, or government's program
0	No formal approval or investiture requirements
1	Formal approval or investiture requirements

Note: Sweden is exceptional in that the prime minister has needed a formal absolute majority since 1975; no sources indicate this was necessary before that year. Austrian governments must present their programs before parliament, but the vote is regarded only as "taking cognizance," not as a vote of investiture.

NDIM Number of ideological dimensions in the party system, as defined by Lijphart (1984)

RESP Responsiveness to election results (Strom 1985, 1990a): proportion of parties increasing their share of parliamentary seats that also entered a cabinet during the subsequent parliament, calculated by decade for each system

VOL Party-system volatility: one-half the sum of the proportional changes in parliamentary strengths of parties from one election to the next

Note: Party strengths are coded "0" if they did not gain representation in an election.

POLAR Polarization of parliament: proportion of parliamentary seats held by extremist parties, as identified by Powell (1982)

Note: Extremist parties are parties that have a well-developed nondemocratic ideology, advocate a fundamental change in national boundaries, or represent diffuse protest or alienation from the political system.

OPPCONC1 Opposition concentration 1: proportion of opposition seats concentrated to the left or right of the government

Note: Based on the same Left–Right scale as in CLOS, with independents excluded.

OPPCONC2 Opposition concentration 2: proportion of opposition seats concentrated in any contiguous bloc on a Left–Right scale (see OPPCONC1), including the middle (i.e., in-between coalition members)

Note: Only twenty-five cases occur in the middle.

NEFFPARL Effective number of parties in parliament (Laakso and Taagepera 1979): the inverse of the sum of the squared party proportions of parliamentary seats

Note: Its inverse is 1 minus the Rae fractionalization index.

NEFFPS   Effective number of prosystem parties in parliament: as in NEFF-PARL, but excluding extremist parties

RN*   Returnability: proportion of government parties entering the next government following a collapse or early termination, calculated by system

Note: All end types except 1, 4, 5, 14, and 15 count as collapses or early terminations.

RW*   Returnability-weighted: proportion of government-controlled seats that are represented in the next government following a collapse or early termination, calculated by system

Note: All end types except 1, 4, 5, 14, and 15 count as collapses or early terminations.

PI   Past instability: the mean duration in years of all governments preceding the present one

Note: The first government per country is missing. Available only for CDS data subset; available in an "all resignations" version only.

The following are standard deviation measures of the polarization of the entire parliament. They are calculated in the same manner as the standard deviation measures of ideological diversity, except that all parties represented in the parliament are included.

POLCM.S   Source: Castles and Mair Left–Right scales
POLVS.S   Source: mean Left–Right self-placements of party supporters in Eurobarometers 6, 24, and Political Action surveys
POLD1.S   Source: Dodd's economic conflict scales
POLD2.S   Source: Dodd's clericalism scales
POLD3.S   Source: Dodd's regime-support scales
POLLD.S   Source: mean of POLD1.S, POLD2.S, POLD3.S

Note: This variable is equivalent to Dodd's degree of cleavage conflict (DCC).

TIME SERIES

This section lists time-based covariates and their associated defining dummy variables. The dummy variables demarcate different portions of noncontinuous time series. For the inflation indicators, a slight noncontinuity is created by the fact that rates are recorded in whole numbers only before 1964; a more serious noncontinuity exists early in the series for a few countries because consumer price data were reported only for capital cities. With respect to unemployment data, discontinuities are created whenever a major change occurs in the method of compiling the data. These discontinuities are indicated in the sources and reflected here in the distinction between more recent and earlier series.

Annual values of the economic variables are recorded for each government from the year prior to its formation until the year of its collapse. In addition, December monthly values for inflation and unemployment are recorded to cover the same time frame; these values were used to interpolate daily rates. Since government durations are limited by the need for periodic elections, the maximum possible number of data points for any one (December) indicator is eight.

CPADMY	Indicator variable for accuracy and reliability of annual consumer price inflation rate (CPA) data)
0	Main series (most accurate available data)
1	Whole numbers only (index values approximate)
2	Limited series, capital cities only
CPA	Annual consumer price inflation rate, main series (CPADMY = 0)
CPACH	Change in CPA over preceding year (365 days)
CPAEXT	Annual consumer price inflation rate, extended series (CPADMY = 0 or 1)
CPAEXTCH	Change in CPAEXT over preceding year (365 days)
CPAALL	Annual consumer price inflation rate, all series (CPADMY = 0, 1, or 2)
CPAALLCH	Change in CPAALL over preceding year (365 days)
CPDDMY	Indicator variable for accuracy and reliability of December consumer price inflation rate (CPD) data
0	Main series (most accurate available data)
1	Whole numbers only (index values approximate)
2	Limited series, capital cities only
CPD	Annualized consumer price inflation rate for December, main series (CPDDMY = 0)
CPDCH	Change in CPD over preceding year (365 days)
CPDEXT	Annualized consumer price inflation rate for December, extended series (CPDDMY = 0 or 1)
CPDEXTCH	Change in CPDEXT over preceding year (365 days)
CPDALL	Annualized consumer price inflation rate for December, all series (CPDDMY = 0, 1, or 2)
CPDALLCH	Change in CPDALL over preceding year (365 days)
AVCPDX	Average consumer price inflation rate per government: calculated by dividing each government's life span into thirty-day intervals and estimating the annualized consumer price inflation rate at the beginning of each interval (based on December values), then averaging these values over the lifespan of the government
SDCPDX	Standard deviation within individual governments of the estimated monthly values of consumer price inflation rate
	Note: See AVCPDX for method of calculating monthly inflation rate values.
FIRCPDX	Estimated consumer price inflation rate in government's first month (thirty-day interval)
	Note: See AVCPDX for method of calculation.
FINCPDX	Estimated consumer price inflation rate in government's last

	month (thirty-day interval)
	Note: See AVCPDX for method of calculation.
JLADMY	Indicator variable for continuity in scope of annual jobless rate (JLA) series
0	Current or more recent series
1	Previous series
JLBREAK	Filter variable for governments that span different unemployment series
	Note: Must be used whenever JL variables that span different series are utilized.
0	Government does not span different unemployment data series
1	Government does span different unemployment data series
JLA	Annual jobless rate, more recent series only (JLADMY = 0)
JLACH	Change in JLA over preceding year (365 days)
	Note: JLBREAK must be used in conjunction with this variable.
JLAALL	Annual jobless rate, both series (JLADMY = 0 or 1)
	Note: JLBREAK must be used in conjunction with this variable.
JLAALLCH	Change in JLAALL over preceding year (365 days)
	Note: JLBREAK must be used in conjunction with this variable.
JLDDMY	Indicator variable for continuity in scope of December jobless rate series
0	More recent series
1	Earlier series
JLD	December jobless rate, more recent series only (JLDDMY = 0)
JLDCH	Change in JLD over preceding year (365 days)
JLDALL	December jobless rate, both series (JLDDMY = 0 or 1)
	Note: JLBREAK must be used in conjunction with this variable.
JLDALLCH	Change in JLDALL over preceding year (365 days)
	Note: JLBREAK must be used in conjunction with this variable.
AVJLDCH	Average change in jobless rate per government: calculated by dividing each government's lifespan into thirty-day intervals, estimating the annualized change in the jobless rate at the beginning of each interval (based on December values), then averaging these values over the lifespan of the government
	Note: JLBREAK must be used in conjunction with this variable.
SDJLDCH	Standard deviation within individual governments in estimated monthly values of jobless rate change
	Note: See AVJLDCH for method of calculating estimated monthly values of jobless rate change. The JLBREAK filter must be used with this variable.
FIRJLDCH	Estimated annualized change in jobless rate in government's first month (thirty-day interval)
	Note: See AVJLDCH for method of calculation. The JLBREAK filter must be used with this variable.

FINJLDCH   Estimated annualized change in jobless rate in government's last month (thirty-day interval)

                        Note: See AVJLDCH for method of calculation. The JLBREAK filter must be used with this variable.

IPC   Annual percent change in gross domestic product, IMF series

IPCCH   Change in IPC over preceding year (365 days)

OPC   Annual percent change in gross domestic product, OECD series

OPCCH   Change in OPC over preceding year (365 days)

Notes

I. INTRODUCTION: THE GOVERNMENT SURVIVAL DEBATES

1. It is true that the rules can be designed to favor this eventuality – for example, by adopting the single-member plurality electoral system, which tends to overrepresent larger parties. Generally speaking, however, there will be a cost; with the single-member plurality system, the cost is a sacrifice in representativeness that may be unacceptable in many democratic societies. As it happens, most parliamentary regimes have opted for some version of proportional representation, thereby making the emergence of majority parties (if not majority coalitions) a less likely and in fact uncommon result.

2. Eckstein (1966) is an exception here since he argued that solidarity could coexist with intense political cleavages if authority patterns are congruent. In addition, the consociationalist school pointed out that some highly divided societies had devised means for preventing social divisions from impairing democratic stability. Both, however, were invoking the special circumstances that exist or existed in just a few societies to overcome what they would agree is the basic tendency.

3. Some time ago, I developed this theme with respect to the French Third and Fourth Republics (Warwick 1978). More recently, I expanded the analysis of the interconnections between ideologism and pragmatism to include Britain (Warwick 1990:3–24).

4. This list includes two systems with influential presidents, Finland and Portugal, and excludes a third, the French Fifth Republic. The distinction between the two situations is that Finnish and Portuguese presidents have largely exercised arbiter or nonpartisan roles (Shugart and Carey 1992:61–5); in addition, the powers of the Portuguese presidency were substantially reduced in 1982. French presidents, in contrast, have tended to dominate the political scene, as reflected in the extent to which partisan politics since 1958 have become aligned into two blocs vying for an electoral majority.

5. This does not mean, of course, that the events in question are uncaused, just that the causes are idiosyncratic and unrelated to any features of the government or the parliamentary arena.

6. The finding that Italian government terminations follow a random pattern was also reported by Cioffi-Revilla (1984).

7. I did, however, make an exception of governments that ran the entire mandated interelection period, since excluding them would have removed all long durations from the sample.

8. In an earlier paper (Warwick 1988), moreover, I showed that the 30% ceiling could be exceeded even under Browne et al.'s definition of valid terminations.

9. The justification is that elections change the distribution of party strengths and hence bargaining power in the parliament that supports the government.

10. As early as 1986, the events theorists acknowledged that combining systematic and stochastic effects should constitute the next step in research, although they continued in their belief that "the dissolution process is dominated by stochastic elements" (Fren-

dreis, Gleiber, and Browne 1986:621). Ironically, the methodology best suited to combine these types of effects (event history analysis) provides no clear means of testing this claim.

11. This data set, which covers fifteen parliamentary democracies over the period 1945–87, is described in Strom (1985, 1990a).
12. This was achieved by showing that no significant improvement accrued to the model from adding a set of dummy variables representing different countries in the sample.
13. At times, the events theorists (Browne et al., 1986:633; Frendreis et al., 1986:622) treat economic downturns as critical events in their sense of the term. This appears to be overgenerous, since these developments are unlikely to be either sudden or unexpected and are amenable to causal analysis.

2. THE QUANTITATIVE STUDY OF GOVERNMENT SURVIVAL

1. The hazard rate is most easily understood in its discrete-time version, where it is the number of government collapses at time t divided by the number of governments still at risk (i.e., still surviving) immediately before time t.
2. King (1988) provides a proof of the well-known result that event counts (the numbers of events or terminations in a time interval) are Poisson processes, from which it can be shown that the distribution of times to termination is exponential. In the following equations, the expression "$\exp(-\lambda t)$" is equivalent to $e^{-\lambda t}$.
3. I use a discrete hazard rate here to avoid needless complexity; the equations describe a continuous model.
4. In an exponential distribution, the mean or expected duration is equal to the inverse of the hazard rate. This relationship reflects the fact that high hazards entail short durations, and vice versa.
5. This can be viewed as a case of "what goes around comes around." Browne et al. (1986:631) had criticized me for excluding certain classes of cases (mainly single-party majority governments) because it prevented "an adequate modeling of the general problem of cabinet duration as it is actually manifested in Western parliamentary democracies"; King et al. were now turning the same criticism – that the whole universe of cases should be included – on Browne et al.
6. In the KABL model, the $\lambda_0(t)$ term is omitted because the baseline hazard is assumed to be constant and therefore is represented by the intercept β_0 in the vector ($\beta'x$).
7. The data set used here is a slightly more recent version than that used by King et al. In addition, two cases that Strom defined as terminated when they lost their parliamentary majorities were recoded to terminate according to Browne, Frendreis, and Mashoba's (1984) criteria, to be discussed below.
8. The coefficients that produced these plots are derived from MLEs, with no independent variables specified. The hazard functions and estimated parameters for the three models are as follows:

Exponential:	$\lambda(t) = \gamma$	$\gamma = .053$
Weibull:	$\lambda(t) = \gamma \alpha t^{\alpha-1}$	$\gamma = .025, \alpha = 1.23$
Log-logistic:	$\lambda(t) = \gamma \alpha t^{\alpha-1}/(1 + t^{\alpha})$	$\gamma = .012, \alpha = 1.72$

All parameters are statistically significant at the .05 level. Needless to say, these distributions are only a few among a large number of parametric possibilities.
9. Models with this property are sometimes referred to as "proportional hazards" models, but this usage can be misleading. In equation (2.9), the overall hazards of any two cases differ only insofar as their values on the $\exp(\beta'x(t))$ term differ. If the x covariates are fixed for individual cases, the ratio (proportion) of their overall hazards will remain constant throughout their durations. When time-varying covariates are used, however, this condition of constant proportionality may no longer hold (Allison 1984: 34–8).

10. An adjustment must be made whenever two or more cases terminate at the same duration time. To minimize the occurrence of identical durations, duration time is recorded in days (rather than the more usual months) in the data set developed for this investigation.

11. These categories were coded on the basis of an examination of the reasons given in *Keesing's Contemporary Archives* (1945–87) for the termination of each government. The coding was then checked by comparing it with Strom's coding of his "cause of resignation," "issue area of resignation," and "mode of resignation" variables. The full coding scheme is presented later.

12. As is normal practice, the definition excludes government reshuffles. Although it could be argued that reshuffles are in some cases the functional equivalent to changes of government, in many other cases – especially those involving single-party governments – they represent an assessment of personnel that rarely implicates the government's immediate viability. Reshuffles may be a worthwhile subject of inquiry in themselves, but they should not be equated with government terminations.

13. Thus, Strom's coding of three successive Craxi *pentapartito* governments in Italy in 1985–7 as one government would not be allowed under this criterion.

14. The idea of external circumstances is consistent with the assumption, made in most event history applications, that cases censored at any time t are representative of cases still at risk at time t or, in other words, that the censoring scheme is independent of the underlying causal processes at work.

15. These sources, of course, do not always agree. In disputed cases, the verdict generally went with *Keesing's* except where a strong current of opinion favored a different interpretation.

3. BASIC ATTRIBUTES AND GOVERNMENT SURVIVAL

1. Minimal winning status and closeness to minimal winning status (Dodd 1976) have also been suggested as potential causes. For reasons that will become evident, these factors will be considered along with ideological diversity in Chapter 4.

2. Strom (1990a:6) defines majority governments to include those controlling exactly 50% of parliamentary seats, on the argument that a tie vote usually cannot defeat a government. While this is true, it is also the case that parliamentary custom often prescribes that governments failing to have their key bills enacted should resign from office. For this reason, this study adheres to the more usual definition of a majority: 50% of seats plus one.

3. Caretaker governments are those expressly formed to occupy power in a caretaker capacity. Governments that fall and then are asked to remain in power until a new government can be formed are not considered to constitute new caretaker governments.

4. Except where noted, all PL analyses reported in this study were performed on the BMDP program 2L (BMDP Statistical Software, 1990).

5. Dividing a coefficient by its standard error gives its t-value. Since each of the covariates in model 1 comes with an expectation as to the direction of its relationship to the hazard, the appropriate test is one-tailed, evaluating the hypothesis that the relationship is different from zero in the expected direction. To meet the $\alpha = .05$ level of significance in a one-tailed test, the t-value must be greater than about 1.645 in a sample of this size. For a two-tailed test, which evaluates the hypothesis that the relationship is simply nonzero, the t-value must be greater than about 1.96. Although most covariates proposed in this investigation come with particular expectations as to the nature of their effects on the hazard, a few either do not or else have elicited contradictory expectations (e.g., formation attempts, to be discussed later) and should be evaluated with a two-tailed test.

6. This is the interpretation Strom (1985:749) puts on the relationship between crisis duration and government survival. (In his model, formation attempts show only a weak and indirect impact on survival.)

7. Strom (1985) found that "electoral salience," a linear combination of "proximity" (the proportion of postelection governments per decade) and "identifiability" (a three-point index of the obviousness of preelection governmental alternatives) was the most important influence on government survival. King et al. (1990:856–7) noted a degree of contamination in this index and replaced it with the separate variables of postelection status and identifiability. Another variable proposed by Strom is "opposition influence," a measure of the autonomy and power of legislative committees; he hypothesized that higher opposition influence would be associated with the formation of minority governments (thus undermining survival). Because both identifiability and opposition influence are subjective assessments based on unspecified criteria and because King et al. found that party-system polarization and fractionalization eliminated any influence they exhibited on survival, neither covariate is included here. The polarization and fractionalization measures are discussed later.

8. Strom makes an exception for single-party majority governments, which are considered responsive regardless of whether the party in question increased its parliamentary size in the most recent elections. I find this position unconvincing and have not incorporated it into this variable.

9. This presumes that their support status reflects a desire not to enter the present cabinet or a refusal of the cabinet to allow them in.

10. Strom (1990a:66) deviated from Powell's criteria in one instance: he treated the Danish Justice Party as nonextremist because it participated in two governments in the late 1950s. Because this decision introduces a different kind of criterion (government membership rather than ideological or policy position), it is not followed in this study.

11. Calculating returnability for each government on the basis of the prior experience of its system would have been preferable but would have generated an unacceptable level of missing data. For example, six countries had no noncensored terminations during the decade of the 1950s and hence no calculable returnability rates for that period. In addition, many calculable returnability values would have been based on very small numbers of noncensored terminations. A returnability measure based on decade averages, the tactic used for the electoral responsiveness index, might have alleviated the second problem but would have run afoul of the first. There was thus little choice but to calculate system values across the entire period and hope that they reflect system propensities known to parties throughout the period.

12. Significance is determined by a χ^2-test, where the χ^2-value (at one degree of freedom) associated with the presence of a covariate in the model is equal to twice the increase in the log-likelihood produced by the inclusion of that covariate.

13. One situation in which the criterion would go awry is where a covariate contributes no significant improvement to the log-likelihood yet is significantly related to the hazard. This could happen if the part of the hazard's behavior accounted for by the covariate in question could also be accounted for by other covariates in the model. Although the overall explanatory power of the model is not enhanced by including the extra covariate, it may be that the covariate must be included for a correct specification of the causal process. All stepwise procedures reported in this study have been examined for effects of this sort.

14. In the case of the number of formation attempts, the t-value is 1.78, which would be significant in a one-tailed test. However, a two-tailed test is more appropriate for this relationship since opposite expectations have been advanced concerning its direction.

15. This result is also at odds with Taagepera and Shugart's (1989:101–2) finding that duration is related weakly to effective government size but strongly to effective party-system size. Nevertheless, the present result holds even when the two independent variables are squared in order to conform more closely to the functional form of the relationship proposed by Taagepera and Shugart. The discrepancy may be due to the fact that their analysis was conducted at an aggregate level (countries) and included no other potential causes.

16. Majority status has an alternative version that takes into consideration parties that agree to abstain in favor of the government. This version will be considered along with other definitions of government membership in Chapter 7. As for effective party-system size, an alternative representing the simple number of parties in the parliament will not be considered because it would be very misleading: most parliaments contain an assortment of very small parties that have no discernible effect on government survival.

17. Model 1 of Table 3.3 differs from the model 4 of Table 3.1 because it is based on a larger number of cases. Missing values for some of the covariates tested in the stepwise procedure that produced the latter model account for this discrepancy.

18. A government is considered to be reelected if it has the same head of government and the same party composition as its preelection predecessor. The outcome of this analysis is unchanged when the reelected government dummy is replaced by a covariate measuring the duration of the earlier period in office of the reelected government or if reelected governments are defined in terms of similarity in party composition alone. Reestimating the model with the reelected governments (either definition) excluded leads to the same conclusion.

4. THE ROLE OF IDEOLOGY

1. A fourth possibility would be to use the ECPR Party Manifestos Project's coding of party platforms (see later) to generate measures; however, these data are less appropriate for this purpose because they frequently exclude the more extreme parties, particularly when they are not large.

2. With this as with the other scales used in this chapter, there are inevitably some parties that are not included. Whenever possible, I have attempted to estimate positions for these parties based on information from other sources (including other scales) so as to produce as complete a set of party positions as possible. Details of these adjustments to the scales are available on request.

3. For the Netherlands, the Left–Right position of the Christian Democratic Appeal, a union of three formerly separate clerical parties that postdates the Eurobarometer 6 survey, was also taken from Eurobarometer 24.

4. This methodology differs from Sani and Sartori's in that they took most of the data from the Political Action surveys and supplemented it with Eurobarometer 6. All three data sets were supplied by the Inter-University Consortium for Political and Social Research. Neither it nor the surveys' principal investigators bear any responsibility for the uses made of their data in the present study.

5. Moreover, the puzzle is compounded by the fact that a variety of other polarization measures, based on alternative sets of ideological scales to be discussed later, met with the same fate.

6. Ethnicity or language is often considered a fundamental dimension, but governments comprising parties with distinct ethnic orientations are in fact fairly rare in the sampled countries. Meaningful scale positions on this dimension would be very difficult, if not impossible, to devise in any case.

7. Unlike the polarization variables developed in the preceding section, range versions of governmental diversity can be justified on the grounds that it is highly unlikely that any government member, no matter how small, is irrelevant to the government's functioning.

8. For many countries, the coding does not cover elections beyond the early 1980s. In these situations, the results of the most recent coded election were extended to cover subsequent elections; similarly, where the coding does not extend to the earliest elections, the results of the earliest coded election were extended to them. The most egregious example is the French Fourth Republic, where only the 1958 election was coded. Details of these and other adjustments and extensions are available from the author.

Needless to say, neither the authors of the original data set nor the Norwegian Social Sciences Data Services, which supplied it to me, are responsible for these changes or for the uses made of the data in this study.

9. Since the focus of discriminant analysis is on generating functions that optimally distinguish among categories, it is appropriate for the Dodd and BGM scales, which are derived from five basic categories, as well as for the cleavage dichotomies. The CM scales will be excluded because they do not have this property. Practically speaking, regression might also have been used; although its assumptions concerning the dependent variable are not met, regression-derived predicted party positions for the BGM scale correlate at .98 with their discriminant counterparts.

10. A PL analysis was also performed separately for the nondiscriminant versions because these versions are available for a greater number of cases. (Utilizing the PMP data has the effect of reducing the number of valid cases.) The result was the same: the range version of Dodd's clerical–secular diversity proved to be the strongest determinant of government survival.

11. Although the first set of scales registers party scores at a time close to the middle of the period covered by the data set, the second set was created because postmaterialism is alleged to be gradually increasing, and public opinion at the time Eurobarometer 6 was administered may not have reflected the phenomenon fully.

12. As noted, the use of the PMP version results in an appreciable loss of cases. However, so does the addition of economic covariates in Chapter 5. Since these losses largely overlap, the number of lost cases that are uniquely attributable to the PMP data ultimately amounts to just twenty-four.

13. Although the selection of covariates in model 7 stems from a two-stage process, virtually the same model would have emerged if all ideological diversity measures had been entered along with the other covariates in a single forward-entry stepwise procedure. The only difference is that a clerical–secular diversity measure based on the clerical–secular dichotomy would have replaced the alternative derived from Dodd's scales. This turns out to be due to the fact that although the Dodd measure clearly outperforms its dichotomy-based alternatives in the full data set, the reduction in cases caused by the inclusion of PMP-enhanced covariates weakens its explanatory power disproportionately. Since the goal is a model specification that is appropriate for the full universe of cases, the Dodd clerical–secular diversity measure is the one that will be retained for further analysis.

14. The same result is obtained when the alternative indexes are based on averages rather than totals.

15. Expert Left–Right diversity receives a PL coefficient of 0.035 ($t = 0.550$) when entered separately and 0.108 ($t = 1.176$) when entered along with the other covariates in the model. The corresponding estimates for PMP Left–Right diversity are 0.016 ($t = 0.228$) and 0.074 ($t = 0.883$).

16. Majority status was included in model 3 because it represents a major conditioning variable for ideological diversity; without it, the effects of the ideological diversity covariates could be obscured by minority governments, which tend to have both shorter durations and lower levels of ideological diversity than do majority governments. As for the other variables in model 2, they were left out to avoid the appearance of "stacking the deck" in favor of the ideological diversity hypothesis by using weights that already allow for the effects of these other covariates. The pattern of results to be reported here would be the same if the weights had been taken from a full model.

17. Remember that government membership is defined here to include cabinet members plus formal and declared support parties.

18. The role of another bargaining-environment indicator, formation attempts, which was found in Chapter 3 to fall just below the .05 level of statistical significance, also turns out to be confined to minority situations, presumably for the same reason.

19. Laver and Schofield (1990:94) note a distinction between minimal winning coalitions and minimum winning coalitions, the latter being minimal winning coalitions that have the smallest possible weight (parliamentary size). The distinction has not been consistently followed in the literature; Dodd (1976:117), for instance, uses "minimum winning" to refer to all coalitions that cannot afford to lose a member without losing their majority. Following common practice, the more inclusive concept of minimal winning status is utilized in this study.

20. A more restrictive version of the same basic idea is De Swaan's (1973) hypothesis predicting the formation and durability of minimal winning coalitions that are of minimal ideological range on a Left–Right scale. This hypothesis met with only limited success in De Swaan's own analysis and will not be tested here.

21. This conclusion also holds when MCW governments are tested. Moreover, for both types of government, the effect persists when the other relevant covariates are included in the models.

5. ECONOMIC CONDITIONS AND GOVERNMENT SURVIVAL

1. In an earlier work, Robertson (1983a) does relate changes in the rate of government collapse in various countries to changes in their unemployment and inflation rates. Individual governments, however, do not constitute the unit of analysis.

2. The BMDP program 2L provides a highly convenient facility for interpolating time-varying covariate values.

3. The simple (bivariate) PL coefficient for the actual monthly inflation rate is 0.056 ($t = 3.25$), while that for the pseudomonthly rate is 0.068 ($t = 3.81$). This pattern holds up when the other covariates of the full model (see later) are included in the analysis. In these tests, the actual monthly data attribute a given monthly rate to each day of that month; the interpolated data attribute the estimated value for the first day of a month to each day of that month. Because of the enormity of the coding task this analysis entails, it was performed only on the 202 cases for which complete data are available. The test is inappropriate for unemployment because actual monthly unemployment rates are contaminated by seasonal effects.

4. The PL analysis linking inflation to the hazard rate, controlling for majority status, produced a coefficient of 0.009 ($t = 1.22$) based upon the post-1963 consumer price series, versus a slightly stronger 0.011 ($t = 1.87$) based upon the more extended series. As for the version of the covariate derived from daily interpolations of December data, the corresponding coefficients are identical: 0.014 ($t = 1.63$) and 0.014 ($t = 1.75$), respectively. A further extension can be achieved by adding data on consumer prices for certain capital cities in the immediate postwar period, but these versions of the covariate performed markedly worse (as one might expect) and are not utilized in this study.

5. This could happen, for example, if economic downturns tend to produce majority governments. Since majority governments typically last longer than minority ones, unfavorable economic indicators might appear (spuriously) to be associated with longevity in office. It should also be noted that other factors may also be affecting the relationships reported in the table. Although uncontrolled here, they are taken into account in the subsequent analyses.

6. The criterion is not foolproof because any of the relationships reported in Table 5.2 could be suppressed by other factors. For this reason, the final model developed in the next section was reestimated using the various alternative indicators of the economic covariates in the model. In all cases, the significance levels declined when the alternatives were employed.

7. The ideological diversity index in model 2 uses weights for the ideological diversity covariates derived from a PL analysis of this smaller data set ($N = 202$); the weights are therefore somewhat different from those used in the index in model 1.

8. Among minority governments, the PL coefficients for inflation and the change in unemployment are -0.001 ($t = -0.217$) and 0.251 ($t = 1.781$), respectively. For majority governments, the corresponding coefficients are 0.048 ($t = 1.724$) and 0.300 ($t = 3.471$).

9. The addition of inflation alone reduces polarization's coefficient only slightly from 3.88 ($t = 2.35$) to 3.69 ($t = 2.11$) for minority governments; for majority cases, the coefficient changes from 1.02 ($t = 1.10$) to -0.61 ($t = -0.41$). Neither of the latter two coefficients is significant, but they do suggest that inflation may be taking up some residual variance attributed to polarization in majority situations.

10. These analyses, incidentally, do not confirm Gleiber, Frendreis, and Granger's (1992) assertion that ideological diversity works only in the middle period, 1965–75. In the earliest period, the principal effect is from clerical–secular diversity; in the latter two periods, the other two measures take over. In all three periods, however, there are statistically significant effects from ideological diversity.

11. The term "saliency" is preferable to "seriousness" because, as Figure 5.1 shows, inflation remained quite high for much of the 1976–89 period as well; its impact on government survival, nevertheless, was negligible.

12. The ideological orderings were based largely on Castles and Mair's (1984) Left–Right political scales, supplemented by the Browne, Gleiber, and Mashoba (1984) socioeconomic scales and by country-specific sources where appropriate. Mean economic indicator values for each government were derived by dividing the government's lifespan into intervals of thirty days, calculating the interpolated value at the start of each interval, and averaging these values over the intervals of the government's life. Thirty-day intervals were used to facilitate computations and to approximate the monthly intervals for which economic data are usually reported.

13. Of the thirty-nine governments in the former period that can be classified into either type (i.e., leaving aside mixed governments), 38.5% were socialist. The corresponding percentage for the forty-eight classifiable governments of the latter period is 35.4%. Thus, the 1965–75 period shows only a slightly greater frequency of socialist governments than does the 1976–89 period.

14. The final month values in Table 5.6 include both noncensored and censored cases (i.e., interrupted governments). The conclusion remains the same, however, when only noncensored cases are considered.

15. One way to avoid ideological types would be to create interaction terms between the economic covariates and a more accurate measure of ideological position, such as expert Left–Right position; these terms would convey the idea that the economic covariates have an impact to the extent that the government in question is left-wing or right-wing. When tested, however, neither of the interaction terms entered the model significantly, suggesting that the use of types is appropriate here.

16. The classification of governments terminating early and under pressure consists of end types 2, 8, 9, 10, 11, and 13 (see Table 2.2). Of the 202 cases utilized in the full model, the 95 that terminated in these circumstances had mean rates of inflation and change in unemployment of 7.5% and 0.4%, respectively. The corresponding values for the other cases are 5.3% and 0.0%. *T*-tests indicate that the differences between the two groups are significant at the .01 level in both instances.

17. This was determined by adding interaction terms composed of the product of each economic covariate and the ideological diversity index to the model. Neither of the interaction terms, whether entered singly or together, proved to be significantly related to the termination rate. In fact, even single-party majority governments, which might be

supposed to be immune to economic fluctuations, show vulnerability: although there are only thirty-one such governments with valid data on all relevant covariates, the inflation rate continues to be significantly related to the rate of termination of these governments.

18. The entire issue of the linkage between the ideological orientations of governments and macroeconomic performance remains a matter of controversy among political economists. See Hibbs (1992) for a recent assessment of the state of the literature.

6. THE UNDERLYING TREND IN GOVERNMENT SURVIVAL

1. The possible presence of this type of effect is explored in Chapter 7.
2. The relative simplicity of the Gompertz model makes it a convenient choice for this type of situation, although others (such as the Weibull) could have been used in this example.
3. The hazard estimates used here are Nelson–Aalen estimates, calculated by the RATE statistical package (Tuma and DMA Corporation 1992) and the associated smoothing program SMUNAHAZ.
4. Spain is excluded because of the paucity of cases (4).
5. This result, as with all other MLEs in this study, was produced using RATE (Tuma and DMA Corporation 1992).
6. In addition, the sign of the γ coefficient for one country (Austria) has become negative as a result of the sample reduction.
7. The integration is made necessary by the censoring procedure. As noted in Chapter 2, censoring entails the estimation of a case's contribution to the overall likelihood by means of the survivor function S. Estimation proceeds on the basis of the relationship $\ln S(t) = -\int_0^t \lambda(t)\, dt$. In the PL technique, this part of the likelihood function is ignored.
8. The results of this reestimation are presented in model 2 of Table 6.5.
9. The interaction terms are defined as

$$z_n = d_n\{\ln(t) - \ln(c)\},$$

where d_n is the country dummy for country n, t is duration time, and c is the mean duration for the sample as a whole. This test is described in Blossfeld, Hamerle, and Mayer (1989:147–8).

10. Greater numbers of cases per country might have produced statistically significant differences, but the important point here is whether there are differences that need to be taken into account in the present data. Note that these tests, although affected by the numbers of cases per country, differ from the earlier duration dependence tests in that all cases in the sample are included in each test.
11. This evidence is not conclusive, however, since we do not know that the baseline hazard is *identical* for all cases. In the next section, we shall find reasons for challenging this assumption.
12. This type of model is known as an "accelerated lifetime model."
13. Because duration is measured in days, the values of the interactive covariates tend to be relatively large and their coefficients correspondingly small. To make the empirical results easier to read, all second-vector coefficients in Table 6.6 and subsequent tables have been multiplied by 1,000. The original values for these coefficients can be obtained simply by moving the decimal point three places to the left.
14. Inasmuch as we have expectations concerning the direction of the first-vector relationships, a one-tailed test is appropriate; for the interactive effects, no definite prediction can be made (except that one of them, at least, must be consistent with a rising hazard). The t-values for all three γ coefficients fall just short of the cutoff value of 1.96 for a two-tailed test.
15. A stepwise procedure for eliminating insignificant covariates is not available in the RATE program. Deleting variables one at a time according to their significance levels

produces the result shown in model 2. The same result is also produced if interactive terms for all nine covariates are entered initially, then deleted one by one in this fashion.

16. The returnability interactive term does indeed appear to have been a red herring: it does not enter significantly when either of the two economic interactive terms is excluded, or even when both are excluded.

17. This follows from the fact that 947 times -0.000468 (the second-vector coefficient) is approximately equal in absolute value to the first-vector coefficient, 0.443. At durations longer than 947 days, the negative interactive effect will therefore outweigh the positive first-vector effect.

18. Note that inflation is included in the first vector of model 2. This is because, with the inflation interactive term omitted, inflation itself becomes a significant factor in the first vector. The coefficient for the unemployment interactive term changes only modestly to -0.288 ($t = -1.24$), however, if inflation is left out entirely.

19. Analyzing the pre–oil crisis and post–oil crisis periods separately also generates results that are consistent with those reported in Chapter 5 (Table 5.4). In the precrisis period, only inflation shows a significant effect, albeit in the second vector. The postcrisis period reproduces the basic pattern of signs found in the overall model, but those associated with unemployment are much stronger, while inflation (negligible in the earlier results) shows a second-vector effect that just achieves statistical significance. Although there are a larger number of significant economic covariates in the later period – suggesting a heightened saliency of economic concerns in government survival – the fact that the unemployment effects tend to offset each other means that the net effect of economic conditions may not be any greater than in the earlier period.

7. MODEL ADEQUACY

1. Note, however, that the assumption appears to have done little harm, since the coefficients for all covariates except the economic ones are only slightly affected by the introduction of a second vector (compare model 1 of Table 6.5 with model 3 of Table 6.6).

2. This is also true when the specification is restricted to fixed covariates in order to preserve a greater number of cases (including those of Finland).

3. The first government formed after an election need not reflect the electorate's verdict in a noticeable fashion. This suggests that the trend might be even more pronounced with respect to those governments that do clearly possess this quality.

4. There is nothing, however, in model 4 to suggest that the censoring scheme could not be used if it is preferred on theoretical grounds: all coefficients significant in model 3 remain so in model 4.

5. It is important to remember that the log-likelihoods listed in Table 7.2 cannot be used to assess the various censoring regimes. As discussed in Chapter 2, log-likelihoods tend to increase in proportion to the number of censored cases, regardless of the validity of the censoring criterion.

6. This is not completely true of investiture since Sweden adopted the practice in 1975, but the small amount of intracountry variation introduced by the Swedish case is not sufficient to overcome the collinearity between investiture and the country dummies.

7. These means are calculated on the basis of the 202 cases for which all covariates are available (in the CDS data subset); they therefore differ somewhat from the values listed in Table 1.1.

8. The coefficient for the Italy dummy falls from 0.93 ($t = 2.37$) to 0.54 ($t = 1.35$); for Sweden, the coefficient declines from -2.19 ($t = -3.00$) to -1.71 ($t = -2.35$).

9. The coefficient for the U.K. dummy drops from 1.24 ($t = 2.86$) in the CDS data subset to 0.54 ($t = 1.16$) in the C data subset.

10. Austria is the excluded country. Note that because the country dummies are multiplied by duration time, collinearity with the returnability and investiture covariates is reduced, and there is no longer any need to exclude three countries.

11. For country dummies entered in the first vector, the coefficient for Italy is 0.85 ($t =$ 1.87), for Sweden -2.68 ($t = -1.81$), and for Britain 1.27 ($t = 2.13$). The corresponding second-vector coefficients are 0.00033 ($t = 0.35$), 0.00084 ($t = 0.42$), and -0.00007 ($t = -0.08$), respectively.

12. Denmark's first-vector dummy receives a coefficient of -0.98 ($t = -1.52$), while the coefficient for its second-vector dummy is 0.00214 ($t = 2.17$).

13. All first-vector covariate coefficients increase in magnitude. As for the second-vector covariates, the removal of the relatively long-lived SPM governments presumably curtails the rising baseline hazard and thereby diminishes their impact.

14. The only other country showing a rate of termination that is noticeably above average if investiture is not taken into account is Britain. That this has to do with the implications of the CDS definition of government membership for the Callaghan government is sustained by the fact that the same analysis performed on the C data subset produces a negative coefficient for the Britain dummy covariate.

15. Since durations are recorded in days, the covariate was divided by 1,000 to produce more presentable results. Dividing any duration-lagged coefficient by 1,000 will produce its original value.

16. These results hold up when party compositions alone define identical governments and when the C, or cabinet-only, definition of government membership is utilized.

8. CONCLUSION: AN ALTERNATIVE PERSPECTIVE ON GOVERNMENT SURVIVAL

1. The standard method is simply to make preference an inverse function of distance; an alternative is to allow the saliency of policy dimensions to vary, which has the effect of making distance in some directions affect preferences more than does distance in other directions.

2. This is true by definition: Laver and Schofield (1990:156) describe stable bargaining environments as those in which dramatic changes in party positions or strengths are required to alter the bargaining logic. Destroying a core would clearly alter the bargaining logic. Hence, a core in a stable bargaining environment must be a strong one.

3. In reality, things are seldom this simple. For example, a core party may prefer to shuffle allies as its policy priorities change in order to preserve or enhance the credibility of the government. Nevertheless, the existence of a strong core ought to be more conducive to durable governments, ceteris paribus, than its absence.

4. This ordering of countries by mean duration is very similar to that produced by the data used here, as a comparison with Table 1.1 reveals. Note that Table 1.1 shows all systems categorized as multipolar to be less durable than those identified as unipolar or bipolar.

5. Denmark is listed as unipolar and multidimensional in the discussion of formation theories (Laver and Schofield 1990:136) but as multipolar in the discussion of duration theories (159).

6. Baron's model requires party leaders to perform complex calculations that involve (1) the probability of the party itself being asked to form a government (assuming the head of state has some discretion in this matter), (2) the probabilities of being asked by other parties to participate in government, and (3) the payoffs associated with all potential governing coalitions – both at the present and at future stages of the coalition formation game. These calculations are demanding even in fairly simple situations and escalate in complexity as the bargaining system becomes more complex.

7. In fact, by 1976 the DC had declined in parliamentary size to the point where it no longer occupied the median position in the Left–Right dimension.

8. This is not a totally satisfactory test because the exclusion of antisystem parties affects the de facto majority criterion: the larger the antisystem party presence, the higher the proportion of prosystem votes required for majority support. Since this revised majority criterion is a linear transformation of the size of the antisystem party presence, however, its effect is subsumed under the polarization variable, discussed later.

9. Parties, to be sure, differ in the degree to which they cater to voters or rely on extraparliamentary organizations. Strom (1990b) suggests factors that may account for these differences and identifies means employed by some parties to ensure that extraparliamentary organizations are influential in party decision making.

10. In reality, other members of the coalition may not be annoyed at all, since they can be reasonably sure that the coalition government will be re-formed and they know that the same option is available to them in the right circumstances.

References

Allison, Paul D. 1984. *Event History Analysis: Regression for Longitudinal Event Data.* Beverly Hills, CA: Sage.

Almond, Gabriel, and Sidney Verba. 1963. *The Civic Culture: Political Attitudes and Democary in Five Nations.* Princeton, NJ: Princeton University Press.

Axelrod, Robert. 1970. *Conflict of Interest.* Chicago: Markham.

Barnes, Samuel, et al. (1979). *Political Action: An Eight Nation Survey.* Ann Arbor, MI: Inter-University Consortium for Political and Social Research.

Baron, David. 1991. "A Spatial Bargaining Theory of Government Formation in Parliamentary Systems." *American Political Science Review* 85:135–64.

Baron, David, and John Ferejohn. 1989. "Bargaining in Legislatures." *American Political Science Review* 83:1181–1206.

Black, Duncan. 1958. *The Theory of Committees and Elections.* Cambridge University Press.

Blondel, Jean. 1968. "Party Systems and Patterns of Government in Western Democracies." *Canadian Journal of Political Science* 1:180–203.

Blossfeld, Hans-Peter, Alfred Hamerle, and Karl Mayer. 1989. *Event History Analysis.* Hillsdale, NJ: Erlbaum.

BMDP Statistical Software. 1990. *BMDP2L – Survival Analysis with Covariates.* Los Angeles: BMDP.

Browne, Eric C, and John Dreijmanis, eds. 1982. *Government Coalitions in Western Democracies.* New York: Longman.

Browne, Eric C., John P. Frendreis, and Dennis W. Gleiber. 1984. "An "Events" Approach to the Problem of Cabinet Stability." *Comparative Political Studies* 17:167–97.

  1986. "The Process of Cabinet Dissolution: An Exponential Model of Duration and Stability in Western Democracies." *American Journal of Political Science* 30:628–50.

  1988. "Contending Models of Cabinet Stability: A Rejoinder." *American Political Science Review* 82:930–41.

Browne, Eric C., Dennis W. Gleiber, and Carolyn Mashoba. 1984. "Evaluating Conflict of Interest Theory: Western European Cabinet Coalitions, 1945–80." *British Journal of Political Science* 14:1–32.

Budge, Ian, and Hans Keman. 1990. *Parties and Democracy: Coalition Formation and Government Functioning in Twenty States.* Oxford University Press.

Budge, Ian, David Robertson, and Derek Hearl. 1986. *ECPR Party Manifestos Project.* Oslo: Norwegian Social Science Data Archive.

Budge, Ian, David Robertson, and Derek Hearl, eds. 1987. *Ideology, Strategy and Party Change.* Cambridge University Press.

Castles, Francis, and Peter Mair. 1984. "Left–Right Political Scales: Some 'Expert' Judgments." *European Journal of Political Research* 12:73–88.

Cioffi-Revilla, Claudio. 1984. "The Political Reliability of Italian Governments: An Exponential Survival Model." *American Political Science Review* 78:318–37.

Conradt, David. 1980. "Changing German Political Culture." In Gabriel Almond and Sidney Verba, eds. *The Civic Culture Revisited,* pp. 212–72. Boston: Little, Brown.

Cox, David R. 1972. "Regression Models and Life-Tables (with Discussion)." *Journal of the Royal Statistical Society* B 34:187–220.

1975. "Partial Likelihood." *Biometrika* 62:269–76.

De Swaan, Abraham. 1973. *Coalition Theories and Cabinet Formations.* Amsterdam: Elsevier.

Dodd, Lawrence C. 1976. *Coalitions in Parliamentary Government.* Princeton, NJ: Princeton University Press.

Eckstein, Harry. 1966. *Division and Cohesion in Democracy: A Study of Norway.* Princeton, NJ: Princeton University Press.

Frendreis, John P., Dennis W. Gleiber, and Eric C. Browne. 1986. "The Study of Cabinet Dissolutions in Parliamentary Democracies." *Legislative Studies Quarterly* 11:619–28.

Gleiber, Dennis W., John P. Frendreis, and Greg Granger. 1992. "Governmental Lifecycles in Post-War Parliamentary Democracies: Continuity and Change." Presented at the Annual Meeting of the Western Political Science Association, San Francisco, CA.

Grofman, Bernard. 1989. "The Comparative Analysis of Coalition Formation and Duration: Distinguishing Between-Country and Within-Country Effects." *British Journal of Political Science* 19:291–302.

Hibbs, Douglas. 1992. "Partisan Theory After Fifteen Years." *European Journal of Political Economy* 8:361–73.

Inglehart, Ronald. 1977. *The Silent Revolution: Changing Values and Political Styles Among Western Publics.* Princeton, NJ: Princeton University Press.

1990. *Culture Shift in Advanced Industrial Society.* Princeton, NJ: Princeton University Press.

International Labor Organization. 1946–63. *International Labor Review* 51–88. Geneva: International Labor Office.

1964–70. *Bulletin of Labor Statistics.* Geneva: International Labor Office.

International Monetary Fund. 1970–90. *International Financial Statistics* 23–43. Washington: International Monetary Fund.

1979–89. *International Financial Statistics Yearbook.* Washington: International Monetary Fund.

Jouvenel, Robert de. 1914. *La république des camarades.* Paris: Grasset.

Keesing's Contemporary Archives. 1945–89. London: Keesing's Publications.

Kiefer, Nicholas. 1988. "Economic Duration Data and Hazard Functions." *Journal of Economic Literature* 26:646–79.

King, Gary. 1986. "How Not to Lie with Statistics: Avoiding Common Mistakes in Quantitative Political Science." *American Journal of Political Science* 30:666–87.

King, Gary. 1988. "Statistical Models for Political Science Event Counts: Bias in Conventional Procedures and Evidence for the Exponential Poisson Regression Model." *American Journal of Political Science* 32:838–63.

King, Gary, James Alt, Nancy Burns, and Michael Laver. 1990. "A Unified Model of Cabinet Dissolution in Parliamentary Democracies." *American Journal of Political Science* 34:846–71.

Laakso, Markku, and Rein Taagepera. 1979. " 'Effective' Number of Parties: A Measure with Application to West Europe." *Comparative Political Studies* 12:3–27.

Lapalombara, Joseph. 1987. *Democracy Italian Style.* New Haven, CT: Yale University Press.

Laver, Michael. 1974. "Dynamic Factors in Government Coalition Formation." *European Journal of Political Research* 2:259–70.

1989. "Party Competition and Party System Change: The Interaction of Electoral Bargaining and Party Competition." *Journal of Theoretical Politics* 1:301–25.

Laver, Michael, and W. Ben Hunt. 1992. *Policy and Party Competition*. New York: Routledge.

Laver, Michael, and Norman Schofield. 1990. *Multiparty Government: The Politics of Coalition in Europe*. Oxford University Press.

Leites, Nathan. 1959. *On the Game of Politics in France*. Stanford, CA: Stanford University Press.

Lewis-Beck, Michael. 1988. *Economics and Elections: The Major Western Democracies*. Ann Arbor, MI: University of Michigan Press.

Lijphart, Arend. 1984. *Democracies: Patterns of Majoritarian and Consensus Government in Twenty-one Countries*. New Haven, CT: Yale University Press.

McKelvey, Richard. 1976. "General Conditions for Global Intransitivities in Formal Voting Models." *Econometrica* 47:1085–111.

Organization for Economic Cooperation and Development. 1980. *OECD National Accounts I: Main Aggregates, 1950–78*. Paris: OECD.

1990a. *OECD Economic Outlook*, May. Paris: OECD.

1990b. *OECD Main Economic Indicators. Historical Statistics, 1969–88*. Paris: OECD.

1990c. *OECD National Accounts I: Main Aggregates, 1960–88*. Paris: OECD.

Paldam, Martin. 1981. "A Preliminary Survey of the Theories and Findings on Vote and Popularity Functions." *European Journal of Political Research* 9:181–99.

Pedersen, Mogens. 1979. "The Dynamics of European Party Systems: Changing Patterns of Electoral Volatility." *European Journal of Political Research* 7:1–26.

Plott, Charles. 1967. "A Notion of Equilibrium and Its Possibility Under Majority Rule." *American Economic Review* 57:787–806.

Powell, Bingham. 1982. *Contemporary Democracies*. Cambridge, MA: Harvard University Press.

Pridham, Geoffrey, ed. 1986. *Coalitional Behaviour in Theory and Practice: An Inductive Model for Western Europe*. Cambridge University Press.

Rabier, Jacques-René, and Ronald Inglehart. 1978. *Eurobarometer 6: Twenty Years of the Common Market*. Ann Arbor, MI: Inter-University Consortium for Political and Social Research.

Rabier, Jacques-René, Hélène Riffault, and Ronald Inglehart. 1986. *Eurobarometer 24: Entry of Spain and Portugal*. Ann Arbor, MI: Inter-University Consortium for Political and Social Research.

Rae, Douglas. 1971. *The Political Consequences of Electoral Laws*. New Haven, CT: Yale University Press.

Robertson, John D. 1983a. "Inflation, Unemployment, and Government Collapse: A Poisson Application." *Comparative Political Studies* 15:425–44.

1983b. "The Political Economy and the Durability of European Coalition Cabinets: New Variations on a Game-Theoretic Perspective." *Journal of Politics* 45:932–57.

1983c. "Toward a Political-Economic Accounting of the Endurance of Cabinet Administrations: An Empirical Assessment of Eight European Administrations." *American Journal of Political Science* 28:693–709.

Sanders, David, and Valentine Herman. 1977. "The Stability and Survival of Governments in Western Democracies." *Acta Politica* 12:346–77.

Sani, Giacomo, and Giovanni Sartori. 1983. "Polarization, Competition, and Fragmentation in Western Democracies." In Hans Daalder and Peter Mair, eds. *Western European Party Systems: Continuity and Change*. Beverly Hills, CA: Sage.

Sartori, Giovanni. 1976. *Parties and Party Systems: A Framework for Analysis*. Cambridge University Press.

Schofield, Norman. 1993. "Political Competition and Multiparty Coalition Governments." *European Journal of Political Research* 23:1–33.

Shamir, Michal. 1984. "Are Western Party Systems 'Frozen?' A Comparative Dynamic Analysis." *Comparative Political Studies* 17:35–79.

Shugart, Matthew S., and John M. Carey. 1992. *Presidents and Assemblies: Constitutional Design and Electoral Dynamics.* Cambridge University Press.

Strom, Kaare. 1985. "Party Goals and Government Performance in Parliamentary Democracies." *American Political Science Review* 79:738–54.

    1988. "Contending Models of Cabinet Stability." *American Political Science Review* 82:923–30.

    1990a. *Minority Government and Majority Rule.* Cambridge University Press.

    1990b. "A Behavioral Theory of Competitive Parties." *American Journal of Political Science* 34:565–98.

Taagepera, Rein, and Matthew Shugart. 1989. *Seats and Votes: The Effects and Determinants of Electoral Systems.* New Haven, CT: Yale University Press.

Taylor, Michael, and Valentine Herman. 1971. "Party Systems and Government Stability." *American Political Science Review* 65:28–37.

Tuma, Nancy, and Michael Hannan. 1984. *Social Dynamics.* New York: Academic.

Tuma, Nancy, and DMA Corporation. 1992. *Rate,* Version 2.9F. Palo Alto, CA: DMA Corporation.

United Nations. 1947–90. *UN Monthly Bulletin of Statistics* 1–44. New York: United Nations Statistical Office.

von Beyme, Klaus. 1984. *Political Parties in Western Democracies.* Aldershot, UK: Gower.

Warwick, Paul. 1978. "Ideology, Culture, and Gamesmanship in French Politics." *Journal of Modern History* 50:631–59.

    1979. "The Durability of Coalition Governments in Parliamentary Democracies." *Comparative Political Studies* 11:465–98.

    1988. "Models of Cabinet Stability: A Preliminary Evaluation." Presented at the Annual Meeting of the American Political Science Association, Washington, D.C.

    1990. *Culture, Structure, or Choice? Essays in the Interpretation of the British Experience.* New York: Agathon.

    1992a. "Ideological Diversity and Government Survival in West European Parliamentary Democracies." *Comparative Political Studies* 25:332–61.

    1992b. "Economic Trends and Government Survival in West European Parliamentary Democracies." *American Political Science Review* 86:875–87.

    1992c. "Rising Hazards: An Underlying Dynamic of Parliamentary Government." *American Journal of Political Science* 36:857–76.

Warwick, Paul, and Stephen Easton. 1992. "The Cabinet Stability Controversy: New Perspectives on a Classic Problem." *American Journal of Political Science* 36:122–46.

Index